AUGUSTUS

AUGUSTUS

GODFATHER
OF EUROPE

RICHARD HOLLAND

SUTTON PUBLISHING

This book was first published in 2004 by
Sutton Publishing Limited · Phoenix Mill
Thrupp · Stroud · Gloucestershire · GL5 2BU

This paperback edition first published in 2005

British Library Cataloguing in Publication Data
A catalogue record for this book is available from the British
Library.

ISBN 0 7509 2911 1

Typeset in 10.5/13pt Plantin.
Typesetting and origination by
Sutton Publishing Limited.
Printed and bound in Great Britain by
J.H. Haynes & Co. Ltd, Sparkford.

CONTENTS

PREFACE

On an evening in spring some two thousand years ago an eighteen-year-old student, sent overseas to improve his grasp of Greek language and literature, received an urgent message from his mother: her uncle had been assassinated in Rome by a group of leading politicians. For the student, Gaius Octavius ('Octavian'), the crime meant not only the personal loss of a much-loved relative but the sinister possibility that he might be next on the assassins' list. For the uncle of Octavian's mother was the dictator Julius Caesar, and his death on the Ides of March, 44 BC, threw the Roman world into turmoil.

Rejecting offers of military help, which he knew would have raised the spectre of civil war, Octavian set out for home as inconspicuously as possible. With a few chosen friends he recrossed the Adriatic in a small boat. They avoided the port of Brundisium (modern Brindisi), where Roman troops were stationed, because they assumed that the assassins, led by two judges, Brutus and Cassius, would already have taken over the reins of government during the two or three weeks since Caesar's murder. They ran their boat up a remote beach on the heel of Italy, walked to the nearest town, rented lodgings and made discreet inquiries about the latest news from the capital.

What followed is the stuff of epic. Octavian learnt, to his apparent surprise, that Caesar had adopted him, under his will, to be his son and principal heir. He immediately began to call himself Caesar. He entered the political arena, recruited a private army, won and then lost the support of Cicero and the Senate, marched on Rome with eight legions and enforced his own election as consul. He was still only nineteen when he thus became titular head – if only a temporary and acting head – of the greatest empire the Western world had ever seen, stretching from the Atlantic to the Euphrates, from the North Sea to the Sahara.

Rome did not tolerate the constitutional aberration of a teenage consul for long. But Octavian was merely at the start of his astonishing career. He would gradually outsmart and outlive all his major opponents, bringing unprecedented peace and a degree of plenty to a large segment of mankind. As the Emperor Augustus (a title he himself never used), he would greet the birth of his grand-daughter's grandson and die in bed, kissed by his wife of more than fifty years, surrounded by family and friends and worshipped as a god. It is the stuff of epic, yes – but no great epic has ever been composed about the man himself. Even Shakespeare could only manage to write a bit-part for him, as the supposed kill-joy who drives the lovers Antony and Cleopatra to suicide.

Posterity, which owes Octavian so much, has shown little enthusiasm for this quiet, self-controlled man of outstanding political and administrative gifts. He was loyal to his friends but, at least in the early years, he preferred to kill opponents rather than argue with them. Later, as absolute ruler, lacking any credible challenger, he killed more selectively; but by that time most people thoroughly understood that, unlike Julius Caesar, he never gave anyone a second chance to betray him. The Roman aristocrats – those who survived – learned to adapt their behaviour to his requirements, and the killings dwindled to almost nothing. That, too, was peace of a kind. Nor was it too hard for people to adapt, because he was personally quite amiable and he concealed the reality of his power behind a pretence of restoring the traditional structures of the old republican constitution.

Opinion of him has swung wildly over the centuries. In the era of the empire-building European monarchies he had no shortage of admirers. Even after many of them were toppled in the First World War, adulation of Augustus reached its height among apologists for the fascist regimes of Germany and Italy. Mussolini, in particular, who fantasized about recreating part of the Roman Empire in his area of the Mediterranean, looked to him as a role model. But in the English-speaking world a very different interpretation was emerging; and it received its classic statement in a book by an Oxford historian, *The Roman Revolution*, published only days after Britain entered the Second World War in September 1939.[1]

Its author, Ronald Syme (later Professor Sir Ronald Syme, OM), researched and wrote it during the inter-war period of the great dictators, lower-class men like Hitler and Stalin, who clawed their way to power over the bodies of aristocrats, amid the wreckage of empires.[2] His Augustus is an earlier revolutionary-turned-dictator from a *nouveau riche* plebeian background, who abolishes Roman political freedom and crushes the aristocracy which had made Rome great. His Brutus and Cassius are 'The Liberators', whose assassination of Caesar is a 'heroic' and 'noble' deed, if a futile one. He writes of Brutus: 'He did not believe in violence.'[3] So why did Brutus stab Caesar, lead a huge army against his fellow-Romans, and crucify a slave for being disrespectful to his master and mistress?[4]

Syme's erudition remains unchallengeable, and his book essential reading. But after the lapse of more than sixty years his masterpiece can be clearly perceived as the work of a man who regretted not just the rise of vulgar dictators *entre deux guerres*, but mourned as deeply the passing of aristocratic leadership from contemporary European society in the aftermath of the First World War and its replacement by the era of the common man. *The Roman Revolution* is an unashamed lament for the passing of the old aristocratic leadership from the very different society of ancient republican Rome, and it tends to label as an unprincipled 'demagogue' anyone – but especially the young Octavian – who dared to appeal directly to the voters over the heads of the entrenched senatorial oligarchy. Syme's overall analysis continues, nevertheless, to enjoy majority support among academic historians, although some have questioned his patrician disdain for 'the mob', and for the use of the word 'revolution' to describe a change of government in which one set of rich slave-owners was replaced by another – the new ones, admittedly, possessing rather less social *cachet* than the old.

This present biography tries to steer a middle course between the admirers of Octavian/Augustus (seen by some as a split personality) and his detractors. It does not pretend that Octavian was other than a man driven by the will to power who was prepared, if necessary, to wade through slaughter to a throne. He once ordered a mass crucifixion of 6,000 runaway slaves who had taken up arms, believing it a socially necessary act, *pour encourager les autres*. The overriding problem for Rome, as he found it, was rapacious, inconsistent and corrupt control from the centre by a limited number of interbred families, whose 460-year-old system of rule by constant reshuffling of annually elected magistrates – designed for running a small city state – was hopelessly inadequate for governing a sprawling empire of tens of millions of people of many races, creeds and levels of development.

Octavian's solution was a form of monarchical control, carefully disguised as a team effort. After building up a largely meritocratic 'party', based initially on citizen-soldiers eager to avenge Caesar, he gradually broadened his appeal to embrace all sections of society above the level of enforced servitude, including leaders of the formerly hostile aristocracy who were prepared to accept public office on his terms. He went on to reign longer and more wisely than any of his many successors as Roman emperors, and bequeathed to Western civilization the fabled *Pax Romana* of his 'golden age', whose benefits embraced a literary and architectural revival of epic proportions, and cleared the way (unknowingly) for the future spread of Christianity to a world disfigured by slavery and sadistic spectacle.

It is misleading and anachronistic to label him a 'revolutionary', as though he were an ancient forerunner of Robespierre or Lenin – and positively absurd to describe his earliest aristocratic opponents as 'liberators', when the freedom they sought was for their traditional right to subjugate and exploit all other classes and races. He was a religious man of deeply conservative views, who used Rome's supremacy to impose its peace and his values on large areas of three continents – with proto-capitalist businessmen following behind the legions to introduce some, at least, of his millions of new subjects to such benefits as central heating and flushable lavatories. If comparisons must be made with modern times, one is safe in asserting that no state since the Augustan Empire has ever enjoyed such overwhelming superpower status over all available rivals until the recent emergence of the United States of America, under President George W. Bush, as 'the world's policeman'.

The chief problem for a biographer of Octavian is the varying availability of written sources. Very little is known about his childhood and early adolescence. A flood of material has come down to us for the period between Caesar's assassination in March 44 BC and the regrettable (but richly deserved) demise of Cicero in October 42. Quite a lot of useful material takes the story on to the final defeat of Antony and Cleopatra some twelve years later. For the remaining forty-four years of his life information is at times so sparse that for some years we have no record of his personal activities. For the last few decades, the sources chiefly focus on his struggle to find a dynastic successor. It is conventional to refer to him as Octavian up to the point when he took effective control of the whole empire, and as Augustus thereafter. That simply reinforces the mistaken belief that he was a sort of Jekyll and Hyde character. I try to call him Octavian throughout.

Modern treatments tend to be padded out with chapters on such non-biographical but worthy topics as Augustan literature, daily life, society, art, institutions, and lists of buildings erected under the auspices of the man who, proverbially, is claimed to have found Rome a city of brick and left it a city of marble. Where such matters directly impinge on Octavian I try to include them as part of the chronological narrative of his life. As this book is aimed at the general reader who wants to know about the man himself, his struggle and his momentous achievements, I think it much more important – now that study of the classics is necessarily a minority occupation – to devote enough space to the decline of the Roman Republic to make the actions of the young Octavian intelligible when he bursts on to the political scene as a prodigy and a phenomenon.

My debt to Syme and to many other scholars will be apparent to historians of the period. The bibliography lists chiefly those modern works that I have found especially interesting or readable. All translations are my own, unless acknowledged. My warmest thanks are to the forbearance of my fiancée, Penelope Old, who wisely waited until the book was completed before agreeing to marry me.

Map of the Roman Empire at the death of Augustus in AD 14

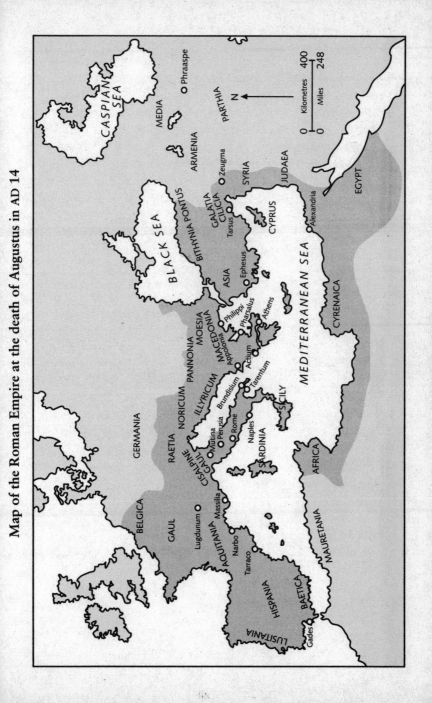

ONE

THE MAKING OF A MASTER RACE

Romans of the early days of empire were encouraged to believe they were descended from Trojans. An elite band of warriors, so the story ran, fought their way out of the burning city of Troy when it was sacked by Greeks after the ten-year siege described by Homer. Led by Aeneas, son of the goddess Venus, the fugitives escaped by ship across the Mediterranean with divine help, and after many adventures landed half-way up the west coast of Italy. They settled in Latium – on other people's land – where, over time, the city of Rome sprang up.[1]

This was a very convenient set of beliefs. They covered in a mythological haze the otherwise compelling evidence that the Romans were originally quarrelsome peasant-farmers who beggared all their neighbours over the course of centuries.[2] There was no shame in their acknowledging that the Trojans had been defeated and driven from their native land, because everyone knew that the ancient Greeks had massively outnumbered the Trojans and that they did not win the battle fairly but by the treacherous ruse of infiltrating their soldiers into Troy inside a wooden horse. In any case, since then, the Romans had beaten the Greeks into submission in 167 BC, and 21 years later (literally) flattened the capital city of their other old enemies, the Phoenicians of Carthage, and ploughed salt into its ruins.

But, above all, the importance of the Trojan legend for the Romans was that it enabled them to invoke a special status for themselves as men following a divinely appointed mission, which both explained their astonishing rise from city state to great power, and justified their vaunted superiority over all other races. With audacious poetic licence, Virgil, supreme figure of the 'golden age' of Augustan literature, voiced their manifest destiny:

> Remember, Roman, that your virtuous art
> Shall be to rule the peoples with your power,
> Impose on them the lawful ways of peace,
> Spare those who shall submit and crush the proud.[3]

In other words, the Romans, as a race endowed with special virtue, had the right and duty to invade any country within reach and reconstruct it along Roman lines. If the inhabitants submitted, their lives would be magnanimously spared; but if they continued to resist they would be killed or enslaved.

It was Gaius Julius Caesar, born in 100 BC, whose colonialist exploits would have provided Virgil with the closest example of such an ideal Roman.[4] During his conquest of Gaul in the decade of the 50s BC, Caesar's legions are estimated to have killed in battle a million Gauls and Germans in the course of taking over the huge territory which today comprises France, Belgium and parts of the Rhineland and north-west Italy. He is reported to have been responsible for enslaving a million more,[5] including a single consignment of 53,000 men, women and children left alive after a long and bloody siege. This is indeed the same Julius Caesar who has been renowned by posterity for his clemency towards defeated enemies – so long as they were Roman citizens. More specifically for our purposes, it is the same Caesar who went on to teach the arts of leadership in politics and war to his sister's grandson, Gaius Octavius, the boy whom he adopted as his son and heir, and who grew up to take Caesar's name and become the founding father of the Roman Empire.

Gaius Octavius (hereafter called Octavian) was born in Rome shortly before sunrise on 23 September in the ominous year of 63 BC, when Italy was stirred up by a revolutionary movement led by a group of Caesar's allies, under a disaffected patrician senator, Lucius Catilina (conventionally known as Catiline). The baby was barely six weeks old when Caesar was lucky to escape being stabbed to death by ardent supporters of the Roman Republic as he was about to leave a meeting of the Senate. It was a bizarre prefiguration of his actual assassination on the Ides of March some eighteen years later. On that earlier occasion he had made a speech seeking to prevent the execution of some of the conspirators; he was suspected of colluding with them because he had earlier supported Catiline as a consular candidate against the optimate oligarchy. A group of armed knights, specially recruited to guard the elected consul Cicero[6] against assassination, drew their swords on the unarmed Caesar, who was saved by the timely intervention of Cicero in person.[7]

Caesar was so alarmed at the narrowness of his escape that he did not show his face again in the Senate until he had been safely installed in office as praetor (the second most senior magistracy in Rome), to which he had been elected by the People several months before the debate on Catiline's conspiracy took place. It is highly probable that during this brief lull in his public life he found time to visit his baby great-nephew, if he had not already visited young Octavian before. The child had been born in a house in the exclusive residential district of the Palatine, just a short step up the hill from the Forum where the Senate met and where Caesar, as *Pontifex Maximus* (chief priest) of Rome, had his official residence. Caesar had no legitimate son; and, in a society where legitimate male bloodlines were of major importance, the arrival of a close male relative could have potential political implications.

At that stage of his career, however, he could still easily have hoped to father legitimate sons of his own. He was only thirty-seven and noted for his sexual prowess among society ladies. Octavian was considerably lower in the social scale than Caesar, who was a blue-blooded patrician of the Julian clan. The boy was the first and (it turned out) only son of a

senator, also named Gaius Octavius, of obscure family.[8]
Gaius Octavius senior was shortly to be elected praetor
himself, but had only an outside chance, at that stage, of
ultimately becoming one of the two consuls who, elected each
year, governed Rome for twelve months only. Achievement of
this post of quasi-monarchical power was considered to
ennoble the holder's family for ever.

The Octavian clan was plebeian, and even those branches
that had lived in Rome for several centuries were not
especially prominent. The family of Gaius Octavius senior
were merely local notables in the Volscian town of Velitrae,
some 25 miles south-east of Rome. Young Octavian's paternal
grandfather was a rich money-lender, who ranked as a knight
(of the equestrian order), and whose wealth had provided his
son with the essential monetary qualification to stand for
election for the junior magistracy of quaestor. Poor people
were ineligible as candidates under the Roman system, which
was deliberately designed to make it almost impossible for
anyone but a rich aristocrat to ascend to the consulship.
Becoming a quaestor was the essential first step on the
electoral ladder, because it automatically brought life
membership of the Senate. It was as an ambitious young
senator looking for a second wife that Gaius Octavius senior
found in his own home town of Velitrae the woman who
would propel him towards the heights.

He offered marriage to Atia, daughter of a rich local
worthy, Marcus Atius Balbus, and of his wife Julia, sister of
Julius Caesar. It may have caused some surprise that his offer
succeeded because his family tree would have barred him
from social acceptance even as a dinner guest in the homes of
some noblemen, if we can believe Mark Antony's claim that
one of the would-be bridegroom's grandfathers was a freed
slave, who had worked as a ropemaker near the town of
Thurii, on the heel of Italy. Admittedly, Antony (Marcus
Antonius) had become an enemy when he made the claim
about the family's allegedly servile origin. Invective of that

4

kind – in this case almost certainly false – was not uncommon in Roman politics. But it is interesting that Octavian's own memoirs draw a veil over the matter, offering no detailed rebuttal but stating simply that he was born into an 'old and rich' equestrian family.[9]

Modern scholarship has failed to establish a direct blood link with any of the original Roman Octavians. That, in itself, proves nothing; but if he had been related to any of the earlier clan members who had served as magistrates he would have said so. A Roman politician's status depended crucially on having magistrates in his family tree. Antony was no doubt correct in asserting that Octavian had none at all apart from his own *nouveau riche* father, but his mendacious smear was designed to raise doubts about where the name Octavius came from. Under the Roman system of nomenclature, a slave who was freed was required to take his master's name to become a Roman citizen with the status of 'freedman'. Antony was thus trying to suggest that Octavian's paternal grandfather was once the slave of a man named Octavius rather than being the legitimate son of a free citizen of that name.

There are, however, other pieces of evidence that fit in with the general proposition that Octavian's family – except for the Caesarian connection – sprang from humble roots. His earliest extant biographer, Suetonius (born about AD 69), came into possession of a bronze statuette of him as a boy; at its base was the name 'Thurinus' in rusty iron letters, difficult to decipher.[10] Thurinus would appear to be a *cognomen* (family surname, which follows the clan name) indicating a person who comes from, or is connected with, the town of Thurii, the origin of the allegedly servile ropemaker. Suetonius believed that the existence of this ornament proved that, as a boy, the future Augustus was called 'Gaius Octavius Thurinus'. The biographer gave the statuette to the Emperor Hadrian (ruled AD 117 to 138), who placed it among the collection of household gods in his palace.

Mark Antony sometimes referred sneeringly to Octavian in

his letters as 'the Thurian', indicating that he was a social interloper from the back of beyond. Suetonius reports that the young man's irritated response was 'I'm surprised that a former name should be thrown at me as an insult.'[11] Octavian clearly wanted to bury the Thurian connection for ever – and that, in turn, throws doubt on the truth of another possible explanation, unconnected with the ropemaker, for the unwanted *cognomen*. When Gaius Octavius senior, as propraetor, passed through the Thurii district before taking up appointment, in 60 BC, as Governor of Macedonia, he defeated a band of runaway slaves; to mark this victory he supposedly adopted the name Thurinus for himself and/or his two-year-old son, as an honoured *cognomen* to be inherited, to distinguish their branch of the Octavian clan from all the other branches.

Among the problems with this explanation is that, during a period of Roman republican history which is well documented, not much fuss is made of that supposed victory. The slaves were presumably a remnant of Catiline's defeated rag-tag army who could not return 'home' without risking crucifixion – the standard punishment for runaways who took up arms. It was definitely not part of a revolt on the scale of that of Spartacus in the previous decade. If Gaius Octavius senior was involved in a pitched battle with them it could scarcely have been a very large one – probably more of a mopping-up operation in which trained soldiers hunted down the doomed survivors of a failed break for freedom.

Antony also mocked Octavian's ancestry on his maternal grandfather's side. Suetonius states unequivocally that Marcus Atius Balbus, who married Caesar's sister, was descended from a long line of senators, but the evidence is shaky; one suggestion is that the biographer has confused Atius Balbus with an Atilius Balbus, who was consul twice in the third century BC. Antony claimed that Atius Balbus's father came to Italy from Africa (the comparatively small Roman province of that name, not the continent) and settled at the town of Aricia, 15 miles south of Rome, where he made and sold perfumes and later operated a bakery.[12] That would have been within living memory, and therefore easily challenged, if Antony had been lying.

Why should any of this spiteful tittle-tattle about his recent forebears matter in the context of the life of a man of Octavian's immense achievements? Modern readers revel in the life stories of people of humble origins who become great national leaders. We do not think any the less of Abraham Lincoln for having been born in a log-cabin – or any the more of Winston Churchill because he was born in Blenheim Palace and could trace his descent from dukes. Most Roman voters took the opposite view. It was a common belief in the ancient world that if a person was born poor or crippled or a slave, it was either because he or she had done something wicked in a previous existence to deserve it or because a god or Fate had ordained it. Equally, if you came from a long line of brave, public-spirited men, you were considered much more likely than not to turn out to be brave and public-spirited too, whether for reasons of destiny or heredity.

The highly complex Roman constitution was geared to arrange for men of distinguished ancestry and conspicuous wealth to take all the top jobs in government and to deny, so far as possible, any opportunity for poor men of obscure families even to stand as candidates, whatever their personal merits might happen to be. Merit did, of course, count in the selection process, but only after the matter of ancestry had effectively reduced the field of candidates to a credible number. Incompatible though that system may be with modern democratic notions, it was undeniably successful for Rome for more than four centuries, until it started to break down during the lifetime of Julius Caesar. It is arguable that without it Rome would have remained just another city state among so many other petty rivals.

The fundamental reason for its long survival may have been that it contained just enough of a democratic element to allow the ruling oligarchy of aristocrats to retain the loyalty of ordinary citizens, who for the most part respected the authority of the Senate, based as it was on a long and proud record of worldly success. Warfare overtook agriculture as the most productive business of the Roman state, and the senators were not just politicians but also the chief officers of the army. Those of appropriate age led the conquering legions into battle, while the overall strategy of the state was determined mainly by the substantial number of retired generals who had served as consuls. Under their guidance, Rome, although suffering occasional setbacks, made war pay. They not only defeated those whom they chose to designate as enemies and milked them for whatever they could get – money, slaves, loot, taxes – but went on to recruit the pick of their able-bodied men to serve in the Roman army, on half-pay, to hold down any other subject peoples except their own.

Officially the nation was ruled by the Senate and People of Rome acting together – the fabled *Senatus Populusque Romanus*, shown on coins and inscriptions by the initials SPQR. But although every citizen had a right to vote, it was not democracy as we know it today or even as the Greeks (who invented it) knew it then. Rather, it was an illusion of democracy, embraced by a conservative-minded people sharing a strong sense of community and loyalty to the state; it served to keep a lid on popular discontents and to permit an hereditary Establishment to retain the substance of power.

Entrenched family privilege was the key. Individuals, of course, changed in line with the natural processes of birth and death, but the same names occur in the lists of ruling magistrates century after century. A patrician named Lucius Junius Brutus led the coup against the last king of Rome that inaugurated the Republic in about 509 BC; nearly half a millennium later a member of the same branch of the same patrician clan, Marcus Junius Brutus, led the group of sixty conspirators who assassinated Julius Caesar on the Ides of March in 44 BC in a vain attempt to save the Republic from reverting to a form of monarchy. The assassins claimed (perhaps correctly) that Marcus Brutus was a direct descendant of Lucius Brutus in the uninterrupted male line because they knew that would increase the validity of their action in the eyes of the populace.

Lucius Brutus had been a member of the royal council which advised the line of elective kings who ruled Rome after the legendary foundation of the city by Romulus, which is traditionally dated to 753 BC. That same council remained in being after the last king, Tarquin the Proud, was ejected. Its first constitutional measure was to arrange for the annual election of two magistrates, later called consuls, who would share between them for one year only the *imperium* (power) that had previously been exercised by the king. The members of the council, which became known as the Senate, were called *patres* (fathers), from which the word 'patricians' is derived. They were called fathers because they were literally the fathers (or, at least, the senior male relatives) of the most important families in the land.

The role of the senators was to advise the consuls, just as it had been the role of the royal councillors to advise the kings. But whereas a king could ignore their advice with impunity, that was not to be so easy for a consul. His *imperium* was nearly as unlimited as a king's had been, but only during his year of office. After he stepped down he would become liable for prosecution for anything he had done while consul; and his judges would be senior members of the Senate whose advice he might have been tempted to disregard. Naturally, if he wished to avoid punishments such as exile or confiscation of his possessions, a prudent consul would take care to win the support of senators in advance of any significant action he might take. In practice, most consuls were willing to fall in with the majority view of the Senate, whatever it might be. They were, after all, members of the Senate themselves, and would resume their senatorial roles with enhanced status as consulars (ex-consuls), whose opinions would in future be sought before those of senators who had never exercised that degree of *imperium*.

The patricians, who exclusively continued to man the Senate in the early years of the Republic, could thus largely circumscribe the activities of the consuls, but they could not stop social change indefinitely. Class war raised its ugly head as leading plebeians agitated for a share in power and the fruits of power. So far as the record shows, nobody was actually killed in this long-running dispute, which was waged by such apparently modern methods as strikes and mass sit-ins. Eventually, a limited number of the richest plebeians were admitted to the senatorial ranks, although it took several more generations before their families were ennobled by winning election as consuls.

But once having joined the patricians in power, the 'plebeian aristocracy' lost interest in advancing the political cause of lesser plebeians, and by the middle of the third century BC there was no perceptible difference of opinion or policy between the two groups of aristocrats. They sank their original differences in the common cause of maintaining their oligarchic power structure, by which individuals within the charmed circle of the senatorial nobility reserved the right to compete against each other in open rivalry for the senior magistracies and military commands, while doing their utmost to block possible competition from outsiders. Intermarriage between patricians and rich plebeians cemented their basic alliance.

What role did the People, as voters, play in all this? Any account of the early voting system would be highly speculative, but it has recently become possible to reconstruct in some detail[13] the strange ways in which Roman voters went to the polls in the last hundred years or so of the Republic – and the even stranger ways in which the ruling oligarchy ensured that those votes rarely counted for much. There were three different forms of assembly at which votes were cast in person by registered citizens, and all three were biased in some degree towards achieving a result acceptable to the government.

All senior magistrates, including the two annual consuls, were elected by the *Comitia Centuriata*, which voted in 'centuries' based on the early organization of the Roman army. Individual votes counted only within each 'century', which in practice might consist of only a handful of men. The majority in each century was worth only one vote in the final tally. There were 193 centuries in all, and no fewer than 180 of them were composed of senators or knights; their votes were counted first and were naturally cast in favour of candidates who would protect their interests – that is, the interests of wealthy property-owners, employers and masters of many slaves. The *proletarii*, lacking a property qualification, were enrolled in only one century, so their participation in the voting would have been merely cosmetic.

Some of the other centuries were dominated by almost equally 'conservative' voters on a social level below that of the knights but well above that of most ordinary citizens. Their votes, added to those of the senators and knights, were almost always enough to ensure that the successful candidates were conventional aristocrats with a long line of former magistrates in their family trees. Very rarely, and in exceptional circumstances, a *novus homo* (new man) might be elected consul, such as Caesar's uncle Marius, a general of outstanding professional competence who reorganized the Roman army, and the gifted lawyer Marcus Tullius Cicero, whose essays on morality can still be read with profit today but whose senatorial career was devoted to maintaining the *status quo* and blocking measures to help the poor.

The Senate had no power either to elect magistrates or to pass laws. The People voted for or against proposed legislation in either the *Comitia Tributa* (tribal assembly for both patricians and plebeians), or the *Concilium Plebis* (Council of the Plebs), where only plebeians were eligible, and from which our word 'plebiscite' is derived. In either assembly they could vote only on what was laid before them by a qualified magistrate. Individual voters could speak in the debate before the vote only if specifically invited to do so by the presiding magistrate, who might not allow opinions contrary to his own to be voiced.

Assembly voting was not by military centuries but by tribes. By Caesar's day the number of tribes had grown to thirty-five. Almost all members of the city proletariat were enrolled in one or other of only four tribes, making their individual votes virtually worthless. Thus, the great mass of citizens living in Rome itself never got their way unless fourteen of the other thirty-one tribes voted with them. Those thirty-one tribes were variously based around Italy, and some of their members lived much further afield – too far from Rome, in any case, for all but a tiny proportion to travel to the city for a vote, which had to be cast in person in the voting arena. The voting process took hours to complete. That made it even less likely that a poor urban citizen who needed to earn a living would turn up to vote.

It must have been intensely boring for any citizen to stand around for the best part of a day in a cramped enclosure, awaiting the turn of his tribe to vote, in an order that was usually decided by drawing lots. He might very well not get the chance to vote at all, because polling ceased once eighteen of the thirty-five tribes had voted in the same direction. A typical voter, therefore, would need to have an unusually keen interest in politics. There were occasions when nobody turned up to represent a particular tribe; and it was normal for the more distant tribes to be represented by only a handful of voters. The system was thus open to the same sort of abuse as the 'rotten boroughs' of eighteenth-century England; a few individuals were in a position to sell their votes to the highest bidder, or at least have their expenses paid by a 'patron' for the cost and inconvenience of travelling to Rome and taking lodgings.

The patronage system loomed large in Roman politics,

although not so large as most modern historians used to believe. A combination of archaeological excavation and arithmetic have demonstrated beyond reasonable doubt that voting was very much a minority occupation.[14] Assemblies of the People were attended, at best, by only a few thousand people; the places where they were held were simply too small to hold larger numbers. Voting involved the physical separation of members of each individual tribe within cordoned-off areas – rather like sheep-pens at shearing time – until they were called to walk in single file over two specially constructed 'bridges' to deposit their ballot. The total electorate of Roman citizens, according to the official census figures, exceeded 900,000 in 69 BC (it rose to about five million under Augustus), but typically no more than one-half of one per cent of them would have voted at any one time, due to physical and temporal restrictions. No doubt there were occasions when that proportion was exceeded, but they must have been rare. There is no longer any need for historians to posit an almost universal system of 'patrons and clients' to explain the otherwise mysterious way in which the government so consistently won the votes of the 'People' for policies that were clearly against the interests of the mass of the population.

The ruling oligarchy among the optimate[15] majority in the Senate did not rig the votes in the *Comitia Centuriata*, which elected the consuls. They were perfectly willing to accept the People's choice of particular individuals, so long as those individuals were of the right class and would not try to introduce reforms in favour of the common people. From time to time they prosecuted successful candidates for bribery – even though bribery was endemic in the system – and thus disqualified a few of those they disapproved of most deeply. As for the Tribal Assembly and the *Concilium Plebis*, they could usually rely on finding one of the ten annual tribunes to veto any legislation against their interest. A further resource, if things were not going their way, was for a consul or priest to declare an inauspicious omen, either in the sky or in the entrails of a sacrificed animal or bird, that would have the effect of negating all official business on a particular day.

Nevertheless, in spite of the obstacles to reform, the aristocracy was vulnerable to attack from within its own ranks. Julius Caesar became the most prominent and notorious of the so-called *populares*, who tried to alleviate the lot of the ordinary citizens in the teeth of senatorial opposition, but he was by no means the first. The need for reform had become urgent by the second half of the second century BC, before Caesar was born. A biting analysis of conditions in that earlier era is provided by the historian Sallust, a Caesarian supporter: 'A few men exercised total control in peace and war. The treasury, the provinces, public office, honours and triumphs were in their hands. The people were burdened by army service and poverty. The generals grabbed the spoils of war for themselves and a few others. Meanwhile the parents or little children of the soldiers were being evicted from their homes by powerful neighbours.'[16]

Sallust's words need some elaboration. As in all pre-industrial societies, the non-military part of the Roman economy was predominantly agrarian. Food could be moved in bulk only by water, so localized famines were a perennial hazard, especially in Italy's many mountainous regions, but also in the city of Rome itself when bad harvests were widespread and piracy common at sea. Trade, except for the sale of their own agricultural products, was not supposed to be pursued by senators, who generally despised it, preferring to make their money from rents, wars and high public office abroad, where they were in a position to exploit the hapless inhabitants of the provinces they took turns to govern. The chief traders were the knights of the equestrian order, some of whom became richer than many senators, notably the *publicani* (of the 'publicans and sinners' mentioned unfavourably in the Bible),[17] who also collected the imperial taxes.

These top two social orders, senatorial and equestrian, together formed the aristocracy and the officer-class; and there was a huge and growing economic gap between them and the mass of the population, most of whom seem to have led a hand-to-mouth existence even in times of comparative plenty. In the early centuries of the Republic, the common foot-soldiers of the army were peasant-owners of smallholdings. Characteristically they sowed their crops at the end of winter, went off to fight one or more of the neighbouring tribes, and returned, if they had avoided death, capture or serious injury, in time to gather in the harvest from their fields, which kept them and their families in rations for the next twelve months.

As Roman-controlled territory expanded through military victories it became necessary to campaign farther and farther afield, thereby extending the fighting season of late spring and summer to encroach into autumn, with risk to the harvest. As the empire spread overseas, the peasant-soldiers found themselves forced to serve abroad for a whole year or more; later still, after huge territorial conquests in such comparatively distant areas as Spain, Greece and parts of North Africa, they were kept away from home for year upon year. There was no adequate state gratuity for a discharged soldier. After walking home for up to a thousand miles, he might find there was no home left to go to.

During his long, enforced absence his wife and children might have died or gone to the city in the hope of avoiding starvation by performing menial or degrading tasks. His cottage roof might have fallen in and his smallholding been taken over by an absentee landowner, who worked it with slave gangs under overseers. If his farm had not already been legally sold, the returned veteran might have no serious alternative but to sell it himself for what little it would fetch, pocket the money and take his chance in the city too, among thousands of others in similar predicaments. As Professor Brunt has pointed out, 'In conquering what they were pleased to call the world the Romans ruined a great part of the Italian people.'[18]

It was, of course, the senators and knights who had been buying or illegally seizing huge swathes of the Italian countryside while the former peasant-owners fought for their country overseas under harsh conditions and for minimal pay. The lot of the Roman peasants in arms was bad enough; that of their allies from other parts of Italy, who were contributing about half the regular legionary troops, was worse. Their pay was even lower and they were subject to a disciplinary regime which including scourgings, from which Roman citizens enjoyed immunity. Many discharged allied soldiers, both Latin and non-Latin speaking, joined the drift to Rome, where they had to compete for jobs with each other and with freed slaves, some of whom were a lot better off financially.

From such elements was to evolve the fabled Roman 'mob', despised by so many comfortable historians for its later reliance on 'bread and circuses',[19] but which was composed not merely of the idle and improvident, who are to be found in all big cities, but of much greater numbers of betrayed old soldiers and other victims of circumstance and exploitation. To lump them all together as an undifferentiated mob is to swallow the oligarchy's line. The first serious attempts from within the aristocracy to alleviate these social evils failed because outraged senators resorted to mass murder to safeguard their vested interests. They would have murdered Octavian, too, for much the same reasons – just as some of them had murdered Caesar – if the young man had not been watched over night and day by armed bodyguards.

TWO

ROMAN MURDERS ROMAN

The man from whom Julius Caesar and the other *populares* derived their earliest inspiration was an ex-army officer whose main concern was the growing shortage of suitable recruits for the legions. Tiberius Sempronius Gracchus had fought in Spain; and on his way back to Rome, as he passed through rural Italy, he had been shocked to see the changes in the countryside due to the mass importation of foreign slaves. Instead of the myriad small farms that used to sustain the peasants and their families, he saw huge new estates run for commercial profit that had swallowed up so many ancestral crofts. Gracchus reasoned that if some way could be found to get the displaced peasants back to farming, on land of their own, they would be in a position to start repopulating the countryside with free citizens of sufficient means to be eligible for military service.[1]

The state owned vast tracts of so-called 'public land' in various parts of Italy, from expropriations in earlier wars. Gracchus, as tribune in 133 BC, proposed to reallocate many small parcels of this land to discharged veterans and other suitable recipients, but the Senate rejected his plan by a big majority. A significant proportion of the 300 senators were from families who had taken the lion's share of the designated land years before – often far more than their legal entitlement – and they had no intention of giving it back. Gracchus provoked a constitutional crisis by withdrawing his bill from the Senate and putting it directly before a People's Assembly. His action was not illegal, but it broke a centuries-old custom. The Senate majority, indignant at his trespassing on what they considered to be as much their political as their geographical territory, instructed another of the ten tribunes to veto his land bill.

The name of the senators' compliant tribune was Marcus Octavius, whom Plutarch says was an ancestor of Octavian[2] (but that is by no means certain). His intervention had such serious consequences that it is plausible to date the beginning of the downfall of the Roman Republic to Gracchus's response to it. What happened was unprecedented and deeply provocative. Gracchus persuaded the Assembly to vote Octavius out of office and then to pass the land bill into law when he could no longer veto it.[3] The issue now was not merely one of agrarian reform but of who ruled Rome. Gracchus had shown that a tribune like himself, working directly through a popular assembly, might bypass both the Senate and the consuls and apparently presume to rule Rome in their stead.

Behind the scenes, moves were afoot to prosecute Gracchus as soon as his year of office ended. To thwart them, he decided to break with tradition again by standing for re-election; and because he feared assassination he went around in the middle of a big crowd of his supporters. An inflamed meeting of the Senate failed to persuade the presiding consul of the need to use force to prevent what they claimed to be an attempted revolutionary takeover of the state by the mob. So the chief priest of the Republic, Scipio Nasica, who bore the ancient title of *Pontifex Maximus* – which is today held by the Pope – led other hard-line senators in a mass walk-out. They armed their waiting followers with wooden staves and clubbed Gracchus to death, along with dozens of his supporters.[4]

Nobody was arrested for these blatant murders. The Senate allowed the Gracchan land law to continue to take effect for a while, because the men with clubs were anxious to demonstrate that they were not challenging the People's right to legislate. To cloak the massacre in legality they held a show trial of surviving Gracchan supporters, convicted them of conspiracy against the Republic and executed them. The *Pontifex Maximus* sat on the jury. Peace was restored, but Rome would never be the same again. It was reputedly the first time in the history of the Republic that men had been killed in an internal political dispute.[5] It would not be the last. Many others, including Octavian, would see to that.

Ten years after the death of Tiberius Gracchus, his younger brother Gaius became a tribune and began to put populist laws through the People's Assembly in cool defiance of the Senate. He lost popularity, however, over his plans to extend Roman citizenship to some of the Italian allies, and he organized an armed group for his protection. That simply gave the Senate an excuse to kill him. A consul led troops against the 'rebels', and Gaius was among an estimated 3,000 who were slaughtered in the one-sided battle, and their bodies thrown in the Tiber.[6]

The Senate thus showed who really ruled Rome when the gloves were off – and it was not the People, it was whoever controlled the army. Octavian was to absorb that lesson under the tutelage of Julius Caesar, who had learnt it in his childhood. We first encounter Caesar in the historical record as a teenage fugitive, racked with fever, in fear for his life, hiding out with whoever can be found to shelter him, trying never to sleep in the same place twice. He had done nothing wrong. He simply found himself on the wrong side of a vicious civil war, some half a century after the death of Tiberius Gracchus, for no better reason than that he was related to opponents of the senatorial dictator Cornelius Sulla. It was Sulla who controlled the army, and it was Sulla's troops who now tracked young Caesar down and arrested him.

An indication of Sulla's character and temperament is revealed by his behaviour at a meeting of the rump of the Senate after his initial purge of its ranks. He had called the meeting at the Temple of Bellona, the Roman goddess of war, where there was a conveniently large open space outside. His troops led 6,000 manacled prisoners of war into this square in long, shuffling lines. As he began to address the Senate, with the doors of the temple open, the soldiers started to kill the prisoners outside. Sulla, who was noted for his graveyard humour, paused theatrically. 'Don't take any notice of them,' he said, acknowledging with a gesture that it was he who had given orders for the slaughter, 'just pay attention to what I have to say.'[7] The screams and groans of the dying, mingled with the vain cries for mercy of those awaiting their turn, continued to ring in the senators' ears while the dictator calmly outlined his policy and proposals until all 6,000 prisoners were dead.

Such was the nature of the person into whose hands Caesar had now fallen. Fortunately, the young man had influential relatives and friends who pleaded for his life, as he had not actually taken up arms against Sulla. Even the Vestal Virgins,[8] guardians of the sacred flame whose perpetual burning in their hearth was supposed to be linked in some way with the continued existence of Rome, joined the chorus of protest on his behalf. Brought before the dictator, Caesar was ordered to divorce his wife, Cornelia. He refused. It was a quixotic response, but it paid off. Sulla had almost run out of adversaries to kill, and he presumably no longer feared for his own safety. As a patrician himself, he perhaps approved of Caesar's refusal to compromise his *dignitas* by such a craven action. But he warned the young man's supporters: 'All right, have it your way – provided you understand that one day he'll destroy the optimate party we have worked for so hard and defended so long.'[9]

Sulla had come to power in the aftermath of a war precipitated by the murder of a tribune who, ironically, generally supported the *optimates*, Marcus Livius Drusus (adoptive grandfather of Livia, future wife of Octavian). Drusus, however, disgreed with them on the citizenship issue: when he tried to make Roman citizens of their chief Italian allies – who supplied essential manpower to the legions – he was stabbed to death in broad daylight among a crowd of witnesses, but nobody was ever prosecuted for the crime.[10] The resentful allies, who were already on the brink of rebellion, responded by declaring war in the name of a new Union of Italia.

The arrogance of the Roman aristocracy towards the Italians is well illustrated in an account preserved by the historian Aulus Gellius of the gist of a speech which Gaius Gracchus made just before his death. The wife of a consul, who was visiting the small town of Teanum Sidicinum, wanted to have a bath (Gracchus said), so everyone was turned out of the local men's bath-house. Afterwards, the wife complained to her husband that the baths had not been cleared quickly enough, and, in any case, were dirty. A town magistrate, who had been ordered to see to the task, was tied to a post in his own market square, stripped and publicly flogged. Later, at Ferentium, a Roman praetor ordered the arrest of two local magistrates for a similar reason. One threw himself to his death off the town wall to escape the humiliation. His suicide had no effect on the decision of the praetor, who went ahead and had the surviving magistrate flogged.[11]

Apart from an enlightened minority, the Senate and People of Rome seem to have been united in resisting extension of the citizenship. The bloody struggle with the allies is conventionally known to historians as the Social War (91–88 BC),[12] but it was in reality the first of the series of civil wars that would ultimately lead to the collapse of the Republic and the emergence of Octavian as ruler of the Roman Empire. The blinkered oligarchs held out for about two years, while thousands of Rome's and Italy's men died pointlessly on obscure battlefields and their wives and children starved through the ruin of harvests. Eventually the Senate agreed to offer citizenship to any of its former allies who would would agree to lay down their arms. Most did so, but by that time the empire was under serious attack from outside. Mithridates, ruler of the Black Sea kingdom of Pontus, had taken advantage of Rome's folly by invading the rich province of Asia (not the continent, but an area which today comprises part of north-western Turkey) and massacring thousands of Roman colonists. It was imperative to send a strong army under an able general to drive Mithridates out.

The Senate appointed Sulla, who had proved his capacity in the Social War. But the Senate's reputation had been severely dented by the fiasco of that conflict, and the people allowed themselves to be persuaded to dismiss Sulla and appoint Caesar's uncle, the elderly *popularis* general Marius, in his place. Sulla told his troops that if they continued to serve under him he would make them rich from the booty of the East, whereas Marius would leave them behind so that the spoils of war would go to his own favoured legions. Sulla thus became the first Roman general to bribe his soldiers to be loyal to him rather than to the Republic. It was a defining moment. All his officers but one deserted him, while the men clamoured for him to lead them, which he did. He led them straight from their camp into the streets of the city, where they killed any who resisted them, set fire to some of the buildings and stole whatever they could conveniently lay their hands on.[13]

Sulla avenged the insult to his honour by killing scores of his political opponents before he and his maverick army marched off to terrorize the East,[14] having demonstrated that Rome was at the mercy of a general with a big enough army dependent on him for its pay. Marius, who had fled the city just in time, proved Sulla's point some months later. After many adventures – including being dragged naked from a swamp by a search party, whom he then frightened by the sheer force of his personality[15] – Marius linked up with another legionary group, led by a *popularis* politician, Cornelius Cinna (soon to become Caesar's father-in-law), recaptured Rome in Sulla's absence and slaughtered his optimate enemies in his turn. Marius died soon afterwards, however, and control passed to Cinna.

Sulla returned home in 83 BC, after five years in the East, at the head of about 25,000 prosperous and battle-hardened veterans, who immediately fought a new civil war for control of Rome. That was the moment when the 23-year-old Pompey (Pompeius Magnus) launched himself on a military career that would lead to his becoming the dominant figure in Roman politics for a period of nearly thirty years. He was already a magnate in the Picenum area, where he had inherited estates from his father (consul in 89 BC). He raised the countryside to revolt, recruited three legions to support Sulla, and thus turned the tide of war. There were now eight legions in the field under this bizarrely assorted pair – Sulla, still with his distinctive yellow hair at the age of fifty-five, his blotchy red face and penetrating blue eyes, and, by contrast, the athletic Pompey, admired for his statuesque good looks and swept-back wavy hair as well as for his precocious military ability.[16]

The city of Rome changed hands once more. Sulla enforced his own appointment as dictator, with powers over life, liberty and property equal to those of any former king. He determined to wipe out, once and for all, the remaining *populares* among the aristocracy, and inaugurated a reign of terror on a scale never before experienced in the sprawling city. Each day in the Forum he posted up lists of names of those of his many opponents he had thus far failed to find and kill.[17] The methodology of those 'proscriptions' was to be copied by Mark Antony and Octavian some thirty-eight years later. Cash rewards were offered to any who tracked down the victims and brought back their heads.

Sulla's long-term plan was to restore the Republic, but in a carefully revised version, that would curb the power of the tribunes and make it impossible for any magistrate to place legislation before a People's Assembly without the prior consent of the Senate. Victims of the proscriptions, whether dead or still on the run, were deprived of all their property; and their sons and grandsons (even if yet unborn) were forbidden ever to stand for public office. Sulla settled his veterans on the land thus seized, and had the surplus auctioned at knock-down prices to his leading henchmen. It was among those disinherited grandsons, bearing ancient names, that Octavian was to find some of his early supporters.

To emphasize his unyielding optimate credentials, Sulla abolished Marius's and Cinna's dole of subsidized grain to the citizens, in spite of the food shortages caused by the civil war. Finally he appointed several hundred of his own supporters to the Senate, whose ranks had been depleted by the death and exile of the *populares*. It was Cicero's view, expressed later, that the activities of the Gracchan brothers, rather than those of Sulla, had divided the People of Rome into two parts. On one side were the *populares*, unprincipled politicians who, through overweening ambition and lust for power, pandered to the mob. On the other side were the *boni* ('the good'), all those with a real stake in society, like the great majority of senators and knights and other property owners. The interests of the *boni* were cared for at the political level by the *optimates* ('the best'), who, according to Cicero, included all those who were not actually criminals or financially embarrassed or 'perverse by nature'.[18]

There is a scintilla of truth in what Cicero says, but it is very far from being the whole truth. It ignores the obvious explanation that the *populares* reflected the views of the great majority of the voters, and that some of them, at least, were prepared to risk senatorial hostility by their active support of those views. We must be on our guard, however, against supposing that the descriptive terms of *optimates* and *populares* bear any relation to political parties in the modern sense. The *populares*, as a minority of individuals among the aristocracy, would have been utterly bewildered if anyone had suggested they ought to campaign electorally for a majority in the Senate.

The *optimates* had a cause for which many of them ultimately died. So did the *populares*. It has been a common misreading of Roman history in the last century of the Republic to suppose that their political struggles were not underpinned, on both sides, by opposing political values as well as by personal ambition. The aristocratic *populares* were not democrats by any definition that would be acceptable today, but in terms of ancient Rome they were much more democratic than the *optimates*, who can scarcely be held to have had any democratic sympathies at all. The *populares*, judged by their actions, stood for the principle that all citizens were entitled to have at least some share in the prosperity that the growth of empire had brought, especially if they had fought for it in the ranks of the legions.

They did not set this out as a specific policy pledge in an election manifesto – there was no such thing in Rome as a general election. What they did assert, time and again, by their actions if not by a formula of words, was the sovereign right of a properly constituted Assembly of the People to decide, with the force of law, any matter brought before it by a competent elected magistrate or tribune, without needing either the prior consent of the Senate or its ratification afterwards. That was fully in accordance with reforms of constitutional law that a much earlier generation of plebeians had won without any recourse to bloodshed.[19] When the *optimates* accused the *populares* of trying to subvert the Republic by appealing to 'the mob' (in this case, the voters) over the heads of the Senate, they were tacitly acknowledging that most citizens opposed them.

It is beyond dispute that ordinary citizens of modest means, as well as the poor and indigent, had good reason to support the *populares* against the ruling oligarchy on specific issues. Not all of them, to be sure, would want to be allocated a distant farm to labour on from dawn to dusk, but they voted *en masse* for cheaper food whenever they were given the chance. The *optimates*, in most but not all recorded instances, opposed land reforms and hand-outs for the poor. As we have seen, they also bitterly opposed tribunes who tried to bypass the Senate, and in the last resort were ready to kill out of hand any who persisted.

Sulla's constitutional changes did not last. Only eight years after his death, Pompey linked up temporarily with Marcus Licinius Crassus, who had also been one of Sulla's subordinate generals; together, as consuls in 70 BC, they repealed much of Sulla's reform package, most significantly his curbs on the power of tribunes.[20] Their underlying motive was to give themselves scope to pursue more active public careers, because the *optimates* had tried to prevent either of them becoming too powerful. Crassus, a patrician, was the wealthiest man in Rome, notorious for saying that nobody could count himself rich unless he could support a legion out of his income. Bankers, businessmen and tax-collectors among the knights looked to him for support in the Senate.

His alliance with Pompey blew hot and cold because he was envious of Pompey's higher reputation, and he was quietly subsidizing with hard cash the unconventional career steps of Caesar, whom he had spotted early on as a natural ally of outstanding political gifts. Pompey followed in Sulla's footsteps by gaining a special military command in the East, where Roman control was once more being threatened. It was during his absence that Octavian was born – and Catiline's revolt broke out. Catiline can scarcely be claimed as a martyr of the populist cause. He was a bankrupt politician who had hoped to restore his wealth by exploiting genuine popular resentments; but he managed to raise the equivalent of two legions to support him, and might well have raised more if Cicero had not been so prompt and ruthless in quashing his rebellion – even to the extent of personally supervising the strangulation of five of his leading henchmen 'in the filth, stench and gloom' of an underground dungeon.[21]

After Catiline's death in battle, Pompey returned from his spectacularly successful punitive expedition to the East, having more than doubled the total revenues flowing into the Treasury at Rome by reorganizing the taxation system in various provinces and finding new places and people to tax. He did not imagine that the Senate would do other than fête him as a national hero and accord him the level of primacy in public respect that his military and diplomatic achievements genuinely deserved. So, exactly as a good Roman should, he disbanded his army and entered the city as a civilian. He had reckoned without the resentment and jealousy of the leading group of *optimates*. Before his return they had been afraid he would enter as a conqueror and dictate his own terms. Relieved of that fear, they reverted to type. They could not refuse him a triumph without risking a public backlash, but when Pompey confidently asked the Senate to settle his veterans on good land and ratify the treaties he had signed, the *optimates* insisted on scrutinizing and debating all his arrangements in insulting detail before rejecting them.

Too late, Pompey saw that they cared nothing for his outstanding exploits and services to Rome. Their overriding concern, as always, was protection of their inherited status. Unlike Caesar, Pompey was not an outsider by choice, but he craved aristocratic acceptance. Even his name was against him, however, as it betrayed his non-Latin origins. He had thought he was impressing his fellow-senators by his bravery and generalship in enlarging the empire, and by channelling such huge sums into the state's coffers instead of taking more of it for himself, as so many of them would have done. But in their view he had obtained his special command in the East by truckling to the 'mob', and their aim was to stop him ever getting such a command again. Far from treating him with respect they were hoping to destroy his reputation with his troops by demonstrating that he was incapable of winning for them the land and gratuities he had promised.

Caesar saw his chance. He came to Pompey with a pledge and a proposal that he knew would cripple the republican system if it were to be successfully implemented. He effectively guaranteed to satisfy his legitimate demands if Pompey, with his veterans, would join Crassus, with his untold millions, to back Caesar as consul. Two elements would be needed for success: command of the streets and money for big enough bribes. Caesar was duly elected consul for the momentous year 59, which ushered in a period of unconstitutional dominance over the state, known to history as the First Triumvirate.[22] Under their secret deal, Pompey and Crassus would get the legislation they wanted, while Caesar's reward would be social measures (partly to keep the plebs on his side) and, at the end of the year, an extended proconsular command so that he could avoid prosecution by the *optimates*. The three would continue to support each other indefinitely afterwards so that their legislation could not be repealed.

It was a formula that could not be fitted inside the republican system of annual magistrates. It relied on violence, intimidation and corruption, the very weapons that had long been in the oligarchy's armoury. When used by the *optimates* they were excused on the grounds of necessity, if without them the republic might falter. That was the true meaning of the Senate's weapon of the non-specific resolution of *Senatus consultum ultimum*, which had originally been devised to defeat Gaius Gracchus. It was the equivalent of 'Anything goes!' The senators, for obvious reasons, drew back from acknowledging publicly that the effect of such a resolution was to clear the way for the consuls and other magistrates to kill as many citizens as necessary to ensure that the traditional aristocracy remained in power. This time the *populares* would be ready for them with a much bigger mob than the *optimates* could quickly muster.

Apart from their specific short-term political goals, each of the triumvirs ultimately wanted to be the most important person in the state. There was no possibility, therefore, of a triumvirate becoming a permanent form of government. At the start, their relative pecking order in terms of status placed Pompey ahead of Crassus, with a bigger gap down to Caesar, who at various times had been merely a junior associate of each of them. It was Caesar, however, who was taking the greatest risks in their joint venture; as it turned out, he was also the one who was to gain the most. Neither of the two ex-consuls were risking anything worse than failure to achieve immediate political goals. Caesar, like earlier *populares*, was endangering both his career and his life – although nobody would have guessed it from his confident demeanour. He relished a fight for big enough stakes.

Unlike Marius and Sulla, none of the three triumvirs showed much inclination to kill off any of their fellow-aristocrats. You don't prove you are a better man than your neighbour by having him strangled in prison. You prove it, if you are Pompey or Crassus or Caesar, by leading Roman armies to victory, in the glorious tradition of your ancestors, and by coming home afterwards loaded down with treasure and buoyed up by fame, and parading through the streets of the greatest city in the world, among crowds of your former rivals cheering themselves hoarse, however envious some of them may feel – perhaps the more envious they are, the better. It was the combined efforts of their optimate opponents to stop any of them achieving these ambitions that ultimately led to a situation where, for Caesar – and for Octavian after him – it became a question of kill or be killed.

The first public indication of the true weight of Caesar's attack on the republican system was the appearance of Pompey and Crassus side by side with him on the rostra[23] in the Forum before a huge crowd of their supporters. Now the secret of empire stood revealed: when the three most powerful men in Rome joined forces to defy the Senate, nobody was able to stop them doing what they wanted – except each other. They had agreed to a self-denying ordinance that none of the three would do anything that either of the other two opposed. Led by Caesar as the operational head of state, and backed by most of the city's tribunes and Pompey's ex-soldiers, the trio were able to legalize their wishes via the massive support of the People voting in their Assembly. Bibulus, the other consul for that year, proved unable to prevent their effective *coup d'état*.[24]

The cohesion of the triumvirate was strengthened by

Pompey's marriage to Caesar's daughter, Julia. At that time Octavian was nearly four years old. Although there is no surviving record of his meeting Pompey, he must certainly have done so, because one of the basic purposes of this dynastic marriage was to bring the two families closer together. We can be sure, therefore, that Octavian attended the wedding along with his mother Atia, who would have been well aware of the political importance of the union. If Julia were to provide Caesar with grandsons (Pompey already had three sons from an earlier marriage), Octavian would naturally become relatively less significant in Caesar's eyes. Given the fact that Pompey was to remain the most powerful man in Rome for some years to come, Atia would have lost no opportunity to keep her son in fairly regular contact with him and Julia.

At the end of Caesar's year of office, he passed from the consulship to being appointed governor for five years of three linked provinces,[25] including the whole of northern Italy (known as Cisalpine Gaul) beyond the Rubicon, and commander of four legions, to which he rapidly added another two by recruitment. Those legions dominated the entire Italian peninsula. The Senate could not build up a countervailing force except by internal recruitment or by shipping in troops from abroad. Neither of those options would be open to it so long as the triumvirs controlled the Roman streets and retained the support of the assemblies through the tribunes. Caesar could, in theory, march at least part of his new army to Rome in a week or two. That time would come. But Caesar's eyes were turned to the north-west. For the next nine years he would be devoted to winning for himself imperishable glory to rival that of Alexander.

THREE

THE BOY WHO MISSED THE WAR

Octavian's father died while Caesar was still consul. It was a heavy blow for the family in political as well as personal terms. Thanks to Caesar's effective control of the levers of power, in partnership with Pompey and Crassus, it had become virtually certain that Gaius Octavius senior would himself have ascended to the consulship. That would have turned Octavian into a member of the nobility, on the definition of one who was a direct descendant of a man who had served as consul. The four-year-old boy would now have to wait for Caesar to confer that honour on him by means of adoption into the Julian clan.

Octavian had probably seen little of his father during his short life. It is evident that he spent most of his early childhood at the family home in Velitrae, where a century later local people took pride in pointing out to respectful visitors the small room that had been his nursery.[1] Some even claimed that Octavian had actually been born there, but that was presumably no more than an attempt to increase the importance of Velitrae and themselves. His father, as praetor in 62, would have spent that year in Rome, perhaps escaping from the city for a week or two in summer to be at home with his family. After his praetorship, he served a year as Governor of Macedonia, acquitting himself sufficiently well to attract the praise of so severe a judge as Cicero. Although it is possible that he took Octavian to Macedonia with him, it is more likely he would have left him at Velitrae in the care of a nursemaid, if only for the sake of the child's health, which was a frequent cause of concern.

Atia did not remain a widow for too long. In view of her uncle Julius's sudden rise to prominence she had become a valuable pawn in the marriage market, through which the aristocracy forged alliances. Certainly nobody could have wed her without Caesar's approval, and there were no doubt many ambitious candidates who were disappointed. The choice ultimately fell on Lucius Marcius Philippus, the wealthy and well-connected son of the consul (of the same name) of 91, who had distinguished himself in the Social War against the former Italian allies. Philippus had a foot in both camps. His daughter Marcia, by an earlier marriage, was the wife of Marcus Porcius Cato,[2] who was Caesar's most determined opponent among the *optimates*. At the same time Philippus managed to be friends with both Caesar and Pompey, to such good effect that he was consul-designate for 56 at the time when he married Atia, after his return to Rome from a year as governor of the frontier province of Syria.

Philippus had the reputation of being a genial and sociable man; he may well have been Atia's own choice among the suitors, even though he was significantly older than the bride. It is hard to imagine Cato's father-in-law as Caesar's first choice for his niece, but he would have been content that the alliance would probably keep both her and her son safe in the event of serious civil strife. There are no reports of any problems within the family as a result of Philippus's arrival, and it is known that he got on well with his stepson when Octavian grew to be a teenager.

By the time Caesar's five-year command was due to expire, the centre of Rome was becoming a dangerous place for law-abiding citizens, thanks to a breakdown in law and order under triumviral rule. Caesar had already brought most of Gaul under Roman domination, having doubled his original four legions to eight, but he needed more time to complete and consolidate his remarkable conquests. He also planned to launch an invasion of a mysterious island in the remote north, which many people in Rome refused to believe existed.

Caesar, however, had gazed across the Channel at Britain's white cliffs and had questioned some of its warriors when they visited Gaul. He knew it existed, and, with characteristic arrogance, he wanted to add it to his trophies of war.

Caesar could not return to Rome without violating the terms of his Gallic command,[3] so he halted on his way south at the Tuscan city of Luca, where Pompey and Crassus met him. They were accompanied by 120 senators and their entourages, who had journeyed from Rome to lend their support and hope for favourable notice, so rapidly had the republican system degenerated.[4] Caesar, of course, wanted his command extended for a further five years – he could not guess how long it would take him and his legions to subdue Britain. In return, he agreed that his two colleagues should each be given commands of comparable authority.

Pompey and Crassus were voted in as consuls for the year 55. Nobody could stop them arranging extensive generalships for themselves, Pompey in Spain and Crassus in Syria. One of the triumvirs, however, had to stay behind to protect the interests of the other two. It could not be Caesar. Crassus was determined to fulfil his long-term ambition to invade Parthia, beyond the Euphrates. So Pompey was left to make sure the centre would hold. Under republican law, as a proconsular general he could not stay in the city itself.[5] So he moved outside the city walls, appointed subordinate generals to go to Spain on his behalf, and used his new home to hold court to visiting senators. Can there ever have been a time in history when such a vast empire was ruled in such a bizarre way? None of the three triumvirs could legally enter their capital city, which was supposedly the seat of government; two of them would invade countries at opposite ends of their 'world' with large armies but only the vaguest idea of the dangers they would face;[6] while the third would stay behind as a general whose army was a month's march away.

Such hubris invited nemesis. It was to come in ample measure to all three, though to Caesar last of all. His luck, for the moment, continued to hold, even though his two invasions of Britain risked the loss of all Gaul along with himself and his men. The first turned out to be no more than a reconnaissance; the second, more carefully planned, nearly ended in disaster when his anchored fleet was destroyed in a storm, leaving him no means of retreat in the face of thousands of angry warriors. With great professionalism he built new ships and fought the natives to a standstill, sailing back to Gaul with hostages and a promise, never honoured, of regular British payments to Rome.[7]

The triumvirate as such came to a sudden end when Crassus lost three-quarters of his army and his own life at Carrhae in Mesopotamia (modern Iraq), in a vainglorious attempt to conquer the Parthians, who were Rome's most powerful neighbours, controlling an empire of their own that stretched as far as India. His quaestor, Gaius Cassius Longinus (the Cassius who was later to assassinate Caesar), made it back to Syria with a remnant of the army, which he regrouped to such effect that he beat off a follow-up assault by the Parthians. At Rome, fate struck another blow at the crumbling regime. Caesar's daughter Julia, who had married Pompey in 60, died in childbirth in September 54. He offered the 52-year-old Pompey an even younger female relative as a prospective wife, Octavia,[8] daughter of Atia and sister of Octavian. Such a match would have made Octavian, then aged nine, Pompey's brother-in-law.

The problem with Caesar's offer was that Octavia was already married to someone else. Her husband was Gaius Claudius Marcellus, a rising optimate senator with powerful connections.[9] It is only too plain that Caesar was more concerned to keep Pompey as a relative by marriage than he was to avoid offending Marcellus. Pompey wisely turned down the offer. The Senate tried to widen the split by appointing Pompey as sole consul to restore order in the city; Caesar was now the paymaster behind some of those responsible for the violence and corruption[10] – and his hold on Gaul was currently being threatened by a mass uprising led by the paramount chief Vercingetorix.[11]

It was not until the summer of 51 that Caesar was finally able to defeat the Gallic hero and pacify more than forty tribes which had rallied to his banner. By then the relationship between Caesar and Pompey, who had married into the patrician Cornelian clan, was deteriorating fast. With general support in the Senate, Pompey had been passing new electoral laws to tighten up procedures without specifically exempting Caesar, who would not now be able to win a second term as consul in Rome until after his Gallic command lapsed. The *optimates* were making plans to destroy him in their courts during the interval when he would be out of office.[12]

Throughout his years in Gaul, Caesar had been careful to ensure that his agents maintained regular contact with his many 'clients' in the Italian peninsula, who included not just locally important individuals but whole towns.[13] He also sent written despatches to the capital, which were made available to ordinary citizens through public readings – and they had sent his reputation soaring. Octavian is bound to have read those texts – like so many other schoolboys since – probably under the guidance of his tutors. He was plainly well advanced in both reading and rhetoric at the age of about twelve when he was chosen to give the funeral address for his grandmother, Caesar's sister, in the Forum.

That would have been his first public appearance before a large audience in the capital he would one day make his own. Such occasions were carefully stage-managed, with retainers of the deceased person wearing the masks (taken in life or death) of family ancestors.[14] We do not know exactly what Octavian said about his great-uncle's sister, but we may be certain that, in addition to the usual Julian family propaganda about their supposed royal and divine ancestry, he would have referred in glowing terms to the exploits of her brother in conquering Gaul and invading Britain.

Caesar himself, unable to return to Rome for the funeral,

was far from idle. He doubled the pay of his troops to tie them more firmly than ever to his side, sent rich gifts to kings and other influential personages around the empire, and began lavish building projects in Rome and other Italian cities, which provided jobs for his supporters among the free workers. He sent his chief lieutenant Mark Antony to stand for the tribunate; once elected, Antony teamed up with Gaius Curio, a gifted orator who had turned against Pompey, and together they protected Caesar's interests by use of the veto and by diplomacy.

Eventually, Caesar offered fresh terms to his enemies in the Senate: he was prepared, he announced, to lay down his command if Pompey, too, would give up his army. When Curio put the proposal to the Senate in December 50 the voting was 370 in favour of Caesar's suggested compromise and only twenty-two against. It demonstrated the almost universal desire for a peaceful settlement and the humiliating lack of support for the die-hard *optimates*. But the minority of twenty-two refused to accept the Senate's verdict.[15] It was, after all, only advice. It fatally lacked the force of law, because executive authority remained with the senior magistrates.

The day after the vote, two of them, bearing a symbolic sword, and accompanied by a crowd of supporters, called on Pompey. Octavia's husband, Gaius Claudius Marcellus, was the consul who was about to retire, and Lucius Cornelius Crus was the consul-designate who was to take his place. They had no mandate from either Senate or People. Marcellus placed the sword in Pompey's hand and told him it was his duty to defend Italy against possible invasion. The great general was unable to resist that dramatic gesture. The memory of how the *optimates* had treated him twelve years earlier evidently faded as they offered him supreme leadership. No doubt Marcellus, in handing over the sword, was also stirred by memory – of how Caesar had tried to steal his young wife Octavia to make a gift of her to Pompey.

The coterie surrounding Cato seem to have believed that

Caesar would back down when faced with *force majeure*. They knew he was encamped in winter quarters at Ravenna with only one legion, having left the other eight on the far side of the Alps. Pompey, with two legions in arms near Rome and huge reserves in Spain and Syria, had boasted he had only to stamp his foot on Italian soil for whole armies of infantry and cavalry to rise up to serve him. Cicero, however, knew that the extreme *optimates* lacked public support even in Rome itself, let alone in the traditional recruiting grounds of the Italian countryside. 'I have not found a single person who would prefer to fight rather than accept Caesar's demands,' he wrote to his friend Atticus on December 17.[16]

Caesar made a last attempt at compromise. He offered to give up two of his three provinces and, ultimately, all but one of his legions, if he could maintain his proconsular authority until the next consular elections. Pompey wavered, on the point of accepting, but Cato told him not to be taken in by Caesar's ploys. The opportunity passed. Caesar was not the man to stay where he was and hope that some of his Gallic legions got through to him in time; he resolved to take his chance against Pompey at once, relying on surprise and speed for a quick victory against the odds. A few miles north of Ariminum (Rimini), at the head of only 5,000 foot soldiers and 300 cavalry, he crossed the Rubicon river, marking the boundary of his province, and headed south. Those few would be enough, under Caesar, to shake the world.

Central Italy panicked. The roads filled with refugees as terrified townsfolk on Caesar's route spread out into the remote countryside. He sent messengers ahead to reassure the people that neither they nor their homes were in danger. Word quickly spread that the invading soldiers were behaving themselves. Throughout the region, the walled towns opened their gates, and their garrisons joined his army. Even Corfinium, packed with Pompeian troops, surrendered without a fight. His clemency to their commander, Cato's son-in-law Domitius Ahenobarbus, who had intrigued to take over the Gallic command, helped to turn opinion in his favour. The general panic subsided and people returned to their homes.[17]

It was at Corfinium that Caesar heard news that astonished him. Pompey had decided not to defend Italy but to cross to Macedonia with all his soldiers and most of the senators.[18] His grand strategy, it transpired, was to assemble the legions of the East and return to Rome at the head of an overwhelming invasion force; it would form part of a giant pincer movement, completed by the simultaneous arrival of his legions from Spain. As a long-term plan it made sense – to Pompey, if not to the baffled *optimates* who had appointed him to lead them. To replace him at that stage, however, would be to hand victory to Caesar on a plate. They could only grit their teeth and follow their leader wherever he might choose to go, abandoning their homes and families to the mercy of the conqueror of Gaul.

Without fighting a battle, Caesar had become master of Italy,[19] but unless he continued to move at exemplary speed he might not remain master for long. He marched to Rome, summoned the Senate and broke open the Treasury which Pompey had unaccountably left intact. Philippus would surely have attended the crucial meeting of the senatorial rump on 1 April, because Caesar needed as many senators as he could find to confer some degree of legal authority on him. Nothing would have been better for his public image than to appear in the capital with members of his family beside him, especially the boy Octavian. Whether Octavia's husband Marcellus was present among the family group is not known. He was certainly still in or near Rome, having refused to follow the other *optimates* abroad. Pompey and his lieutenants were contemptuous of the man who was the first to raise a sword against Caesar and then left them to wield it without him. Caesar evidently forgave Marcellus, but the dishonour, in Roman eyes, would have been indelible.

The following year, having built a fleet, taken over the

Spanish legions and ferried part of his army across the Adriatic, Caesar defeated the combined might of Pompey's forces on the plain of Pharsala in Greece, even though outnumbered two to one.[20] Surveying the piles of bodies, he exclaimed bitterly, 'They brought it on themselves. They would have condemned me to death. Me! Gaius Caesar!'[21] He was particularly upset to think that Marcus Brutus, son of his former mistress Servilia[22] (Cato's half-sister), might be among the Pompeian dead. He formed a search party which eventually found the young man alive. Caesar, embracing him, could not have guessed he was looking into the eyes of his future assassin.

Back in Rome, meanwhile, Octavian became officially a man. He did this through a ceremony shortly after his fifteenth birthday, a year or so earlier than was then usual, by ritually removing the *toga praetexta* of childhood and putting on the *toga virilis*. An obviously made-up story survives that when donning the toga of manhood the garment came apart at the seams and fell around his ankles. Octavian is supposed to have turned this potentially ominous sign to his advantage by declaring that, in future, he would have all the *dignitas* of the Senate at his feet.[23] The story is significant for showing the myth-making process at work, as a flatterer tries to make the future Augustus look preternaturally assured as an adolescent, but succeeds only in casting him unjustly as an insufferable prig.

A more entertaining example comes from a surviving fragment of a lost biography of Augustus by Herod the Great's secretary, Nicolaus of Damascus,[24] commenting on Octavian's appointment at about this period to the priestly college of *pontifices*, to fill the vacancy caused by the death at Pharsala of Ahenobarbus. According to Nicolaus, the 'handsome' Octavian was obliged to carry out his sacerdotal duties after dusk because of the number of swooning society ladies whose presence might otherwise have compromised his chastity. If we may judge by a bust in the Vatican Museum, showing him as an adolescent, the blond Octavian did appear to have had natural good looks, with well-proportioned features, and cheeks so smooth and rounded as to be almost girlish, yet displaying the quiet *gravitas* of an ideal (or idealized) Roman patrician.

Although in a highly favoured position on the Caesarian side, Octavian was by no means the most obvious choice as Caesar's principal heir. The dictator's elder sister, also named Julia, had two grandsons who were just as close to him in blood. Both were older than Octavian. One of them, Quintus Pedius, was actually serving as praetor in Rome in 48 and may well have been present as a distinguished family guest when the boy put on the *toga virilis* that year. To most observers at that time he would have seemed to be the leading contender if Caesar was, in truth, aiming at a dynastic succession. The other grandson of the elder Julia, Lucius Pinarius, appears never to have attracted more than a passing interest on the part of his great-uncle.

The major reason for Caesar's delay in returning to Rome was his unexpectedly serious involvement in the internal affairs of Egypt, after he met Cleopatra.[25] It was his pursuit of Pompey that led him to the Nile. Earlier, Caesar's old rival had arrived off the Egyptian coast near Pelusium, hoping for help from Cleopatra's brother, the boy pharaoh Ptolemy, whose father's claim to the throne he had supported. Instead, Ptolemy's advisers lured him ashore, cut off his head, pickled it and presented it to Caesar, who turned away in disgust at the sight, later bursting into tears when given Pompey's signet ring, which showed a lion with a sword in its paws.[26]

Determined to make the Egyptians pay for the murder of his former son-in-law, Caesar took advantage of the civil war then raging between the boy king and his sister by sending secretly for Cleopatra. She was about nineteen or twenty years of age, and although not perhaps as beautiful as Shakespeare makes out, she was unquestionably alluring and vivacious – and unafraid to use her sexuality to get her way. To enter the palace past the Egyptian guards she wrapped herself inside a sort of sleeping bag made of carpeting material, and was literally unrolled before Caesar by a muscular Sicilian, Apollodorus, who had carried her in. Caesar was charmed, and quickly captivated by her daring and her sharp intelligence. He resolved to support her claim to the throne.[27]

After being besieged in the palace for several months while awaiting reinforcements, Caesar killed the pharaoh in battle, and made Cleopatra queen. Later she was to give birth to a son, Ptolemy Caesar, popularly known as Caesarion ('little Caesar'). He grew to manhood in time to be put to death by Octavian, who, however, spared all her other children. Doubts have been expressed by some modern scholars over whether Caesarion was in truth Caesar's son. Few seem to have doubted it at the time. She and the boy went to live in Rome while Octavian was a teenager, holding court at a sumptuous villa on the far side of the Tiber from the walled city. Whether they met at that time is not known.

When he eventually got back to Rome in the autumn of 47, Caesar sent for Octavian to join his staff for a fresh expedition, this time to retake the province of Africa (Tunisia) where the indefatigable Cato had managed to assemble ten legions. The boy's mother vetoed the move, saying that, at only sixteen years of age, he was not yet old enough. Octavian's disappointment must have been intense, but he obeyed his mother and stayed at home, with Caesar's reluctant acquiescence. Some compensation came when Caesar returned again in July 46 after routing the die-hard *optimates* at Thapsos. He presented military honours to Octavian for the Africa campaign even though the boy had never been there, and later allowed him to ride in his chariot during the triumphal procession. The celebrations went on for days, and culminated in a torchlight ascent to the Capitol at dusk between forty elephants, arranged in two rows as torch-bearers.[28]

Caesar still could not turn his full attention to the long-term needs of Rome and her empire. Cato had committed suicide after Thapsos, but Pompey's sons, Gnaeus and

Sextus, had rallied the remaining dissidents and now held Spain. This time Caesar obtained Atia's consent to allow Octavian to accompany him among his entourage of staff officers, but almost on the eve of their planned departure the boy fell seriously ill. Caesar came to see him on his sick-bed and arranged for him to have the best medical attention available. He could not, however, wait for him to recover. Before the end of 46 he set out for Spain, urging the invalid to follow as soon as practicable.

Octavian was to have a number of apparently life-threatening illnesses in the course of his career, but it is not known for certain what they were. Rome was close to extensive swamps and wetlands, infested by mosquitoes, and malaria was endemic in the city and the surrounding countryside.[29] The malady that now prostrated Octavian was not quickly cured, but Caesar himself was held up by the stubborn resistance of the Pompeian brothers. It turned out to be his last military campaign, and he was lucky to survive it. He had taken the sort of risks that can perhaps best be explained by a combination of overconfidence and impatience to end the long civil war. Pompey's sons came so close to avenging their father that, for the first time in his life, Caesar seriously contemplated suicide to preserve his *dignitas*. He said afterwards that he had never before had to fight for his life as well as for victory.[30]

Meanwhile, Octavian had at last set out from Rome in the hope of joining him in the field, wherever that might happen to be. But his ship was wrecked in a storm, and the seventeen-year-old was washed up on a Mediterranean beach along with a few soldiers. He and his reduced escort managed to pass unscathed through territory still controlled by the enemy. Caesar was delighted at this evidence of his initiative and persistence, and congratulated him warmly.[31] By that time he had already defeated the main forces ranged against him at the decisive battle of Munda on 17 March 45. Gnaeus, the elder of the two Pompeian brothers, died a fugitive, but young Sextus Pompeius escaped to become a thorn in Octavian's flesh for years afterwards.

Talk on the winning side was now all of victory and going home, and of what needed to be done politically in Rome to consolidate the regime. Octavian was present at these discussions; and on the long road back to Italy that summer he shared Caesar's coach for some days, just the two of them together.[32] As it had become evident to all that Octavian was, at the very least, his most favoured political protégé, the conversation must have touched on the serious matters of state that now faced them. We may well imagine that Caesar was also testing his grasp of affairs with pertinent questions, seeking to confirm his earlier impression that the articulate youth would mature into a man worthy to succeed him in ruling Rome.

How far Caesar took him into his confidence we do not know. But it seems plain from the astonishing political maturity and skill displayed by Octavian in the first few months after Caesar's death, less than a year later, that he had been briefed in detail on the men he found himself dealing with at the age of only eighteen. It is true that the dictator's private office, staffed by his most trusted aides, survived the Ides of March and would be on hand to give Octavian excellent support, but they would not be his only advisers. One of the repeated features of his adult career would be his ability to weigh up conflicting opinions offered to him and rarely err in his choice of the course that had the best chance of success.

It was Octavian, certainly, who master-minded the creation of the new form of politics (which academic historians call the Principate, although posterity in general thinks of it as the Roman Empire), but he could scarcely have been in a position to achieve such a radical transformation if Caesar had not blazed a trail. The empire itself, as a geographical entity, was already largely in existence. What Octavian did, in addition to expanding it further, was to change the way it was centrally controlled, from a system of annually elected magistrates advised by a senate of former and current magistrates, to a system of one supreme ruler advised by a senate whose members he was effectively able to appoint or dismiss.

But did Caesar intend to destroy the Republic? Plutarch, the Greek biographer and religious mystic, writing about 150 years after the event, believed that Caesar had planned it from the beginning, and must have been helped by the gods.[33] A close examination of Caesar's career, however, shows that it was full of lucky breaks. It could have turned out very differently. Scholarly opinion is divided over whether Caesar intended to introduce a monarchical system. Most believe that his primary object was simply to become the leading man in Rome, the one with the most *auctoritas*. But his enemies were so determined to stop him that they forced him continually to raise his stakes, until, in the end, he had the choice of either accepting prosecution and risking ruin, or making himself sole ruler by force of arms.

Some who take that view also argue that, at a more fundamental level, the Republic collapsed because it had become anachronistic. Here they are on surer ground. The Republic's complex system of checks and balances was intended to stop any one individual from taking away sovereign power from all the rest. It was much safer for everyone in the original small city state if *imperium* could be shared so that nobody got too much – and when a particular individual did acquire power lawfully he had to give it back after a year. The assassins who stabbed Caesar believed they had only to kill him for the old republican system to resume as before. If Octavian had not proved them wrong, it is claimed, some other powerful figure would have done so.

What the assassins were incapable of realizing, according to this theory, was that the underlying problem was not just Caesar's lust for power but the impossibility of continuing for much longer to run a vast empire to suit the personal interests of a limited group of interbred families, whose individual members spent their public lives trying to score points off each other, while squeezing as much money as they could out of their provincial subjects and continuing to neglect the basic interests of the great mass of their fellow citizens. The empire needed strong centralized leadership, with continuity and probity of provincial administration, or it would fall apart; and for a while it did effectively split into two halves, until Octavian reunited it.

Both these theories fit together and are eminently plausible: the one based on analysis of a specific and unique political system, the other focusing on underlying developments in social, political, economic, military and colonial structures. The snag is that both leave out of account, or brush aside, a significant body of evidence[34] that tends to support Plutarch's belief that Caesar not only wanted to be 'king' but directed his efforts towards that ambition from a comparatively early stage in his career, if not quite from the very beginning. Some of that evidence also suggests that he was grooming Octavian to be his hereditary successor to kingship.

Why should Caesar want to be king when, as dictator for life, he already enjoyed the power of one? For more than four centuries it had been a capital offence in Rome to try to become king. Yet Caesar dressed up as a king in public. He sat on a golden throne. Mark Antony tried to crown him with a royal diadem in front of a festive crowd. Other diadems appeared on his statues; and when two tribunes tore them off and arrested the men suspected of putting them up, Caesar freed the suspects and forced the Senate to dismiss the tribunes. It is difficult not to believe Brutus and Cassius when they claimed to have killed him for his regal ambitions.

When he decided to adopt Octavian as his heir, Caesar began the Orwellian task of re-creating the youngster's background. He judged that the true ancestry of his great-nephew would not bear close examination, so he took measures which effectively wrote the boy's real father out of the script. He needed the acquiescence of Atia, who was evidently persuaded to accept a concocted story of divine intervention. She allowed the belief to circulate, without denial, that Octavian might be a son of Apollo, not of an earthly father. Atia confessed that she had fallen asleep at the ancient Temple of Apollo in Rome during a midnight service. The god himself, in the form of a serpent, slithered up to her while she dreamt, entered her body, and silently slithered away.[35] Nine months later Octavian was born.

Suetonius faithfully reports this tall tale, saying he found it in a book; but Stefan Weinstock, a modern authority on such matters, has no doubt where the tale originated – in the fertile mind of Julius Caesar.[36] As for the boy's discarded father, Gaius senior was recruited from beyond the grave to authenticate the divine connections of his son; during his governorship of Macedonia, the Caesarian myth-makers asserted, he consulted priests at a shrine of Dionysos in Thrace about baby Octavian's prospects. When they poured wine on their altar, a vast flame leapt up above the level of the open roof, a sign previously vouchsafed only to Alexander the Great. 'He will be ruler of the world!', the priests supposedly exclaimed in unison.[37]

What may seem to us a farrago of nonsense was part of a successful campaign to manipulate public opinion. Its object was to persuade people that Octavian was much more than an ordinary mortal: heavenly forces were on his side and it would pay a prudent man to support him. Octavian's image among the masses – but not among the sophisticated aristocracy – changed from that of a rather sickly, nondescript schoolboy to appearing to be a semi-divine figure, descended from an apparently endless line of gods, kings, heroes, statesmen and patriots. His future was predicted to be one of unimaginable glory in which he would follow Caesar in binding up the wounds of his divided nation and ushering in a new age of gold.

For the present, however, Caesar was having to face up to the dilemma of having won an empire too big for him to govern alone under the prevailing system. The war was over, but civil society had been shattered. The aristocracy, whose surviving members had been trained up from youth to run the state and the provinces, were for the most part still his adversaries. As for the ordinary citizen voters, they had little incentive to do other than support the winning side. To vote for its beaten rivals would have been to vote for a resumption of civil war. Caesar made it clear there could be no return to the former regime. 'Rome needs me more than I need Rome', he is reported to have said in exasperation at the persistence of republican attitudes among the *nobiles*.[38]

To a war-weary state his administration, whatever its limitations, had imposed a peace that held out some prospect of reforms to benefit the majority of free citizens; whereas neither peace nor reform were on offer from those who continued to cherish the memory of Cato. Once when Caesar's temper got the better of his discretion, he burst out, 'The Republic is nothing! It's just a name, without form or substance. Sulla was a fool to resign as dictator.'[39] Caesar would arguably have survived longer if he had resisted the temptation to make such remarks, but it was against his nature and his patrician mentality to dissimulate. When the Senate came to him in a body to confer divine honours on him he remained arrogantly seated;[40] Octavian, even at the height of his power, never failed to rise when a consul entered the room.

The plot to kill Caesar was hatched before his return from Spain. Antony, who had ridden into southern Gaul to meet him – and to take Octavian's place in the dictator's coach[41] – did not mention the most significant piece of information he had picked up in Rome. One of the leading conspirators, Gaius Trebonius, an old drinking companion, had sounded him out about joining the plot.[42] Antony refused. It is understandable that he would not want to betray a personal friend, but ominous and sinister that he did not give a specific warning to Caesar or name any of Trebonius's associates.

Meanwhile, Octavian occupied the second coach in the procession returning to Rome, sharing it with Decimus Brutus, who, if he had not already joined the conspiracy, would do so in time to link bloody hands with the other assassins, led by his cousin, Marcus Brutus, on the Ides of March. Decimus, designated by Caesar to become Governor of Cisalpine Gaul (northern Italy) for 44, was no doubt offended to have been kept out of the seat of honour in his commanding general's coach by a seventeen-year-old, who had arrived in Spain too late to fight in the war. Octavian's prominence at so early an age was more appropriate for a prince than a junior officer. For Decimus, it would have raised the question whether Caesar intended to have himself declared king, with Octavian as his successor.

The weight of evidence that he intended to do just that continued to pile up in the last months of his life. First, he moved to secure Octavian's future, so far as he could, in the event of his own sudden demise. It was not simply that he may have feared assassination but that his health was deteriorating. He was fifty-five years old, and the epileptic fits that had plagued him since his youth were becoming more frequent. On his return to central Italy, he bypassed Rome to go to his country estate near Labici, south-east of the capital, where in secrecy he drafted his will, making Octavian his adopted son and heir.[43] Not even he could have guessed that this document, for good or ill, would influence the course of Western history for centuries to come.

Before the end of the year he raised Octavian's social status above the plebeian level of his birth by having him enrolled as a patrician. He selected a leading Greek rhetorician of the day, Apollodorus of Pergamum, to be his tutor, and sent the pair of them to a safe distance on the far side of the Adriatic, to Apollonia in Dalmatia (then part of the province of Macedonia). With them went the advance guard for Caesar's projected expedition to the East, where he planned to train a largely new army by aggressive measures in the Balkans before moving on to his primary aim, the avenging of Crassus's defeat by the Parthians a decade earlier.

The year 44 began with Caesar as consul as well as dictator.

Having exacted from all senators an oath of loyalty to him personally rather than to the Republic, he had himself appointed, in February, as dictator for life. That convinced his enemies that the Republic would never be restored while he lived. On 26 January, after celebrating the *Feria Latina* (a festival commemorating the origins of the Latin-speaking peoples, held at Alba Longa, once their principal city), Caesar returned in solemn procession to Rome, wearing royal robes and the high red boots of the Alban kings. Some of his supporters in the crowded streets and squares hailed him as king of Rome, but objectors to these shouts were sufficiently vocal to make him feel obliged to reply that his name was not *Rex* but *Caesar*.[44]

The most blatant attempt to have himself crowned took place in the Forum on the day of the *Lupercalia*, an ancient and primitive rite during which young men of good family, dressed only in goatskin loin-cloths, got a little drunk and ran around the city centre with hairy lengths of goat-hide, whipping lightly any woman who stood in their path. It was popularly believed that this would increase her fertility and ease the pains of childbirth. Antony, even though his status as consul ought to have precluded it, was one of the runners. A path was cleared for him and, almost naked, he ran to where Caesar was sitting in state on a golden throne. Friends of the consul were waiting under the rostra to lift him up in one swift movement to where he was able to place a king's diadem, entwined with a spray of laurel, on Caesar's head.

Some of the crowd broke into applause, but a larger number booed. Caesar snatched off the diadem and threw it down. Antony picked it up and crowned him a second time. The protests of those opposing this unofficial 'coronation' overwhelmed those who supported it. Caesar again took off the headband and handed it back to Antony. While the mass of the citizens shouted approval at Caesar's reaction, he ordered Antony to take it to the Temple of Jupiter and dedicate it with a written message to say he had been offered the diadem and rejected it. It is inconceivable that Antony would have taken part in this charade if he had not been asked to do so by Caesar himself.[45]

Those who still claim that Caesar genuinely did not want to become king are driven to argue that he deliberately staged the whole thing in order to demonstrate that at heart he supported the Republic in principle. It is also necessary to take into account various honours he was awarded which bolstered his pretensions to some degree of divinity, as was characteristic of contemporary Hellenistic monarchs. His chariot was ordered to be placed on the Capitol in front of the statue of Jupiter; and he himself, according to Dio, was to be called 'Jupiter Julius'[46] and worshipped as such in temples planned for him, with Mark Antony as the *flamen* of his cult. While he was absent in Spain in 45, an ivory statue in his likeness was displayed to the people in company with statues of the gods. It was further decreed that the statue should be placed on a *pulvinar* (a sacred couch of a type found in temples) during public games at the circus or arena. In addition, his golden throne was designated to be positioned in the auditorium at important theatrical performances.

These objects were not intended simply to represent him or in the case of the golden throne – which nobody else would be allowed to sit on – to remind people of his bodily existence elsewhere. As Weinstock remarks, they were intended to indicate a spiritual presence. 'These startling divine honours only make sense if they were planned for Caesar's absence in Parthia . . . While he was fighting in the East his rule in Rome was to be strengthened by religious means.'[47] Other statues of him were reproduced by teams of sculptors and sent around Italy and the provinces to stand in the main squares of large towns.

To the very end, Caesar continued drawing more and more power into his own hands. He was effectively commander-in-chief of the entire Roman army, wherever it might be stationed, with the various legions placed in the charge of subordinate legates, whom he appointed. He nominated unprecedentedly large numbers of his supporters to serve in the Senate, pushing the total up to 900; for the first time, leading men from provinces outside the Italian peninsula were admitted. Caesar took charge of the public revenues and formed what was later to develop into the first permanent 'civil service' of Rome: hitherto, individual magistrates had called on their clients and slaves to form temporary secretariats, which were disbanded once their masters ceased to hold office.

The conspirators who were plotting to assassinate Caesar claimed that he intended to make a further effort to gain the title of king from a reluctant Senate. The rumour went round Rome that one of his kinsmen, Lucius Aurelius Cotta, would report to senators on 15 March (the Ides) that the Sibylline Books – a collection of ancient prophetic writings – laid down that nobody but a king could conquer Parthia. The implication of Cotta's proposed intervention was that Caesar needed to be made king before 19 March, when he was due to leave the city on his Parthian expedition.[48]

On the evening of 14 March, Caesar enjoyed a good dinner, and afterwards sat talking with two of his closest associates, Marcus Lepidus and Decimus Brutus. He asked them what they thought was the 'best sort of death'. Both Decimus, who intended to kill him next day, and Lepidus offered various suggestions. Neither of them agreed with Caesar, who said he would prefer to die suddenly.[49] That night his wife Calpurnia had a nightmare which convinced her it would not be safe for him to attend the Senate meeting that had been called. At first, he agreed to humour her by not going. But Decimus persuaded him he would lose face if he sent a message saying he could not attend simply because his wife had had a bad dream.[50]

Antony was walking at Caesar's side as their entourage entered Pompey's extensive theatre complex, where the Senate was waiting. His old friend Trebonius, who six months earlier had tried to recruit him to the conspiracy, now stepped forward and led him aside, ostensibly to discuss some urgent matter unconnected with the unfolding crisis. While they stood talking by the entrance, Caesar entered the senatorial chamber. As soon as he sat down, the conspirators surrounded him, blocking the view of other senators. One of them, Tillius Cimber, petitioned him for the recall from exile of his brother. He clutched at Caesar's robe as if to emphasize his plea, but in fact to bare his neck.

Casca drew a dagger and stabbed at his throat, but Caesar, suddenly realizing his danger, swerved away and took a flesh-wound in the chest. He jumped up, grabbed hold of Casca and flung him to the floor. It was too late. A second dagger was thrust into his side. Caesar fought like a cornered animal, trying to snatch the murder weapons by the blades with his bare hands. Cassius stabbed his face, Brutus his groin,[51] others his back and sides. The man who, a minute before, had been master of the Western world, sank in his blood to die at the foot of Pompey's statue.[52] The great dream was over.

FOUR

ANTONY TAKES COMMAND

As Caesar's body, spurting blood from twenty-three stab wounds, lay crumpled at the foot of Pompey's statue, the mass of senators who had not been party to the conspiracy fled for their lives. The assassins shouted at them to stop. They meant them no harm, they cried, waving their dripping daggers; they had restored freedom – their only target had been the dictator himself. The rush for the exits continued unabated. Amid a hubbub of incoherent noise, one of the conspirators tried to make a formal speech in justification, to the departing senators' backs. Others called out vainly to Cicero to join them.

Although the assassins had carefully excluded the distinguished elder statesman from their plot, they were well aware that he had privately longed for Caesar's demise as a tyrant who was out to destroy the Republic for no better reason than to feed his own insatiable ambition. That was a view they all shared. But Cicero was not such a fool as to risk his neck by siding straight away and in public with Brutus and Cassius; and he proved himself to be as fleet of foot as the other escaping senators, squeezing out through the crowded doorway with little evident regard for his *dignitas*. Panic-stricken cries of 'Run for it!' and 'Bolt your doors!' gradually died away in the distance, leaving the assassins standing uncertainly in the vacated and silent chamber to consider the implications of their failure to win immediate support for what they had done.[1]

Brutus had made no plans for seizing control of the

government. He had assumed it would only be necessary to demonstrate that the 'tyrant' was dead for all good republicans to rally to his cause. Cassius had warned him not to make the mistake of leaving Mark Antony alive, but Brutus had been unable to reconcile such a move with his rather selective conscience. It was enough, he felt, that he should be obliged to betray the man who had spared his life on the battlefield of Pharsala. His sense of rectitude would evidently accommodate that. A merely personal act of treachery to a benefactor could, at a pinch, be justified in the wider context of restoring republican liberty in the great tradition of his ancestor, that earlier Brutus who had toppled the last of the Roman kings nearly half a millennium before.

Not knowing quite what to do, now that the Senate had voted so nimbly with their feet, he effectively surrendered his token leadership of the group to the onward gallop of events. One thing was certain: they could not remain in isolation at the scene of the crime. Deprived of the Senate's instant approval, which they had so blindly and blithely anticipated, they fell back on the absurd hope of being able to convince the general public that they had acted rightly and for the best. At the same time the disadvantages of such a blatantly public assassination of Caesar began to dawn on them. Everybody of importance now knew exactly who they were and where they could be found. Perhaps, after all, they would have done better to consult Cicero in advance.

For all they knew, Mark Antony, who had vanished from sight in the general panic, was probably already marshalling the resources of the nation against them. As the sole surviving consul he became automatically the temporary head of state under the republican constitution, which they were supposedly championing. Would he try to make himself the permanent head of state, in the manner of Caesar? More immediately alarming, however, was the potential threat posed by Lepidus,[2] Caesar's Master of Horse. Technically, that anomalous position lapsed, also automatically, as there now remained no dictator for him to serve as theoretical second-in-command. But it would be no use their trying to tell that to the 5,000 or more troops still under Lepidus's command, Caesarians to a man, who were encamped not far outside the city walls, on an island in the Tiber.

In the event the conspirators need not have worried about Antony's initial response to the crisis. For the second time in his career the gallant general disguised himself as a slave[3] and went into hiding until the situation clarified itself. Not so, Lepidus. He had not been inside the chamber when the assassins struck, but he had met some of the panting senators on their way home to barricade their doors. Shocked and outraged, Lepidus ran off, too, but in the direction of the army camp, to muster his soldiers for revenge. Brutus, Cassius and the rest would need to act quickly if they were to survive, and they would have to stick together to avoid being picked off one by one. Disguise and concealment would be, for them, a recipe for disaster.

Having finally made up their minds, they strode from the chamber in their bloodstained togas, brandishing their daggers for all to see. Some of the blood was their own. In their eagerness to stab Caesar, several of them had stabbed each other. Brutus himself had a gashed hand, which continued to drizzle blood. As they entered the Forum they shouted slogans about restoring liberty by killing a 'king', but such people as they found there responded with fear, drawing back at their approach. Some support, however, was at last at hand. A few senators who had had second thoughts about what to do now came to join them.

One of them was Cicero's former son-in-law, Publius Cornelius Dolabella, who until then had apparently been a slavish supporter of Caesar's regime, much to the displeasure of Cicero, who had good reason for considering him unscrupulous. The dictator had appointed Dollabella to take over from him as joint consul in Rome with Antony after his departure from the the city on his proposed Parthian expedition. Although his legal right was uncertain, Dolabella did not intend to wait for the appointed date. Brutus, as a stickler for observing republican forms, could not be expected entirely to approve of that, and there is no suggestion that either he or Cassius was prepared at that stage to defer to Dolabella's doubtful claim of seniority. But for what it was worth, the plotters now had their own rival 'head of state' in their ranks to validate their action.

They also had some degree of protection. Decimus Brutus, cousin of Marcus, had arranged for a small group of gladiators to act as their escort – no match, of course, for the legionaries under Lepidus, but enough to see off the official lictors, if need be, or to cope with a popular demonstration against them. Realizing now that it would be dangerous, and probably fruitless, to linger around the Forum in the hope of assembling a favourable crowd, they marched up the steep hill to the Capitol, with Dolabella in their ranks. After giving thanks to Jupiter in his temple, they took up a defensive position behind the stout walls, prepared to sell their lives dearly if it should come to a fight.[4]

By this time messengers were beginning to pass between the assassins up above and some of the uncommitted senators down below. As the day wore on, with no sign of an assault by the Caesarians, a crowd gradually gathered on the ancient summit of the city. Among them was Cicero, who had distanced himself sufficiently from the crime to be in no danger from either side; each now hoped to profit from his supportive oratory and his reputation for probity and patriotism. He was careful, however, not to address the crowd. Instead, he urged Brutus and Cassius to use their authority as praetors to summon the Senate to a meeting there and then. It was sound advice. Had they followed it, the ultimate outcome might have been significantly different.

Most senators distrusted Antony, and many of them tended to have at least some measure of sympathy with the conspirators' motives, if not their precise actions. Given the chance, they might well have been persuaded to vote in their interests, especially if Caesar's closest allies decided it was too risky to come unarmed to the Capitol to attend a meeting of the Senate called by Brutus instead of by the surviving consul, Antony. Brutus was not an inspiring speaker, but as a practised lawyer he could have made out a strong case, on constitutional grounds, to a potentially sympathetic Senate, for what he had done. But for reasons which remain unclear, he passed up this opportunity; instead, he addressed the crowd, and was sufficiently encouraged by the loud applause he received to venture down to the Forum.

There, mounted on the speaker's rostrum, his reception was very different. Unlike the crowd on the Capitol, the gathering in the Forum was not composed chiefly of republican partisans. They heard him out in ominous silence as he explained the constitutional and 'democratic' justification for killing Caesar. They had done it, he said, not in order to seize power but so that every citizen might be free again. The next speaker on the rostra, another praetor, the elderly Lucius Cornelius Cinna, was tactless enough to launch into a tirade against the late dictator, whose body had recently been seen, carried on a stretcher to his home by three slaves, with his bloody and mutilated face exposed and one of his arms hanging limply down beneath an inadequate cover. Cinna's abuse was too gross to be borne. The crowd hurled insults back at him and drove all the conspirators from the Forum with such violence that they retreated back up to the Capitol.

Darkness fell, with the situation still deadlocked. That night, Lepidus led his small army into the city centre and Antony emerged from hiding to join him and other Caesarian leaders in what everyone supposed would be a council of war. Lepidus and Balbus,[5] head of Caesar's private office and a key figure in the dictator's administration, both argued for swift and exemplary punishment of the murderers, using their present overwhelming military advantage to carry it through. But Antony counselled moderation, even if that meant some degree of compromise with the assassins. The first priority, he said, was to ensure that the Senate ratified all Caesar's edicts during his five-year rule. Revenge could come later. He was supported by Aulus Hirtius, consul-designate for the following year, a firm Caesarian but a cautious and conservative man, whose priority was plainly to avoid reigniting civil war.

Lepidus, finding himself opposed where he had expected wholehearted support, eventually conceded the argument, in spite of knowing that his soldiers, like many of the ordinary citizens, were thirsting for revenge. The ancient sources agree that Lepidus lacked strength of character. As the man in direct command of the only substantial body of troops for hundreds of miles, he was in a position to dictate his own terms to the Senate. And as most of the legions in the provinces were under the command of Caesarian loyalists, Antony and Lepidus were hardly likely to have feared future reprisals if they had slaughtered the assassins at dawn. The impetus for that grisly task would now be left to Octavian.

As yet, the teenager was, of course, completely unaware of what had happened. At some point during all the upheaval in the aftermath of the assassination, Octavian's mother sent off a warning message to him. She would, naturally, have been advised by her consular husband, Philippus, who presumably attended the fatal meeting of the Senate on the Ides of March or had at least been in the vicinity. As a relative by marriage of Caesar, and one who enjoyed a solid power base in his own right, Philippus had become one of the most important and influential figures in a city where, after the carnage of the civil war, there were few surviving patricians of his status and breadth of senatorial experience. He would have realized only too clearly the potential danger for his stepson. The message that was about to be carried to Octavian in distant Apollonia must surely have included advice not to do anything rash in reaction to the appalling news.

The young man himself would remain in ignorance of his

great-uncle's murder for another week or two. Apollonia was not far from the coast on the other side of the Adriatic, but communication was slow and difficult. The messenger would need to ride a series of post horses south from the city down the Appian Way, turning east past Campania to follow the mountainous road to Brundisium or a neighbouring port on the Italian coast facing Greece. Then he would have to find passage on a boat and wait for a favourable western wind to blow him to what is today Albania but was then the western extremity of the Roman province of Macedonia. It would take Octavian some time, after receiving the news of Caesar's assassination, to make up his mind, amid much conflicting advice, about what to do. Such a measured response would become characteristic of him.

Octavian was not studying alone or performing his occasional army duties without friends of his own age around him as his daily companions. Two among them would later become prominent and powerful figures during the course of his rise to the top – Marcus Vipsanius Agrippa and Salvidienus Rufus. Both men were from humble backgrounds, the first of the 'meritocracy' on which Octavian would chiefly rely during his long struggle with the old aristocracy. One would stay faithful to the end and marry into the imperial family, the other would seek to betray him and would pay the inevitable price. But for the present, these were his closest friends, to whom he would turn for counsel in the moment of crisis that was now slowly but inexorably approaching him.

Back in Rome, the political situation was passing through a series of bewildering changes that nobody could have predicted. Antony, having secured the reluctant acquiescence of Lepidus, succeeded in seizing the initiative for himself. That same night Antony called on Caesar's grieving widow, Calpurnia, and persuaded her to hand over to him all her husband's political papers and most of the princely hoard of gold coins kept under guard at his home.[6] As dawn broke next day, the assassins looked down on a Forum packed with

Lepidus's armed soldiers and heard the news that Antony had called a meeting of the Senate for the following morning. Few in Rome were surprised when Brutus and Cassius, in spite of a guarantee of personal safety for the occasion, forwarded their apologies for absence.

The events of that first night, followed by Antony's masterly performance in the Senate on the morning of 17 March, ought to have buried for ever the popular belief, which still prevails, that he was just a plain, honest soldier who loved Caesar as a friend and who strained every nerve to avenge him. Antony had seen a safer and more congenial route to personal pre-eminence, one that need not involve killing his childhood friends, so long as they were prepared to cooperate. At the age of thirty-seven or thirty-eight he was still in the prime of life, and for several years he had been widely regarded as Caesar's natural successor. He must often have thought about how he would act if the dictator's death should suddenly pitchfork him into leadership of the Caesarians.

Antony evidently believed himself to be Caesar's main heir,[7] as he had been, apparently, before the secret switch to Octavian. It is likely that Calpurnia believed it, too, or she would scarcely have parted so readily, and in the middle of the night, with such a vital part of Octavian's inheritance. Caesar's motives for secrecy need little explanation. He did not want to turn Antony into an enemy or endanger Octavian's life by revealing the precise terms of his new dynastic arrangements. If Antony had known about the new will, in which he was named merely as a secondary heir in the event of the pre-decease of Caesar's great-nephews, he would surely have used his power to demand the document from the Vestal Virgins, or, at the very least, would have tried to block any move to have it read in public.

Some of the conspirators were initially in favour of asking Antony to join them in assassinating Caesar.[8] They would hardly have risked exposure and execution in that way if they had not been reasonably sure of his approval, if not his actual participation. Their tentative proposal to kill Antony as well as Caesar was made long after he had rejected their earlier approach; and Brutus, in spurning such a move, must have taken into account the fact that Antony had not betrayed them, when he could easily have done so. Antony would never have plunged his own dagger into Caesar's back. Such infamy would have offended his deepest instincts as well as his aristocratic code of honour, in addition, probably, to arousing fears of divine or human retribution. He was not a sophisticated intellectual like Brutus, who could rationalize an act of base personal treachery into heroic service for the state. But he did not conceive it to be his duty to carry tales to Caesar about what some of his friends might be up to. And he was able to reckon on profiting more than any other single individual from the dictator's death.

As an experienced staff officer, used to expecting the unexpected on the line of march or the field of battle, Antony must surely have prepared, at least in his head, a fall-back plan in the event of the conspiracy succeeding. He may even have known the probable date when the attempt would be made. Rumour of it had reached the ears of some other senators, much less well informed than he, well before Caesar left home on the morning of the Ides of March to walk to the Senate meeting, with Antony among his entourage of supporters and lictors. In any case, as everyone knew that Caesar planned to leave Rome four days after the Ides and would probably not return for three or more years, any senatorial attempt on his life would have to be made within that brief timescale, before he resumed active service as a general, guarded by a permanent escort of armed soldiers. Antony had already been detailed to stay behind in Rome for the rest of the year, thus allowing Octavian the prospect of a clear run for sharing Caesar's anticipated military glory.

In three or four years' time, depending on the outcome of his expedition, Caesar might decide to return to his capital as an all-conquering sovereign, and turn the Republic into a monarchy, just as Brutus and Cassius feared he would. By that time he might also have promoted Octavian to an unassailable height as his lineal successor. The boy of eighteen would have become a man of twenty-one or twenty-two, trained in the art and science of war by the master exponent of his era. In either or both of those events, Antony's path to the top would be blocked. We cannot, of course, know for certain what thoughts passed through Antony's mind in the period leading up to the assassination, but we may be sure that he knew better than anyone else the true extent of Caesar's ambitions. Was Antony not the man who, only a month before, felt obliged to prejudice his *dignitas* as consul by stripping to a loincloth in public and offering to 'crown' his master before an excitable crowd in the Forum?

Antony had been born into a distinguished senatorial family – plebeian, it is true, but ennobled by generations of senior magistrates. As a young officer with an excellent military record and comparatively modest means, he had joined Caesar in Gaul not because he agreed with his general's politics but in order to make a career for himself and to share in the spoils of war. He was noted for womanizing, hard drinking and extravagance; but on the battlefield, strictly sober, he proved a resourceful and intrepid tactician. Caesar seems to have regarded him as a man after his own heart, and it may well be that he saw something of his own earlier self in Antony's open and confident personality, and his glorying in the thrill of battle, heedless of personal risk. Promotion to the innermost circle of his trusted confidants came quickly; and Caesar, lacking legitimate sons of his own, plainly encouraged him to believe that, in the fullness of time, he would be his heir.

There is no evidence to suggest that Antony supported Caesar's programme of social reform out of personal conviction. His earlier posturing as a tribune of the People had been for Caesar's benefit and his own, not for that of the populace at large. Like others of his class, he was a soldier-politician who, in the circumstances of the time, had chosen to follow Caesar rather than Pompey, and had been richly rewarded for doing so. If he had any sympathy for the plight of poorer citizens he does not appear to have shown it. On the contrary, when left in charge of Rome during the dictator's absence he massacred 800 of them while putting down a popular riot over high interest rates and the crushing burden of debt. Even allowing for the typically exaggerated round numbers of the historical sources, that surely represents an excessive response.

In short, Antony had far more in common with Brutus, Cassius and the rest of the conspirators, most of whom he had known since adolescence, than he would ever have with the common people. His own priority, in line with traditional aristocratic ambitions, was to preserve and increase his public status with a view to becoming the unchallenged 'first man' of the state, without, in his case, being overscrupulous about whether or not that might subvert the old republican constitution. Judging by his actions in the first few days after the assassination, it is hard to believe that avenging Caesar was high on his list of priorities – if, indeed, he gave it any serious priority at all.

With Caesar dead, and the culprits effectively at his mercy, he evidently saw no necessity for further bloodshed to boost his *auctoritas*. Having secured the cooperation of Lepidus, he had no reason to suppose there was any other serious rival on the horizon. Dolabella, now recognized as his consular colleague, was bribed into acquiescence by having his substantial debts paid out of the money Antony took from Caesar's widow. Over Octavian he would not have lost a moment's sleep. What, after all, could an eighteen-year-old student, whose only experience so far of active military service consisted in being late for a battle, hope to achieve against a Roman consul and senior general, wielding the power of the state, who had already taken over a major portion of Caesar's legacy and had no intention of giving any of it back.

Now that all the important cards, so far as he knew, were in his possession, he was ready to act the role of magnanimous statesman in the manner of his former master, dispensing forgiveness and favours with one hand while obtaining a long-term proconsular command for himself with the other. The expeditionary army that Caesar had assembled would be his for the taking, and could be used to enforce his will in Rome. Civil war would not be necessary, and he would be careful not to provoke it by calling himself dictator or seeking the status of king. Having neither the taste nor the talent for day-to-day politicking in the capital, he evidently saw himself winning glory in foreign fields to rival the conquests of Caesar and Pompey, but without arousing too much republican hostility.

He had demonstrated in their own blood his opinion of the legitimate concerns of the Roman 'mob', so he plainly had no fear of being unable to cope with any popular backlash which his unexpected policy of *rapprochement* with the assassins might provoke. As for the sensibilities of the soldiery, he was sure he would inherit their support by honouring Caesar's promises to pay bonuses and resettle them on good farmland after discharge. It was therefore in the supposition that he alone, at this moment of crisis, had both the *de jure* authority to opt for violence or restraint, and the *de facto* power to carry it through, that he called the Senate to meet at the Temple of the goddess Tellus, only a few steps from his own closely guarded home and out of range of the Capitol. Just to make sure, in the cynical tradition of those of his predecessors who had similarly quested for supremacy, he saw to it that Lepidus's army also 'guarded' the assembled senators.

He had a further persuasive argument to use, but he saved it up until after the most senior apologists for the absent assassins had identified themselves publicly. The distinguished ex-consul Tiberius Claudius Nero, husband of Octavian's future wife Livia, proposed that Brutus, Cassius and their colleagues, far from being arraigned for murder and treason, should be congratulated and awarded special honours for having restored the Republic. Other *optimates* called for Caesar's decrees to be repudiated. It may have been on this occasion, too, that one extremist apparently said that the dictator's body should be denied burial and be cast into the anonymous waters of the Tiber.[9]

Now Antony intervened. Avoiding any expression of praise or blame, he pointed out in a matter-of-fact way that if even one of Caesar's edicts were to be set aside on the grounds that he had been a tyrant who had seized power unlawfully, then all of his *acta*, without exception, would have to be similarly rejected. Twisting the knife, he added that this would apply equally to all the many appointments Caesar had made by personal fiat over the past five years and also for three or more years into the future. The senators stared at him, and then at each other, in undisguised horror. More than half of them were sitting in the Senate chamber only because Caesar had appointed them. Unless they voted to ratify all Caesar's decisions they risked forfeiting their seats and being obliged to seek re-election.

Many of them were from remote parts of Italy which had never before been represented in the capital. A few were even from the provinces, where Caesar had identified them as potentially valuable supporters. City wits had been joking, at the expense of the Gauls, that if you spotted a man wandering around Rome in trousers rather than a toga it would be a kindness to point the simple fellow the way to the Senate House. Dismissed senators would need to seek re-election under a voting system that was so biased in favour of the local Roman aristocracy that most would stand little chance of ever returning to their prized benches. Even long-serving, properly elected senators had been counting on filling certain top posts, including potentially lucrative provincial governorships, for which Caesar had designated them, in some cases for years ahead, to take account of the time he had expected to be absent in Parthia.

No more was heard of cancelling Caesar's decrees. The Senate voted not only to ratify them all but, in addition, to validate and support those he had intended to promulgate, but which, because of his assassination, he had been unable to see through to the desired end. This played straight into Antony's hands, as he had no doubt intended it should. He alone possessed Caesar's official papers – and he would be careful not to let anyone else read them. That enabled him for some weeks ahead to take any measures he chose, including announcing new appointments and milking state funds, by claiming that the proposals were not his but Caesar's. There was a sweetener for the more ardent republicans at the end of the debate in the form of a motion for general amnesty, proposed by Cicero, accepted by Antony as presiding consul and passed comfortably.[10] At a stroke, the sixty conspirators ceased to be wanted criminals.

Antony and Lepidus had already sent their sons up to the Capitol as hostages in an attempt to persuade the leading assassins to come down. After the debate Brutus and Cassius felt perfectly safe to do so. Brutus was welcomed in person by Lepidus, to whom he was related by marriage, and the two of them enjoyed a relaxed dinner. Antony opened the door of his home to Cassius, presumably still unaware that the 'lean and hungry' praetor had plotted to kill him at the same time as he and his friends had killed Caesar. They too dined together, in apparent harmony and good-will.[11] Just three days and two nights had passed since Caesar had been slaughtered like an ox. Next morning the Senate met again and carried a vote of thanks to Antony for having averted a resumption of civil war. To the ordinary people of Rome it must have seemed as if the aristocracy had stitched up the brief reign of Caesar – but neglected his gaping wounds.

The political situation, however, was more complex and unstable than surface appearances might suggest. The differing aims of Caesareans and *optimates* would soon lead to a new rift. Antony, having conjured up a diplomatic solution that effectively spared the lives of the assassins, was not disposed to let them interfere with his plans for personal supremacy. The conspirators, having risked their lives to thwart Caesar's ambition, were even less inclined to permit Antony to take over the late dictator's role. Few apart from Cassius and Cicero seem to have realized the danger inherent in proposals by Caesar's father-in-law, Lucius Calpurnius Piso, for Caesar to be given a public funeral and for the text of his will to be read aloud to the Senate. Brutus loftily agreed to both measures, cutting the ground from under the feet of his allies, whose rejected advice was once again to be proved correct.

Senators recognized that, for Piso, his insistence on the funeral and the reading of the will was basically a matter of maintaining family honour. He had good reason to be angry at Antony's cavalier disregard for the due process of law in removing Caesar's possessions to his own home as if they were already his personal property. As the father of Calpurnia, he plainly believed it should have fallen to him to look after the inheritance until the will had been proved. Although he did not accuse Antony of not trusting him to carry out this task honestly, Piso's speech to the Senate was sharp with indignation and pique. He was evidently aware that Caesar had changed his will, but it is unlikely that he knew much about its contents.

The Vestal Virgins now surrendered up the explosive document, and the Senate learnt at last that Caesar had left three-quarters of his vast estate to Octavian, with the remaining quarter split equally between Pedius and Pinarius, his other great-nephews. Antony was to get nothing. He would have stood to gain only if Octavian had died before Caesar. His disappointment and embarrassment must have been intense. Ironically, Decimus Brutus and some of the other assassins were listed with Antony among the potential secondary heirs. Both Suetonius and Dio report that Caesar also named Antony and Decimus to be Octavian's guardians;[12] but, if so, there is no evidence that they ever tried to exercise a guardian's rights. In any case, Philippus, as his stepfather, would have expected to take precedence over them.

Even more sensationally, the will declared Octavian to be Caesar's adopted son, a move which would require him to take Caesar's name, becoming Gaius Julius Caesar Octavianus. As there appears to have been no sound precedent for such a method of posthumous adoption, lawyers have questioned ever since both its legality and efficacy, but Octavian was ultimately able to resolve the anomaly to gain general acceptance. The will further directed that each citizen should be given 300 sesterces (for comparison, 900 sesterces was a legionary soldier's annual pay after the Augustan reforms); that implied that Octavian, or all three of the primary heirs acting together, would be personally responsible for seeing that it was paid. In a final burst of patrician generosity, Caesar bequeathed his extensive gardens along the banks of the Tiber to the city, for the free enjoyment of all citizens.[13]

News of the bequests radiated swiftly outwards from the Senate chamber and brought crowds onto the streets. Antony, however, made no move to disgorge the treasure he had seized, confident in his power to resist expropriation. In any case, he needed the money urgently to resettle Caesar's veterans. It was the army, of course, on which his power was, in the final analysis, actually based, not on his temporary possession of the consulate, which protected him from legal action for as long as he held it. The people's subsequent realization that they would have to wait for Octavian before any of them could hope to get their hands on their individual cash payments helps to explain some of the warmth of his reception when he eventually reached the city.

Five days after the Ides, Caesar's body was brought in state to the Forum, through a vast crowd of mourners. No Roman had done more than he to extend and increase the power and prestige of city and empire, although Pompey, arguably, had done as much. Antony gave the funeral address, the traditional panegyric in which the dead man's achievements were listed in the presence of his fellow-citizens and his 'ancestors', represented by death masks worn over the faces of family retainers. But this was to be a funeral like no other before or since. While the corpse lay shrouded on a couch, a wax effigy of Caesar was raised above it and suspended there in full view of everyone present. During Antony's speech, a mechanical contrivance caused the waxwork to revolve slowly, displaying all the twenty-three wounds on his face and body.[14]

As the crowd moaned and wept, Antony aroused them further by pointing out some of the more prominent wounds and lifting up the toga he had worn – still stiff with caked blood – to show where the daggers had gone in. The people could stand it no more. They broke out in spontaneous riot and took over the proceedings. Dragging tables, chairs and anything else that would burn from nearby shops, they constructed a huge pyre and placed Caesar's body on top. As the fire engulfed him, women cast their jewellery into the flames. The hottest heads among the crowd snatched up blazing brands and went on a rampage, vowing to kill his assassins and burn their houses to the ground. Brutus and Cassius, however, had sensibly absented themselves, and other senators left the scene as quickly as they could. Robbed of their chief prey, the rioters found a substitute victim in the person of a tribune and poet called Cinna, who bore the same *cognomen* as the conspirator and praetor, Lucius Cornelius Cinna, who had enraged the crowd on the afternoon of the Ides by his abuse of Caesar from the rostra. Vainly protesting his innocence, Cinna the poet was torn to pieces on the spot.[15]

Over the next days the beleaguered assassins began to leave the city and take refuge where they could find it. Some stayed on for several weeks behind locked doors, hoping to weather the storm of public anger as 'prisoners in their own homes' – the phrase is Cicero's[16] – afraid to venture out except after dark. In the Forum a man calling himself Amatius, and claiming to be a grandson of Marius, set up an altar to Caesar on the ashes of the funeral pyre. People flocked there, and he quickly recruited a gang which roamed the streets in search of stray assassins, intending to impose their own rough justice in place of the decree of amnesty voted by the Senate.

Antony allowed the street violence to continue for a short while. It suited him to have the more extreme optimate leaders effectively removed from the political centre, where they might have made it difficult for him to extract the maximum benefit from his possession of Caesar's official papers. The Senate had, in fact, moved to appoint a committee to inspect them with a view to assessing priorities, but Antony ignored it. He knew he would be safe from future prosecution once he had obtained a long-term military command, and he was fast preparing the way for that, as well as for the expensive process of resettling Caesar's veterans.

He moved against the rioters to prevent a total breakdown of public order, but not before they had sufficiently terrorized the assassins. Having discovered that the gang leader 'Amatius' was a Greek imposter named Herophilus, he had him executed without trial and punished enough of his followers to restore some degree of calm.[17] Antony could feel well pleased with his first weeks at the top, in spite of his setback over the will. His dominance was now virtually total. He had persuaded the Senate to sanction all Caesar's acts, along with the opportunity to invent future ones of his own. By conciliating the assassins he had effectively marginalized them. And his position as consul combined with his secure hold on Caesar's papers enabled him to drain ever more wealth from public coffers, recruiting troops of his own to add to those of Lepidus. If the Senate should attempt to thwart him he could turn to the popular assemblies for support.

Cicero might well complain to his old friend Atticus about the menace posed by the new regime now that *libertas* had supposedly been restored but without the necessary republican freedom to make it effective. 'Our heroes' (Cicero means the assassins) 'acquitted themselves most gloriously and magnificently. . . . We need money and troops for what remains to be done, but we haven't got any.' Still harking back to the Ides of March, he asks with a rhetorical flourish: 'Don't you remember that first day on the Capitol when I cried out for the praetors to call a Senate meeting up there? By the immortal gods! – what might they not have been able to do while all good men, even some not-so-good, were rejoicing!'[18]

Late in March, almost certainly after the funeral riot, Decimus Brutus wrote to his cousin Marcus Brutus and to Cassius complaining bitterly of Antony's 'treachery'. All three conspirators were still in Rome but evidently unable to meet without difficulty because of mob violence. Decimus was the current Governor of northern Italy (Cisalpine Gaul) but had not yet taken up his post; now he was being threatened with dismissal. 'Antony says he can't see his way to giving me my province,' he writes, advising that they should all leave Italy while they could.[19] He suggests, treasonably, that they could join either Sextus Pompey, who continued to hold out against Roman forces in his Spanish stronghold, or the maverick optimate Caecilius Bassus, who controlled a legion in Syria.[20]

Antony was, of course, trying to deprive Decimus of his governorship because he wanted it for himself. The two legions stationed in northern Italy formed the biggest single concentration of troops on the peninsula, and direct control of them would cement Antony's hold on the capital, which they could reach faster than any of the other provincial armies. We do not have a record of a reply by Brutus and Cassius to this letter from Decimus, but we can guess their answer from what happened next. In mid-April Decimus slipped out of the city, not to follow his own advice by going abroad, but to head north for his legitimate command before Antony could finalize his plans to take it away from him by a vote of the People. Brutus and Cassius were plainly behind his move. The counter-attack by the *optimates* against the dominant Caesarians had already started before Octavian reached Rome.

FIVE

THE YOUNG PRETENDER

Octavian was about to sit down to dinner when his mother's messenger arrived at Apollonia with the news of Caesar's assassination. The messenger must also have spread his tidings around the town, because during the course of the evening various prominent citizens called at his door to express their condolences and wonder out loud what he might be proposing to do about it. His feelings may be imagined. Most of the vistors left after being thanked for their trouble, but Octavian invited to his table some of the more experienced among them – experienced in war as well as in politics. Their animated discussions went on into the early hours of the following morning.

Opinions were strongly divided. Agrippa and Salvidienus were apparently among those who advised him to go to the headquarters of the Macedonian army, which his great-uncle had assembled, and appeal for their immediate support in avenging his murder. Others were much more circumspect. They felt that while it would be appropriate and sensible for him to address the soldiers and win their sympathy, it would be premature, as well as treasonable, to call for an invasion of Italy before he had more information about what had happened since the Ides of March. For all they knew, Caesar had already been avenged. He ought not to risk starting a new civil war against unknown odds and for a cause that might no longer exist.[1]

Octavian showed maturity in accepting this more cautious line of argument. After he had slept on the problem, he resolved to organize a small reconnaissance mission, led by himself, to seek out the facts and assess the strength of public opinion. Were the assassins now in control in Rome? Was he designated to be their next victim? Alternatively, had Antony and Lepidus, as the senior Caesarians on the spot, brought them to trial and execution? As yet, he did not even know the extent of his own status under Caesar's will, nor even whether that will would ever be honoured, although he must have been assured he would be in some degree a beneficiary. No doubt his legal advisers would have told him that if the Senate had approved the assassination, then Caesar's will, along with all his other political and financial arrangements, would very likely be set aside. It was possible that the entire estate would be forfeit to the Republic if Caesar were to be officially deemed a tyrant.

The young man did not need to go to the Macedonian army headquarters. A significant part of the army came to him, in the form of a deputation of centurions and men who had served under Caesar, to offer their services and assure him of their support.[2] Octavian had, of course, been on training exercises with these highly professional soldiers, and it was in a spirit of comradeship that he praised their loyalty to Caesar and said he would certainly call on their help when he needed it. That meeting, with its exchange of firm pledges, was to have important consequences in the difficult and dangerous months ahead. He would need them in a dark hour, and they would not fail him.

Octavian was apparently able to take a few of them with him, presumably on leave of absence from their legions, when he finally crossed to Italy, probably in the first week of April. He also took a fairly large sum of money, for he was able to pay the way for all of them from the moment of landing on a deserted beach well to the south of the garrison port of Brundisium. It had been a rough crossing of many hours, and he and his small escort would have been in no condition for immediate strenuous action. They made their way on foot to the little town of Lupiae, where he rented lodgings. It was either on arrival there, or the next day, that he learnt for the first time that Caesar had adopted him. At the same time he would have discovered the ominous news of the Senate's vote of amnesty for the murderers.

With characteristic caution he sent a few men on ahead to Brundisium to make sure no traps awaited him. As soon as the soldiers there heard that Caesar's heir had returned to Italy, they marched out from the town to meet him and escort him back, hailing him by his new name of Caesar.[3] It was a heady moment. Octavian was in a position to see clearly now what a glittering future might open up to him if he had the courage and will to seize his opportunity with both hands – but also the spectre of death and disaster for himself and his friends and family should he fail. Abandoning much of the secrecy that had so far shrouded his movements and motives, he proclaimed that he was going to Rome to restore the honour of his 'father' and to claim his inheritance. But he wisely avoided any public threats against the assassins, whatever he may have said about them in private.

Men flocked to him, and money, rather mysteriously, seems to have followed in their wake. Caesar had been building up a war-chest for his Parthian expedition, so public funds, presumably for the most part in the form of silver, gold and bronze coins, would have been passing between Rome and Brundisium, for shipment to Macedonia, to pay the troops and purchase supplies. Other cash flows, for the same purposes, may equally have been passing through Brundisium in the charge of tax-farmers, returning from other eastern provinces. What is certain is that by the time he arrived in Rome, Octavian was in control of a large fortune.

Part of the explanation for its existence may be connected with the fact that when Octavian reached Naples he was greeted by Lucius Cornelius Balbus, who for several years had managed Caesar's business and political affairs (in close association with the knight Gaius Oppius). It was Balbus, a

Spaniard, believed to be of partly Phoenician descent, who had supported Lepidus's proposal on the night of the Ides of March to set his troops onto the heavily outnumbered conspirators. In the recent past, Balbus would have needed direct access to the dictator's extensive funds simply in order to carry out his day-to-day work. He is unlikely to have made any of it available to Antony after the consul's decision to compromise with the assassins.

Balbus seems to have been deeply impressed by Octavian's resolute behaviour, and he became a dedicated partisan in his cause. Although there is no direct evidence, it is not unreasonable to suppose that he made over at least part of whatever Caesarean funds he controlled, without waiting for the will to be legally proved. There would have been no question of Balbus trying to hold on to the money for himself. He was already one of the richest men in Rome, having been adopted by Theophilus of Mytilene, a leading adviser of Pompey during that general's highly profitable campaigns in the East. Balbus had been originally a Pompeian, who helped to broker the agreement that led to the 'First Triumvirate' of Pompey, Caesar and Crassus. Later he switched his allegiance to Caesar, perhaps because of growing *optimate* jealousy at his advancement.

His career is important for demonstrating how reformers such as Caesar and Octavian were prepared to reward merit by promoting gifted and capable non-Romans to the highest level in the administration of affairs. It also shows the complexity of personal networking around the empire among people of different social and racial groups. Less than three years after his confidential meeting with Octavian in Naples, Balbus was to become the first foreign-born consul in the history of Rome. That does not, of course, prove conclusively that he gave Octavian access to substantial funds at a crucial early point in his independent career, but it is extremely suggestive.

Balbus, hot from that meeting with Octavian, hurried to

Cumae, near Puteoli, on the northern extremity of the Bay of Naples, where Cicero had retreated to one of his various villas[4] to escape the violence and uncongenial atmosphere of Antonian Rome. The two men were old campaigners, if not exactly friends. Cicero had successfully defended Balbus in a court case some thirteen years earlier, and they had continued to keep in touch, as each was a useful source of information to the other. Balbus's mission was evidently to try to reassure the ageing statesman about Octavian's intentions, with a view to gaining his support. He confirmed that the young heir had definitely decided to claim his inheritance but expected to encounter major problems from Antony. Cicero, however, had already expressed in a private letter to Atticus his suspicion that Octavian might be attempting a *coup d'état*[5]. He was not yet ready to help.

By coincidence, Octavian's mother and stepfather had a villa near Cicero's, in the Puteoli area, and it was there that the young man called a few days later after engaging in what were probably essential public relations activities in Naples, designed to increase his political profile and win him more support. Atia, his mother, had already expressed her fears to him over the dangerous enmities he would provoke in pursuit of his inheritance, which she and Philippus had advised him to reject. Whether that advice was meant seriously, or whether it represented no more than an attempt by the cautious Philippus to insulate himself and his wife from the potentially catastrophic consequences of failure, is not known for certain. Octavian is on record as having told them that as Caesar had thought him worthy to take over both his fortune and his name, it would be wrong for him to settle for anything less.[6] At that point, it seems, Atia and Philippus were moved to pledge their full support, as a united family.

Philippus, after his many years close to the heart of power, would have been fully aware of the immensity of the task. Octavian was already quite an accomplished orator, trained to speak *extempore* at public meetings, but there was an obvious limit to what his words alone could achieve. Nevertheless he would have had a significant number of potential supporters in the big, bustling city of Naples, and it was essential for him to meet and speak to as many of them as possible before resuming his journey to the capital. Although Naples was originally a Greek foundation, and the language was still widely spoken there, many Roman veterans of the legions had been officially settled as colonists in the Neopolitan region of Campania on Caesar's initiative, and more were waiting for land grants to be approved.

We have no detailed record of what he may have said to them at this time, or what they replied, but we may be certain that numbers of them considered themselves to have been effectively in the position of 'clients' in their relationship to Caesar, and wanted vengeance against his killers. The bond between a patron and his clients in late republican Rome was essentially one of mutual self-interest. For the system of aristocratic rule to work with reasonable efficiency and a wide enough measure of public support, it was necessary for those below the level of aristocrats, but usually above the level of the poorer citizens, to have a means of access, even if indirect, to the men making the more important decisions that affected their lives. Clients relied on such access for protection as well as for the occasional fruits of patronage, such as appointments and contracts. In return, the clients pledged political and, if need be, physical support to their patron.

Leading senators commonly inherited their clients from a retired or deceased member of their family or clan, and used the status this gave them to attract more. Their clientele would typically include men of lesser senatorial rank, knights and other 'opinion-formers' in their local neighbourhoods. They would greet their patron respectfully on a fairly regular, even daily basis, and turn out in force to support him on important public occasions, such as a prepared speech to an assembly in the Forum, when they would be expected to applaud. These lesser senators and knights would, in turn, have their own sets of clients, each of whom relied on them for protection and for lower-level forms of career advancement.

In earlier times, these hierarchies of chiefs and clients had spread down into the very roots of Roman society. But since the widening of the franchise to much of Italy after the Social War, the mass discharge of pauperized peasant-soldiers and the increasing manumission of elderly slaves who were no longer considered worth their keep, a huge underclass had been created which lacked even the unofficial, informal links to political power represented by the client system. The information gap between optimate senators and resentful underclass no doubt explains the conspirators' surprise at finding that their assassination of Caesar, far from being popular with ordinary citizens, roused them to murderous violence.

Nevertheless, the patron/client relationship had underpinned political actions and attitudes across a fairly wide social spectrum throughout Caesar's career, when it would have made no sense for him or for his aristocratic rivals and enemies to have acted for purely ideological reasons unconnected with the needs of their hierarchical interest groups. Cicero may have bequeathed to Western civilization his voluminous writings on morality and government, but as a practising politician his aim was to maintain the balance of an interest-group system of chiefs and clients which he himself had manipulated to his own advantage, and which he came to identify, like so many politicians since, with the advantage of the state. Brutus and Cassius might claim to have assassinated Caesar for noble reasons, but their daggers were also guided to his heart and loins by the cumulative personal interests of their many clients, who looked to them for that flow of beneficial patronage of which the sudden pre-eminence of Caesar had largely deprived them.

Caesar had had an exceptionally large and varied list of clients long before he became dictator. They included not only senators, knights and other individuals hoping for advancement by serving his interests, but whole towns, tribes, garrisons, islands, even substantial regional areas of Italy and Gaul and some other provinces, embracing citizens and free non-citizens alike. When Caesar died, all those individuals and groups would have tried to attach themselves to a new patron as soon as practicable, and their choice would naturally have been likely to favour the more prominent Caesarians over the *optimates*.

Octavian thus had many respectable support-groups to appeal to, in addition to the 'mob', but as he was only eighteen he would have been unable to offer them the direct influence at the centre of power that would be available to a mature man of consular rank. Many of them would already have tried to achieve a client-patron link with Antony, as the Caesarean successor actually wielding power and most likely to retain it. In order to accumulate clients of his own, and of a sufficiently high calibre to enable him to achieve his goals, Octavian would need to find politicians of some standing who were willing to back his cause in the Senate, for which he himself was ineligible. But he would not be able to put himself in the normal position of a client to any one of them without prejudicing his own chance of detaching existing Caesarian clients from leaders such as Antony or Lepidus.

Octavian had never been consul or led an army, yet success would depend on his acting as though he already possessed the *auctoritas* that those two positions conferred. Antony was right when he said later than Octavian owed everything to a name.[7] That name was 'Caesar'. The young pretender would have to bury the name he was born with. In a sense he would have to become Caesar – even to be Caesar – in the eyes of other people. Not for him the slow progression over twenty or more years through the traditional *cursus honorum*, that long career ladder on which a man climbed up by such steps as election to quaestor, aedile and praetor before finally reaching the top, as consul, if lucky, by the age of forty-two. That had been Caesar's route. A few, like Mark Antony, had reached it earlier, but only by bending the rules. The idea of a teenager becoming consul was unthinkable. Yet it would happen, and relatively soon.

We can now see clearly, what otherwise might have been puzzling, why Octavian took the best part of a month to travel from Brundisium to Rome. Like a modern politician on a whistle-stop campaign, he was showing himself to his potential supporters and arousing their hope that all that Caesar stood for was not yet lost. He did not need to swear bloody vengeance on Caesar's murderers; often enough, the people themselves called out to him, as a son, to avenge his adoptive father as a matter of duty. By the time he reached his parents' villa at Puteoli he was able to say to them with passion, and in the original Greek of Homer, what the hero Achilles had declared over the body of his fallen comrade Patroclus: 'May I die this very hour, who failed to save him from death!'[8] According to the Greek historian Appian, who had a fine pen for the theatrical gesture, Octavian's mother thereupon embraced him joyfully as the one who alone was worthy of great Caesar, her uncle.[9]

Perhaps the most important of Octavian's achievements on this journey was to have sown the seeds that would lead to his future alliance with Cicero. Initially it proved to be stony ground. They met for the first time at the proconsul's villa, where Balbus was staying as a guest in company with Hirtius and Pansa, the consuls-designate for the following year. 'Octavian has just stepped over from Philippus's villa,' Cicero wrote to Atticus; and he added, perhaps with tongue in cheek: 'He's utterly devoted to me *(mihi totus deditus)*!'[10] Next day Cicero provided a more serious and considered judgement after a longer visit by Octavian, who, by a mixture of deference and youthful charm, was apparently hoping to win the active friendship of a senior statesman old enough to be his grandfather. 'His entourage call him Caesar, but Philippus doesn't, so we won't, either. It's just not possible that he can be a good citizen. He's surrounded by a crowd of people who claim they can't tolerate the present situation, and so they menace our friends with death. What do you suppose will happen when the boy gets to Rome, where our liberators, who have won fame for ever, can't even stay?'[11]

Most of the conspirators had in fact left Rome voluntarily by that time. Brutus and Cassius, as serving praetors, suffered the further indignity of having to ask Antony's permission, which he was pleased to grant. Antony had meanwhile cemented his relationship with Lepidus by two important moves. First, he gave his daughter in marriage to Lepidus's son. Secondly, he arranged for Lepidus himself to be installed as Chief Priest of Rome *(Pontifex Maximus)* – partly in order to exclude Octavian from that influential office, which Caesar, the previous holder, had wanted to bequeath to him.[12] Such a bequest had no basis in republican law because the office was not hereditary.

With his most dangerous enemies out of the way and the city streets temporarily calm, on 21 April, by coincidence the same day that Octavian first called on Cicero, Antony now felt it was safe for him, too, to leave Rome. Antony needed a month or so to travel south to Campania and oversee the resettlement of large groups of Caesar's veterans, whose clamour for revenge on the assassins might now, he hoped, be stilled. Again, he calculated that it was safer to move these former soldiers out of Rome on a permanent basis, amid rumours that some were planning to murder Brutus, if they could only find him. Brutus and Cassius had, in fact, taken refuge not far distant at Antium, on the Latium coast, from where a day's ride would take them back to the city. It was a ride they would never make.

In Antony's absence, but before Octavian's arrival, pro-Caesarian violence erupted once more in and around the Forum. Followers of the executed impostor Herophilo put up a column in place of his destroyed altar, and rioted after some of Caesar's statues were removed by the authorities. One demonstrator led them to a shop where the statues were being dismantled. This was not an especially uncommon practice. Often enough, the trunk and limbs of a statue would be saved in order to put some new leader's head on them. The enraged mob, however, burnt the shop to the ground. Dolabella, now the only resident consul, called for troop reinforcements. They pulled down the column and inflicted horrifying reprisals. Any who resisted were killed. Of the survivors, Dolabella crucified those who were slaves and threw to their death over the Tarpeian Rock those who were freedmen.

Cicero was exultant. In a series of letters from Puteoli and later from another of his villas in Pompeii, he praised his former son-in-law to the skies. 'O, my wonderful *(mirificum)* Dolabella – now I can say he is really mine!' he wrote to Atticus on May 1. 'Down from the Rock with them! Up onto the cross! Away with their column! . . . It's positively heroic!'[13] To Cassius, he wrote of the new optimism he felt after Dolabella's actions, advising the arch-conspirator that it ought now to be safe for him to return to Rome.[14] Cicero himself, however, was already planning to go abroad, to spend the summer and autumn in the relative safety of Greece.

He had received a letter from Antony a few days earlier, asking with great politeness for a personal favour, but including the warning, 'Although I am certain, Cicero, that your good fortune is beyond all peril, nevertheless I judge that you would prefer to act out your old age in tranquillity and honour rather than in worry.'[15] Cicero, now in his early sixties, could take a hint. He replied that he would always be ready to do whatever Antony might wish.[16] The same day, 26 April, he wrote to Atticus, prophesying a massacre *(caedem maximam)* of all who had wanted Caesar dead, unless they were prepared to escape to Sextus Pompey's camp or to Decimus Brutus, now in Cisalpine Gaul with its two legions and, for the moment, safe.[17]

It was in the immediate aftermath of Dolabella's savage repression of the riots that Octavian finally reached Rome.

According to the chroniclers, a large halo surrounded the sun in a multicoloured glow as the young man entered the city gates,[18] supposedly a favourable sign from heaven. In order not to show hubris or otherwise give the wrong impression, he had parted from the main body of his followers and walked in with only the minimum number of attendants consistent with his personal safety from street ruffians. He was coming, after all, as a suppliant in the first instance, to ask the praetors' court to formalize and register his adoption as Caesar's son, a move too important to risk its being blocked if an open display of power on his part should antagonize any of the magistrates. He was also, of course, hoping to conciliate Antony in the hope of persuading him to hand over, without a fight, the money he had acquired from Calpurnia on the night of the Ides. As for Caesar's papers, he can hardly have expected to get them in any circumstances.

Antony returned to Rome in mid-May. His entrance to the city was in marked contrast to Octavian's. The consul was accompanied by 6,000 armed men, the equivalent of a legion at full strength – a rare enough occurrence in itself, as a legionary commander usually had to reckon on getting by with only 5,000 for most practical purposes. When people asked what the 6,000 men were intended for, Antony stunned the city by saying they were his personal bodyguard.[19] A more blatant demonstration of unconstitutional power could scarcely be imagined. Caesar never went that far. It must have convinced the *optimates* that his assassination had not restored republican *libertas* but had provoked a further step in the opposite direction, towards rule by the use of military force.

As Cicero put it, the despot had been removed but the despotism remained.[20] Antony now had a bigger force in Rome than Lepidus, who, in any case, was leaving the city at about this time to take over the two huge and only partly tamed provinces to which he had been appointed as governor, one in Gaul, the other in Spain. From now on it became plain that Antony's objective was to acquire as big an army as possible before he ceased to be consul at the end of the year. What would he do with such an army? Cicero had no doubt: Antony would use it to make war on his enemies and ultimately to take over the state.[21]

Balbus had visited Cicero again on 11 May to tell him that Antony was not simply resettling veterans in Campania but getting them and other former comrades to swear an oath to support Caesar's edicts. In addition, he had instructed them to keep their weapons to hand, and in good condition, against the time when they would be needed. Cicero lamented to Atticus that the killing of Caesar had been carried out with the spirited courage of men but the planning capacity of children; they had made the mistake of leaving an heir behind.[22] In this instance, Cicero was clearly referring not to Octavian but to Antony as the (political) heir in question – clear evidence that he did not yet see the younger man as a serious contender.

Octavian applied for a private interview with Antony on the consul's return to Rome. When it was granted he was kept waiting for what he considered an insulting length of time at the entrance to Pompey's Gardens, where the meeting was to take place. Antony is said to have spoken haughtily *(superbe)*, while Octavian was polite but persistent in pressing his demands for his full inheritance, including the money removed from Calpurnia's custody. In reply, Antony said bluntly that he no longer had the money, because he had already spent it in the interests of the state; in any case they would need to work out how much of it, if any, really belonged to Caesar and how much comprised public funds. Further discussion was stifled by his assertion that, as consul, he was not obliged to account for his actions to a young man like Octavian, who lacked any official position. He advised him to give up his quest, as the inheritance would be a heavy burden to him, in view of the amounts Caesar had promised as gifts to the citizens. He promised, however, to do what he could to see that an appropriate *lex curiata* was passed to validate his adoption.[23]

Octavian remained polite to the end of the brief interview, but he left Pompey's Gardens more determined than ever to get his way and see justice done. He began by selling large amounts of family property to try to raise enough to honour Caesar's bequest of 300 sesterces to each citizen. Philippus helped by sales from his own extensive property interests; and, more surprisingly still, Pedius and Pinarius pledged to him their shares of one-eighth each in Caesar's estate.[24] They, at least, must have had confidence in Octavian's ability to win it all back for them in the end. He and his agents meanwhile spread the news among the citizens of how Antony had taken the money that Caesar had earmarked for them, but that Octavian would make good the pledge. Within a short time his popularity soared while the consul's slumped.

Antony resorted to menaces. He warned his new rival to stop ingratiating himself with the People or he would have him thrown into prison.[25] Octavian called his bluff. Balbus was no doubt on hand to advise him that Antony could not afford to be seen locking up Caesar's lawful heir, because of the probable adverse reaction of the 6,000 soldiers who were guarding him. The worst he could do, short of murder, was take him down a peg or two. This led to a number of petty incidents. Once, after they clashed during legal proceedings because Octavian tried to address him from a dais instead of from the floor, Antony ordered his lictors to pull him down and remove him from the court.[26] He also reneged on his promise to help push forward the adoption process, by arranging behind his rival's back for some compliant tribunes to postpone the hearings indefinitely.

Nothing daunted, Octavian took to moving around the city in the middle of a crowd of supporters, who evidently acted as a sort of unofficial bodyguard to protect him from the possibility of being roughed up by the many street thugs in the pay of his enemies. Every so often, when he spotted a likely audience of citizens or soldiers, he would leap up on a wall or some other elevated position to harangue them. His standard message was that he was not seeking their support for himself but in order to defend Caesar and his legacy against the attacks of his detractors; he insinuated that otherwise they would never be safe in their enjoyment of what Caesar had left them. He called for Antony to stop helping himself to Caesar's money until all the citizens had been paid their share; then he, as Caesar's true heir, would be content to let Antony keep the rest.[27]

This was transparent rabble-rousing, with his valid complaints intermingled with flights of eloquent insincerity. Oratory of that sort was not, however, peculiar to Octavian. Professional speakers, including Cicero, practised similarly shameless techniques and taught them to their pupils. Hyperbole ruled. The Roman voters were so used to it that they no doubt discounted the less plausible statements of Octavian, but his direct appeal to their self-interest would have struck home. It was common gossip that Antony, having embezzled the money from Calpurnia, was now raiding an even larger cache of Caesar's, at the Temple of Ops, ancient goddess of plenty.[28]

To help restore his credibility among the veterans as a loyal Caesarean, Antony began to shift the emphasis of his public pronouncements away from his earlier policy of conciliation. He attacked verbally those who had plotted against Caesar, but without going so far as to call for their prosecution. The bipartisan truce which Antony had initiated on 17 March was thus beginning to show signs of breaking down, and the ripples spread out from Rome to alarm all those many conspirators who had fled the city and were longing to return. Cicero, believing that war was imminent and he himself too old to fight, now applied to Dolabella for a place as a legate on the team he would be taking to Syria later that year as governor-designate;[29] he would be able to join up with them as they passed through Greece, where he already planned to go. Briefly he became so despairing of the future that he could no longer take comfort from the Ides of March: whatever Caesar had done to subvert the Republic, he had not been 'a master one had to run away from'.[30]

The *optimates*, and especially the assassins among them, had every cause to worry about the turn events were taking. Various actions of Antony were now being perceived as a calculated plan to achieve personal supremacy by manipulating the constitution during the remainder of his year as consul. Two or three weeks after the Ides, the Senate had allotted Macedonia and Syria to Antony and Dolabella as their respective proconsular provinces for 43. Before the end of April Antony changed his stance. He still wanted the six legions that Caesar had sent to Macedonia but he no longer wanted the province that went with them. Instead, he wanted two other provinces, those of northern Italy and of Gallia Comata ('long-haired' Gaul).

His ostensible reason was that, at least for the time being, the six legions were no longer required for their original purpose, and most of them ought therefore to be redeployed where they might be urgently needed if, for example, some of the restless tribes of Gaul should take advantage of the turmoil caused by Caesar's death and foment a new revolt against Roman rule. It was certainly not unreasonable to fear that eventuality, nor for Antony to consider himself the best-qualified person to take on the responsibility of ensuring that Gaul remained loyal. Equally, it would be prudent to start moving some legions back across the Adriatic as early as practicable. He called a meeting of the Senate for 1 June to discuss a proposed *lex permutatione provinciarium* to make the necessary changes of provincial governorships for the next consular year, but effectively handing him immediate control of the six legions.

The *optimates* were hardly likely to accept these dispositions at face value. If they were carried through they would place Antony in a position similar to that of Caesar just before he crossed the Rubicon – except that Antony would not have to march on Rome because he would already be there. Six infantry legions of about 5,000 men each, plus their associated squadrons of cavalry, companies of archers and other light-armed troops represented an overwhelming force to add to the 6,000-strong 'bodyguard' Antony had recruited. Waiting in the wings would be Lepidus, with some of the remaining Gallic legions, blocking the north-western land route into Italy, and Publius Vatinius, a staunch Caesarian in command of at least three legions in Illyricum, covering the north-eastern approaches. That would leave the two legions in northern Italy under Decimus Brutus hopelessly outnumbered; and Decimus would be legally bound to hand over his command to Antony in 43.

In order to lull the Senate, Antony introduced a law making it a capital offence for anyone even to suggest appointing a dictator, let alone striving to become one. The senators voted eagerly in favour, but the ploy was not sufficient. They had seen enough of Antony by now to realize that he was quite capable of assuming the role of a tyrant without bothering about the precise title he might choose to hold. It must have become plain to him before the date set for the debate, 1 June, that he would not win a senatorial majority for his proposed change of provinces. Like so many *populares* before him, he decided to turn instead to an Assembly of the People. The bipartisan arrangement of 17 March faced collapse after only two-and-a-half months.

The vote of the People, however, was by no means a foregone conclusion. They, too, had seen the tyrannical side of Antony's behaviour when he had crushed the rioting by debtors during Caesar's absence from the city. There was also widespread popular disapproval of the way he had compromised with the assassins but shown unremitting hostility to Octavian. This disapproval was felt particularly by Caesar's many former veterans in and around Rome, including the senior officers of Antony's own bodyguard, who had been pressing him to offer the hand of friendship to

Caesar's heir. He evidently decided it would now pay him to do so, if only until after the votes were counted.

In an interview with the military tribunes of his bodyguard – their rank is conventionally deemed to be roughly equivalent to that of colonel in modern times – Antony offered a reasoned explanation of his attitude towards Octavian, in terms they would be likely to approve of. The young man, he claimed, had shown arrogance and a general lack of respect towards his elders, including himself as consul. It was the sort of behaviour that deserved a reprimand. However, in view of the concern which they had expressed, he would be prepared to observe friendly relations with Caesar's heir, so long as he, for his part, would stop being so presumptuous. The colonels immediately arranged a meeting between the two rivals, and after some initial sparring, for form's sake, they agreed to cooperate.[31]

The stage was now set for the Senate to be bypassed and hoodwinked. The *optimates* were apparently led to believe that the vote would be taken in the *Comitia Centuriata*, where they were strong enough to anticipate victory. Instead the measure was put to the popular Assembly, voting in tribes rather than in centuries, where the newly united Caesarians under Antony and Octavian would have a much better chance of achieving a majority. Security was tight to the point of menace. Those tribunes who were bribable had already been bribed; any who remained did not dare to interpose a veto. No magistrate stepped up to the rostra to protest that the meeting had been called without sufficient notice, effectively disfranchising those who would not have had time to reach the city or might not have heard about it.

On Antony's orders the Forum was surrounded before dawn on 2 June and roped off into a number of separate sections where voters from particular tribes could assemble before filing to the ballot boxes. The comparatively small size of the old Forum implies that turnout must have been low, especially in conditions where people would be afraid of an outbreak of violence. Octavian stood by the ropes urging them to vote 'yes'.[32] It was, to be sure, a defeat for the *optimates*, but he must have known that the result would clear the last legal hurdle on the consul's path to supreme power. Evidently, at that stage, Octavian realized that he had more to gain by cooperating with Antony than by opposing him. That feeling was not reciprocated. After the vote, Antony cynically dropped him and resumed hostilities.

Octavian was forced to start again. He might be only a slender teenager, barely 5ft 6in tall, but be now, after just a few weeks, he had the nucleus of a 'party' working for him. It was not, of course, the equivalent of a political party in the modern sense, but it had a leader and a cause, experienced advisers, substantial funds and popular support. It needed no slogan but the single, charismatic name which Octavian now bore: *Caesar!*

SIX

OCTAVIAN FIGHTS BACK

Octavian needed to get his message across to the widest possible audience in the shortest possible time, before public outrage at the assassination of Caesar faded into a reluctant acceptance of the *status quo*. In Rome that meant going to the races at the Circus Maximus, or to the smaller arenas, permanent or temporary, in and around the capital. It would be impossible to address the crowd at the bigger events and hope to be heard by any but those nearest to him, so he needed to achieve publicity by some other form of personal projection. He could, perhaps, cause a stir by entering among a disciplined group of supporters, all shouting out for him in unison; but he and his advisers thought of a better way. They made arrangements to display Caesar's gilded throne in a prominent position at such events, so that Octavian could stand beside it and take the salute from the crowd.

The law permitting the throne's exhibition on various kinds of public occasions – passed during Caesar's dictatorship – had not been repealed. In theory, at least, formal permission from the authorities would not be required. The first major opportunity to arise would be at the *Ludi Cerialis*, the annual games in honour of the goddess Ceres (Demeter), whose favour guaranteed the growth of crops. An aedile named Critonius, a middle-ranking magistrate who was probably acting on Antony's instructions, refused to allow the throne to be carried into the arena where the games were about to take place. Octavian promptly haled Critonius before the consular court for allegedly breaking the law.

Antony, from his judgment seat, said he would refer the matter to the Senate for decision, knowing that the senatorial majority, anxious to preserve the still shaky peace, would not support a move to stir up public opinion against the assassins. The young man retorted that the law was clear enough already, and that he would therefore exhibit his adoptive father's throne while the measure remained in force, like all the other acts of Caesar that Antony had advised his fellow-senators to maintain without exception. Antony then lost patience and used his prerogative as consul to forbid Octavian's plan out of hand.[1] That would cost him further loss of popularity within the Caesarian party, which he claimed to lead, but he was no doubt correct in assuming it would be worse to allow his rival so many recurring opportunities to whip up the masses against his policy of *rapprochement* with those who had supported Caesar's murder.

More than fifty days a year were set aside for public games. Only a small proportion featured gladiators and exotic wild animals; apart from the immensely popular chariot racing, there were also a number of important *ludi scaenici* ('scenic games'), which consisted chiefly of theatrical performances but might also include some form of institutionalized violence as well, to draw in the crowds. Just such an event was due to be given by Brutus early in July, whose aim in organizing it was similar to that of Octavian, to rally his supporters and demonstrate to Antony's regime the extent of his *auctoritas*. Octavian's partisans, thwarted over the *Ludi Cerealis*, resolved not to let the chief assassin get away with trumpeting his cause in the heart of the city less than four months after stabbing Caesar.

Antony was evidently content to allow Brutus's games, the *Ludi Apollinares*, dedicated to the god Apollo, to go ahead without interference – so long as Brutus himself was not present as a focus for popular discontent. Indeed, the consul's biggest mistake that summer was not so much his second rejection of Octavian's support and friendship, expensive though that was to prove, but his evident belief that Brutus and Cassius were no longer a significant threat to his plans for personal supremacy in the Republic. Three days after the People effectively voted him his extended command of six legions, he had arranged for the Senate, on 5 June, to appoint the two chief assassins to worthy but junior posts supervising overseas corn supplies to Rome.

Believing that he had all the cards safely in his own hands, Antony thought it would do no harm to give them an honourable pretext for leaving Italy during the remainder of their praetorial year, while at the same time, from his point of view, keeping them out of mischief. Like Caesar, he was making the mistake of thinking he could do a deal with them, that they would be grateful to him for smoothing their path after the assassination, when he could have used his power to kill them. They plainly found his clemency patronizing, even insulting; as in the case of Caesar, it indicated to them that he no longer feared their opposition.

Cicero, too, had lost confidence in their ability, and his own, to achieve any serious progress in the optimate cause while Antony remained consul with full republican *potentia* and *auctoritas*. On 7 June, having stayed out of Rome but kept himself informed of the Senate's debate two days earlier, he went to see Brutus and Cassius at the coastal resort of Antium, south of the capital, to advise them to fall in with Antony's plan by accepting the Corn Commission posts, so that they could be sure of living to fight another day.

The house where they met belonged to Brutus's mother, Servilia, who was so entrenched in the upper reaches of the aristocracy that she was also the mother-in-law of Lepidus and Cassius, as well as half-sister of the dead republican hero Cato, and former lover of Julius Caesar. Her affair with Caesar had been sufficiently notorious and long-lasting that he was popularly rumoured, quite falsely, to have been Brutus's father. In Caesar's consular year of 59, they at last became free to marry, but he failed to pop the question. Instead, he married the teenage Calpurnia, no doubt supposing she would give him a better chance of begetting male heirs. Did Servilia react like a woman scorned? We do not know. What is plain, however, is that at the meeting at Antium she showed herself totally committed to the support of her son Marcus, who had so publicly stabbed her ex-lover to death.

Cicero's report of the meeting,[2] conveyed in a letter to Atticus, is uniquely precious. Not only does it throw a flood of light on a vitally important juncture in the downfall of the Republic, but it is the only genuinely contemporary account from that era, written down almost immediately afterwards by a participant, which shows women operating behind the scenes to influence and change political decisions at the highest level. We have to read between the lines because even Cicero himself is not fully aware of what is going on in front of him. The letter can only be adequately interpreted with the benefit of hindsight: later that summer Brutus and Cassius would sail east to raise armies to fight a new civil war. At Antium they picked his brains but decided not to take him into their confidence.

When Cicero arrived, Servilia's house was already full of her relatives and partisans, talking among themselves. During the course of the meeting he was given clues, without realizing what they portended, because he was so concerned to project his own preconceived views, harking back to the past and to what they might have achieved if only they had followed his advice. Servilia herself was flanked by two other women, her own redoubtable daughter Tertulla (Junia Tertia), wife of Cassius, and Portia, Cato's child, the sensitive and vulnerable wife of Brutus. It was Brutus who greeted Cicero on his arrival, and Cassius, 'looking like a warrior', who walked in later during a Ciceronian oration to the roomful of aristocrats.

Completely misreading the situation, Cicero was trying to persuade Brutus to accept his appointment to the Corn Commission for Asia. Servilia evidently considered it to be nothing more than a pretext to get her son out of the way.

Cassius agreed with her. He, too, had been offered a similar post to import Sicilian corn. 'Do you think I should have accepted an insult as though it were a favour?' he demanded scornfully of Cicero, making it plain that he was going not to Sicily but to Greece, with the unspoken inference, probably clear to everyone else in the room, that he would be looking for support there against Antony.

Cicero evidently failed to pick up the hint. It would become apparent later that Cassius, no doubt with the backing of Tertulla, was hoping to persuade Brutus to go east with him to try to take over the many legions there that had never served under Caesar. At the meeting, Brutus gave the appearance of being unsure what he was going to do next. Ought he to go to Rome, he asked, as he was giving the games for Apollo that might boost his reputation with the citizens? Cicero urged him emphatically not to go: his life was too precious to be risked there at present. 'But if it were possible to be safe there,' Brutus persisted, 'would you agree?'

With his reply to this question, Cicero snuffed out any remaining likelihood that Brutus and Cassius would take him into their confidence at that stage. He repeated his advice to stay out of Rome, adding, 'Nor should you go to a province – either now or after your praetorship ends.' In view of what had gone before, Cicero clearly did not mean that Brutus should not go to the province of Asia to oversee the corn supply. He meant he should not risk going abroad where legions were stationed in what, to Cicero, must have seemed the delusory hope of subverting the soldiery. It was intended as a discreet but friendly warning from an elder statesman.

Cassius quickly changed the subject to talk about lost opportunities. That encouraged Cicero to relaunch himself into a speech about how, on the Ides, Brutus and Cassius should have summoned the Senate after the assassination and taken charge of the Republic before Antony emerged from his hiding place. Servilia, angry at this implied criticism of her son and son-in-law, exploded, 'Well, I'll be . . . ! I never heard such stuff!' The great orator suddenly lost his voice. *'Ego me repressi,'* he wrote afterwards.[3] 'I held myself back.' Servilia wound up the debate, having had quite enough of Cicero's advice. She announced imperiously that she would arrange for the two appointments to the Corn Commission to be excised from the Senate's resolution. Nobody present seems to have doubted that this was within her power and influence to achieve.

Cicero, who intended to escape to Greece until Antony's consular year ended, left the meeting dissatisfied and gloomy, consoled only by the thought that he had at least done his duty by being present, even if nobody had taken his advice. Brutus, Cassius and their associates, he wrote, lacked a coherent plan, and no way of carrying one out *('nihil consilio, nihil ratione, nihil ordine')*. Nothing could indicate more clearly that Cicero had failed to understand what the meeting had been called for. Not only did they have an excellent plan, but one that would work spectacularly well, later that summer, when they sailed abroad in separate flotillas to put it into effect.

Before they did so, Brutus suffered a public humiliation at the *Ludi Apollinares*, which he had financed lavishly through buying a variety of wild beasts well before the Ides of March. A huge crowd of citizens turned up to watch the animals hunted to death in the arena, or matched against each other and provoked to fight. Brutus, who did not dare to show his face, paid a group of men to shout out for his recall to the city, along with that of Cassius and the other conspirators. But the agents of Octavian had evidently done their work well in placing enough of his supporters there to encourage most of the crowd to shout back. They brought the games to a halt in protest and they did not resume until Brutus's claque had been cowed into silence.[4]

When a vacancy next arose on the tribunes' bench, Octavian thought at first to nominate his own candidate, but then changed his mind – no doubt prompted by his team of advisers – and announced that he himself would stand for election. This alarmed the *optimates*, who had experience since the days of the Gracchus brothers of the damage that a determined tribune could inflict on their vested interests. Octavian, if elected, would be in a position to bring before a popular assembly any matter he chose – and the rumour was that he would move to prosecute Caesar's assassins, thereby negating the Senate vote of 17 March for an amnesty. After the massive public demonstration at Brutus's games of support for Octavian and revulsion towards the assassins, there could be little doubt of what the outcome would be if no other tribune could be found hardy enough to risk vetoing the proceedings.

Antony reacted swiftly and effectively to thwart him. Although Octavian had been born a plebeian, his adoption into the Julian clan made him a patrician and so, at least theoretically, ineligible to serve as tribune of the People. Antony, sure of the overwhelming support of the senators, threatened the full force of the law against him unless he withdrew his candidature. Octavian had to back down. To prevent him from fielding his own 'Caesarian' candidate, Antony then used his consular power, against precedent, to cancel the election on the provocative grounds that Rome had enough tribunes already and did not need another one for the time being.[5]

The next important games scheduled for Rome, organized and paid for, with the help of friends, by Octavian himself, were the *Ludi Victoriae Caesaris*, lasting for ten days from 20 July. This grand event had originally been intended by Caesar to serve as a showcase for his entire regime, and few of the leading *optimates* are likely to have supported it, except with reluctance. Caesar's former partisans, especially his veterans, packed the stadium. Yet Antony once again intervened to prevent the display of the golden throne – perhaps because he feared that Octavian might try to sit on it and accept the plaudits of the whole crowd, as if he were truly Caesar himself.

The tables were turned by what we must consider to be a tremendous stroke of luck, but which the Romans understandably took to be a sign from heaven. During the course of the games, a comet appeared at dusk, trailing fire in the northern segment of the sky, where it remained visible for some nights.[6] It was hailed as Caesar's spirit flying to his eternal home among the gods. Octavian seems to have accepted it as an authentic indication that the gods were on his side. The psychological boost this gave him should not be underestimated in our less credulous times – nor the effect it had in increasing his own already growing popularity and status. He arranged for a representation of a star to be fixed to Caesar's statue in the Temple of Venus, which the dictator had built in honour of his divine ancestress. Caesar's cult, previously stamped out amid the ashes of the funeral pyre in the Forum, thus got off to a new and literally flying start, carrying Octavian's reputation along with it.

Shortly before the appearance of the comet, Antony had been trying to reassure the optimate majority in the Senate, who, in line with Cicero, had become jittery about the imminent prospect of the Macedonian legions marching to Rome. What guarantee could there be that he would not use them to take over the state like Sulla, Marius and Caesar before him? Antony probably regarded himself as being most vulnerable to assassination in the waiting period before the 30,000-strong army arrived. In a speech to an open-air assembly in the Forum, which any citizen had the right to attend, he softened his previous line of principled opposition to the conspirators[7] and announced that he was calling a meeting of the Senate for 1 August. This encouraged the dual belief that he was clearing the way for important concessions, and that these would be formalized through the medium of Senate and People, rather than the People alone.

Rumour enlarged and expanded on these vague hints of a coming thaw, so that by the time the news reached Cicero on 6 August, *en route* to Greece by sea, it was being suggested that a diplomatic settlement was imminent under which the assassins would be allowed to return peacefully to Rome and resume their public careers. By a coincidence which may have seemed to him to be the work of providence, Cicero's ship had already left the toe of Italy 30 miles behind him when it was forced back to port by sudden contrary winds. Although it was nearly a week since the crucial meeting of the Senate, the travellers who reported the news to him had left Rome before the end of July, so it was well out of date. But they told him, accurately, that Brutus had sent out letters from Naples to all former consuls and praetors urging them to attend the debate.[8]

Cicero decided there and then to abandon his plan to seek safety abroad, but to return home instead, knowing that another meeting of Senate had been called for 1 September. He was unaware that the political situation in the capital had suffered a total reversal. The reason is not entirely clear, but it may well be that the upsurge in public feeling provoked by the advent of Caesar's comet was a contributory factor in forcing Antony to revert to his previous stance. In addition, Brutus and Cassius had done their cause no good by issuing a public statement, as serving praetors, justifying their actions on republican grounds; although they offered to go into permanent exile if that should prove to be the only way to maintain peace, they added that wherever in the empire they might find themselves, there the Republic would live on also.[9]

The arrogance of this announcement infuriated the senior officers of the Rome garrison, who once again confronted Antony over his treatment of Octavian, but this time their objection took the form of a warning rather than a plea. Their continued support was crucial for the consul, who could not afford the risk of their switching allegiance to Octavian and taking many of the junior officers and other ranks with them. He published an edict accusing Brutus and Cassius of making clandestine preparations for civil war by sending their agents to try to suborn the Macedonian legions.[10] Whether the two men were actually doing so at that time is not known, but Octavian was certainly trying to ensure that those troops would not act against him, by reminding them discreetly, through his friends, of their promises before he left Apollonia and holding out the prospect of better pay and conditions if he should ask them to join him.

That was treason. Octavian was now playing a very dangerous game. It was one thing to attack Antony in public for not punishing Caesar's assassins and blocking his inheritance – currently mired in legal wrangling in the courts – but quite another to try to induce state troops to desert a consular army and transfer their allegiance to a private individual. No doubt he was careful to keep his distance, so that he could claim to know nothing of what was being done in his name. While that might save him if he appealed to a People's Assembly against conviction in a senatorial court, it would scarcely protect him from any rougher justice which Antony could be expected to mete out, glad of a genuine justification for eliminating this awkward rival.

Octavian, however, managed to evade immediate detection, although he would soon enough begin openly recruiting his own private army in Antony's absence. He no doubt justified these activities to himself by reflecting that it had been much more blatant treason that the assassins had used against his adoptive father. His outward manner was plausible enough to make even the sceptical Cicero begin to wonder if he might not, after all, be susceptible to reasoned persuasion about the motivation of 'our heroes', Brutus and Cassius. 'I perceived in Octavian enough of intelligence, enough of spirit, that it seemed to be the case, with reference to our heroes, that his feelings will be as we would wish,' he had written to Atticus just before leaving Pompeii for Greece. 'But what credence we should place in someone of his age, name, heredity and educational upbringing, is a matter requiring great deliberation. The stepfather [Philippus], whom we saw at

Astura, thinks none at all. However, he should be cherished and, if nothing else, separated from Antony.'[11]

The Senate met, as planned, on 1 August, when Antony had to suffer a direct attack on his latest change of policy from Calpurnius Piso, whose status as Caesar's father-in-law would protect him from possible reprisals. No other senator was brave enough to support him. Antony, however, was still hoping to keep the peace process alive, at least until his legions finally arrived in Italy. Having failed in his ploy to reduce the *auctoritas* of the two chief assassins by giving them minor supervisory jobs in the corn supply system, he now persuaded the Senate to appoint them as governors of provinces where they could do no serious harm, Brutus to Crete and Cassius to Cyrene. But this new gesture proved to be no more successful than the first.

The breach became final after an exchange of letters. Brutus and Cassius, signing jointly, wrote from Naples on 4 August: 'We have read your letter, which is very much like your edict – insulting, menacing and below the level of dignity appropriate to a letter from you to us.' They continued in this vein at some length, denying allegations of tampering with his troops and accusing Antony of threatening them, as legally elected praetors, with armed violence. 'Our freedom is more important to us than your friendship,' they declared. And, in case their warning was not clear enough, they added a sharp reminder to Antony of the comparative brevity of Caesar's period of unconstitutional power.[12]

The gloves were off. From now on there would be no talk of compromise between Antony and his supporters on the one hand and the optimate-backed assassins on the other. The irony is that their open breach may have been an unintended consequence of Octavian's actions, both in campaigning at Rome for avenging Caesar's murder and in sending his agents to Macedonia with promises of hard cash for any soldiers who might be prepared to take the risk of changing sides. There is no reason to doubt the word of

Brutus, at least, when he and Cassius denied having tried to suborn the Macedonia-based legions that Antony had ordered to join him in Italy. Antony knew that someone was tampering with the men's loyalty, and may have jumped to the obvious but mistaken conclusion that it was part of an optimate plot to remove him from power before the end of his consulate and prevent him securing the special five-year command voted to him by the People.

Cicero got the news from Brutus himself on 17 August, when the two men met for the last time at Velia, south of the Bay of Naples, as the former consul was returning to his Pompeii residence after abandoning his proposed visit to Greece. Brutus did not, apparently, discuss his own future plans in any detail, although the ships and men he had with him must have indicated clearly enough that he was preparing to leave Italy. Instead, he reproached Cicero for having sought to abandon his country at a time when his presence was sorely needed in the Senate. Cicero evidently assured him of his continued moral support, but wrote to Atticus that he would not be returning to Rome to take part in politics, because he could not see that it would be any use.[13]

Something must have happened quite suddenly to change his mind, because Cicero in fact made an elaborately publicized entry into the capital on the last day of August, fully aware that Antony had called a meeting of the Senate for the next day, 1 September. The fact that large crowds of citizens came out from the city to greet him shows only too clearly that he had advertised his approach well in advance, and was thus testing the strength of his underlying political support. The citizens apparently begged him to stay on in order to defend their interests in the Senate. Antony, too, was adamant that Cicero should attend the next day's meeting, when he was going to propose, as consul, posthumous honours for Julius Caesar, including a one-day holiday dedicated to him each year as if he were indeed a god. To Antony's fury, Cicero declined to attend, excusing himself on the grounds that he needed to rest after his journey.[14]

Cicero's motive, of course, was to avoid having to vote for or against Antony's proposal, or to abstain publicly. He could not vote in favour without conceding, by implication, that Brutus and the other assassins were treacherous criminals rather than liberators. He could not vote against without risking being set upon by Caesarean troops as he left the meeting, and beaten up or perhaps even killed out of hand – an eventuality which Antony would ostensibly deplore while secretly rejoicing that he had got rid of a dangerous adversary without serious risk to his reputation. Cicero's third alternative, abstention, would show vacillation and cowardice, injuring his standing among his peers, his clients and the ordinary voters. Antony apparently considered sending lictors to Cicero's house to bring him by force to the debate, if persuasion failed, but was dissuaded by his friends.

The following day, 2 September, the Senate met again. This time Antony was absent on other business. Cicero, having enjoyed his day of rest, joined the debate and made a powerful speech, his so-called 'First Philippic'[15] against Antony, in which he tore to shreds the consul's political record. It would, admittedly, have been more impressive if he had delivered this carefully reasoned attack to his opponent's face, but Antony was sufficiently disturbed by reports of the speech, and of its reception by other senators, that he drew back from any threat of open violence against the great orator, and spent more than two weeks composing a reply. It was not until 19 September, after Cicero had left Rome, that the consul returned to the Senate to make his considered riposte, in which he accused the absent orator of being the true originator of the conspiracy to assassinate Caesar.[16] And it was not until 20 December, three months later, that Cicero summoned up the courage to attend another meeting of the Senate; he spent his time composing further 'Philippics', mostly circulated in manuscript form, that strayed so far from pure politics as to accuse Antony of moral depravity, sexual inversion, theft, fraud, drunkenness and tyranny.

Why had Cicero decided to burn his boats so comprehensively? The most likely explanation is that between his meeting with Brutus and the delivery of the First Philippic, he had received information which encouraged him to believe that, during his absence from Rome, opposition to Antony's regime had grown enough to make a political fight-back a less risky prospect than it had appeared to be in the early summer. It was perhaps at about this time that he received an offer of a secret deal on Octavian's behalf from two of the young man's most senior relatives; both were ex-consuls, his stepfather Philippus and his brother-in-law Marcellus, husband of his sister, the younger Octavia. It was the same Marcellus who had handed the symbolic sword to Pompey – and then himself refused to fight against Caesar. The deal was that if Cicero would use his influence and his undoubted talents as a public speaker to support Octavian both in the Senate and in the People's Assembly, the young man would guarantee his safety from Antony through the enormous prestige he enjoyed among the soldiers as Caesar's heir.[17] Cicero was not yet ready to cooperate so closely, but the dangerously attractive idea of playing Aristotle to Octavian's Alexander the Great had been sown in his mind to excite his vanity.

Meanwhile, Antony had once again felt it prudent to yield to the pressure from his city-based troops to patch up his long and counter-productive quarrel with Octavian. A public reconciliation took place on the Capitol before crowds of enthusiastic Caesareans,[18] who could see no logic in the consul's persistent opposition to Octavian's principled campaign against the assassins, especially when they were rumoured to be conspiring once more, this time to return to Rome at the head of an invading eastern army. Antony flaunted his new credentials by erecting a statue to Caesar in the Forum, inscribed to a 'parent', thus seeking to claim filial feelings to match Octavian's. He followed this up on 2

October with a speech from the rostra – evidently with the new statue beside him – in which he effectively accused Brutus and Cassius of treason.[19] It seemed that he and Octavian now stood shoulder to shoulder in firm alliance. But half a week was a long time in politics, even in ancient Rome. Three or four days later Antony accused his young rival of plotting to kill him.[20]

Octavian hotly denied the charge – but Cicero, for one, believed in his guilt. 'People think Antony invented it in order to get hold of the young man's money,' he wrote to a friend. 'But good men *(boni viri)* believe it's true, and approve of it . . . Great hopes are riding on him.'[21] Antony had claimed, no doubt accurately, that Octavian had tried to suborn some members of his bodyguard. We know that Octavian had already tried the same technique on the legionary soldiers still in Macedonia, and would do so again. It seems highly likely that at least part of the recent agitation among Antony's large bodyguard for the *rapprochement* between the consul and Caesar's heir had been fomented with the help of Octavian's substantial funds. But was he really guilty of conspiracy to murder the joint head of state? Did his agents exceed their instructions? Or was Antony cynically trying to ruin him by exaggerating the offence?

It is impossible to be sure. With the benefit of hindsight, however, it is obvious that Octavian would have had much more to lose than to gain by killing him. He could not have hoped to take over Antony's place in the way that Antony had taken over Caesar's. Such an assassination, presumably by his own consular guard, would have benefited the *optimates* rather than the Caesarians. As events were soon to prove, Octavian would need a live and powerful Antony within the next twelve months to protect him from what would otherwise have been the overwhelming military superiority of Brutus and Cassius. His senior advisers ought to have told him as much, and probably did so. Seen in that perspective, Octavian must be entitled to the benefit of the doubt.

In any case, Antony did not pursue the matter for more than a few days. The evidence of skullduggery cannot, therefore, have been very strong, and only a few members of the bodyguard were seriously punished. The main result of the affair, no doubt to the delight of the *optimates*, was distrust between the two more bitter than before. That caused them both to raise the stakes dramatically. On 9 October, Antony left Rome for Brundisium to take direct command of four legions that had just disembarked from Macedonia. He had already announced they would be bypassing Rome on their way to Gaul, but it is most unlikely that he intended to send them further away than northern Italy. Cicero was not alone in fearing that the consul planned to march the 20,000 Caesarean soldiers straight to the city and 'bring them down on our necks'.[22]

Once again, however, Antony had underestimated the resourcefulness and daring of his much younger rival. Octavian was about to pay him back, with interest, for the latest insult to his *dignitas*.

SEVEN

THE TEENAGE GENERAL

Antony had good reason for haste. During September and early October the strategic situation had begun to shift perceptibly against him, although he still remained much the strongest individual contender for power. News was slow to reach Rome from the East, but as the scattered information drifted in it became evident that Cassius was creating havoc with Antony's provincial arrangements, which were designed to ensure that most, if not quite all, of the various legions stationed in that region were under the control of loyal Caesarians. Syria, where a maverick ex-Pompeian was still holding out in a besieged city, was especially vulnerable to the blandishments of Cassius because of his military prowess there nearly a decade earlier, when he had saved the province from Parthian invasion after the death and defeat of Crassus.

In the province of Asia, Cassius would also find a firm ally in its governor, Gaius Trebonius, the conspirator who had deliberately kept Antony talking outside the Senate's door while Caesar was being murdered inside. In Egypt, where Cassius's arrival was expected, there was rioting by legionaries, although the cause is not clear. Official despatches to Antony were now being rivalled by secret messages, carried chiefly by slaves or freedmen, to Marcus Scaptius, Brutus's resident agent in Rome, for onward transmission to reliable optimate leaders. Those apparently included Servilia, who passed at least some of this military intelligence on to Cicero.[1]

Brutus himself was in Athens, apparently inactive, but in reality waiting for the Caesarian legions to be posted back

to Italy before making his own planned move to take over
Macedonia and Illyricum, at rather less personal risk than
Cassius was currently shouldering. For many weeks Brutus
was to be seen prominently in public, watching theatrical
performances, giving dinner parties and having long
discussions with Greek philosophers. Out of the public eye
he was engaged in extensive correspondence with his
supporters in the Senate, including Cicero, whom he would
come increasingly to criticize for cooperating with Octavian
– a dangerous young man, in Brutus's opinion, who could
not be trusted to work within the constitution.[2]

The implications of a possible major optimate revival in the
East, leading to renewed dominance in Italy and the West,
were alarming for Antony, and scarcely much better for
Octavian. At best, Caesar's heir would then be obliged to
pursue his political career at a level appropriate to his age,
which implied some years of trailing around in the wake of
his proconsular stepfather, and filling junior posts in the
entourage of a provincial governor or army commander.
Under such a regime, he would have to wait until he reached
his thirties before he could become eligible for election as
quaestor, which conferred membership of the Senate; and he
would have to attain the age of forty-two before he could
stand for election as consul. At worst, however, he could be
killed – or perhaps haled before a senatorial court, convicted
of offences against the state, stripped of his possessions and
even the right to call himself 'Caesar', and banished from
Italy to live in closely monitored obscurity.

Antony's response to the new situation was to make
immediate use of his fresh legions, now at Brundisium, to
bolster his otherwise temporary position as master of the
capital, knowing he would not be able to count on the Senate
once his consulship expired at the end of the year. If he
tamely ordered those troops to march beyond the Alps into
the heartlands of Gaul, in line with his earlier stated
intentions, the effect might be to hand Italy on a plate to his

optimate enemies, should Brutus and Cassius succeed in uniting the East against him. He must already have been aware that Decimus Brutus, another of the assassins, was unlikely to yield northern Italy (the so-called Cisalpine Gaul) to him, as one of his future proconsular provinces, even if he waited for the official date of the handover on 1 January. Decimus had taken command of the two legions already stationed there when he arrived in April, and since then he had recruited more troops at his own expense. He was training these raw recruits in the optimate cause by sending them out on brief punitive expeditions against neighbouring Alpine tribes, to give them practice at killing people in battlefield conditions.

Antony had been a little slow to realize the danger that posed. He would need the continued support of Lepidus and his legions (based in Spain and southern Gaul), but he knew that, as Marcus Brutus's brother-in-law, Lepidus had an important foothold in the optimate camp. The other western generals, Plancus (Gallia Comata) and Pollio (southern Spain), were even less reliable as potential allies unless Antony could convince them of his own superior power. To be sure of doing that, he would need to oust Decimus from his key position controlling the north-western passes leading into and out of Gaul, so that he could not block or seriously delay a conjunction of nominally Caesarian forces.

Cicero would soon be feeding Decimus a novel constitutional doctrine, which he had just refined to his own satisfaction, by which it was permissible for a governor to disregard an official edict transferring his command to a legally named successor if he considered it contradicted the true will of the Senate, at a time when the Senate was too afraid to express it.[3] Decimus was happy to take him at his word. As for Hirtius and Pansa, the moderate Caesarians who were due to become consuls on 1 January, they had been sufficiently alienated by Antony's manipulation of the constitution to have offered their future support to Cicero if he would consent to stay near Rome until their term of office began. They had no intention, at what ought to have been the crowning moment of their careers, of knuckling under to Antony if he tried to make himself, effectively, a new dictator – without, of course, actually assuming that now forbidden title.

Pompey's surviving son, Sextus, had recently ceased to be an officially designated public enemy, having accepted terms negotiated by Lepidus, which permitted him to keep his motley armed forces of soldiers and sailors – no longer rebels, of course, but hardly stout republicans, and certainly not Caesareans. Sextus had no reason to love Antony, and family feeling suggested a preference for the assassins, but it was unlikely he would intervene on either side until he had tested in the courts his true chances of recovering what could still be salvaged of his father's former estate, which had been confiscated and sold off under Caesar's regime.

Ranged against Antony in mid-October, therefore, were most of the important interest-groups in the state, comprising a majority of senators, all of the *optimates*, the resurgent assassins, those many thousands of soldiers and veterans, even in his own ranks, who supported Octavian's mission to avenge Caesar, and, last but not least, the mass of the ordinary citizens of Rome, who now blamed him for risking a fresh outbreak of civil war for the sake of personal ambition, just as they had earlier blamed Brutus and Cassius for destabilizing the state by murdering Caesar. They saw that if Antony were to take over the capital with a mere four or five legions, it might not be long before a rival combination of much larger forces invaded the country to turn him out.

Antony, however, had by now recognized his mistake in allowing Brutus and Cassius to slip the leash so easily: he accepted that he might be involved in a race against time to rebuild his fractured coalition before they reassembled theirs. When he left Rome for Brundisium on 9 October he was clearly intending to rally his reinforcements to the cause of depriving Decimus, one of their 'hate' figures, of his North

Italian command before the due date. If Decimus agreed to go quietly as governor, so much the better; if he resisted, Antony would be justified in recruiting Caesarean reserves among the many veterans in the south to swell his army and force the issue, executing Decimus as an example to the rest.

The way, and the necessary motivation, would then be clear for Lepidus, Plancus and Pollio to join him and place their legions under his overall command. Meanwhile, Antony was sending his consular colleague, Dolabella, to take command in Syria before Cassius could usurp legal authority in the region. If Antony had actually succeeded in these various ventures, clearing Decimus, Cassius, Brutus and Trebonius out of his path, he might well have reverted to his earlier policy of establishing a *modus vivendi* with the more moderate *optimates*, who were anxious for peace. That would have enabled him to follow the earlier example of Caesar: rather than being obliged to immerse himself in the daily grind of politics in Rome, he could lead a great army of conquest for five or ten years to win glory for himself, and further extend the boundaries of the empire.

As an aristocrat by birth and upbringing, Antony was probably conditioned to preferring that more glamorous and exciting route to the very top, but one that did not preclude the exemplary crushing of any who might threaten to take up arms against him. In time he would have been able to arrange his own triumphant return to the capital for extended consulships and, no doubt, settle down to enjoy a uniquely honoured position, underwritten by the presence of his army, as the principal senator whose opinion was always sought first and could not be effectively overruled. Being more ruthless than either Pompey or Caesar in his dealings with his fellow aristocrats, he would have been less likely to make the mistakes that had brought those two great men to untimely deaths.

Whatever Antony's precise intentions, however, Octavian had already taken steps to thwart them some days before the consul left the capital. He sent his agents to Brundisium ahead of his older rival to offer unprecedently large bribes to the legions from Macedonia if they would defect from Antony and serve him instead. Each man would get an initial payment of 2,000 sesterces, with a promised bonus on final victory of 20,000 sesterces (perhaps in annual instalments) to retire on.[4] Those were princely terms to the long-suffering, underpaid legionaries, and it is not surprising that, on arrival at Brundisium, Antony found himself in the thick of a rancorous disagreement with these long-idle troops over money and conditions.

Meanwhile, Octavian, with a massive war-chest, went in person to Campania, accompanied by Marcus Agrippa and their opulent friend Gaius Maecenas, and recruited thousands of Caesar's discharged legionary soldiers, who would otherwise have been available to join Antony against Decimus.[5] Treason, of course – but Octavian and his advisers, who may by now have included Hirtius and Pansa (if not yet Cicero), must have reckoned he had little to lose by recruiting an illegal private army. It was plain that once Antony arrived in Brundisium he would learn from both officers and men the extent of Octavian's efforts to subvert them. Caesar's heir had instructed his agents to get their message across by word of mouth, but they also handed out and pasted up numbers of leaflets in the barracks. These must have been deeply incriminating, and it is not clear on whose instructions they were written and distributed. With such evidence in his hands, Antony would not have found it difficult to have Octavian declared a public enemy and hunted down.

Raising his own army, as a private person with no official standing, was the biggest calculated risk Octavian would ever take in his life, and it was only by a sudden turn of fortune at a critical juncture that he survived it. He had no trouble recruiting men, as another team of his partisans had been preparing in advance the target area of Campania, south of Rome, where there were big concentrations of Caesar's veterans living in early retirement beside the Appian Way, close to the major town of Capua. By offering each former infantryman the same down-payment of 2,000 sesterces, he soon assembled a force of about 10,000 fully experienced soldiers, including centurions of the highest calibre, who naturally qualified for even more money. Before Antony had time to retrace his steps, Octavian marched 3,000 of them to Rome under arms early in November and took over the Forum.[6] Civil war had thus effectively begun, and it was Octavian, just six weeks past his nineteenth birthday, who had started it.

Antony was probably unaware of the rebellion behind his back when he entered Brundisium to a frigid welcome from his new troops. They made it clear they blamed him for conciliating Caesar's assassins instead of prosecuting them, and, contrary to normal tradition on receiving a new commander, they declined to applaud him when he mounted the platform in their barrack square. Antony made matters worse by losing his temper and telling them they should think themselves lucky to have been transferred back to Italy instead of having to spend years away from their homes fighting the Parthians. He also demanded they name and arrest Octavian's agents; he would in any case, he claimed, discover the guilty parties for himself.

But Antony's cardinal error was to offer them a mere 400 sesterces as a future reward for serving him against Decimus. They broke their stony silence by laughing him to scorn. That amount was only one-fifth of the sum on offer, straight away and in hard cash, for switching their allegiance to Octavian – and there had been no mention at all by Antony of a terminal bonus. The laughter turned to booing, the consul became enraged and the meeting broke up in tumult. Storming off the platform he shouted, 'You'll learn to obey my orders!'[7] and then proceeded to demonstrate the extent of his vindictiveness by summoning the military tribunes, the 'colonels' of the legions, to draw up their own lists of all those whom they considered insufficiently loyal. Some hundreds of men, including a number of centurions, were brought before him, and he chose a proportion of them by lot to be put to death.

The executions of these unlucky soldiers, which took place in public before Antony and his wife Fulvia,[8] aroused their comrades more to hatred than to fear. They were well aware that their new general, although acting within the strict terms of military law, had exceeded the traditional bounds of his authority by such an act, especially when it was doubtful whether they were on active service at the time or merely being transferred from one posting to another. The Senate had not declared war on Decimus, and Antony was not yet aware of Octavian's rebellion. The consul's method of punishment fell far short of a full-scale decimation, but it was rarely employed, and then only for grave offences such as cowardice or disobedience in the face of the enemy. Antony's victims, it could be said, had died for misplaced laughter and bad manners. The solidarity of the rest of the soldiers in their hostility towards their commander was such that, in spite of his repeated threats, combined with promises of rewards to informers, not a single man came forward to identify any of Octavian's agents or those who had collaborated with them.

When Antony heard of the scale of Octavian's recruiting campaign in Campania his attitude changed. He called a hasty meeting of his legions and said he was sorry to have felt obliged to punish some of their comrades in the interests of military discipline. To show he was not cruel or mean, he added, he would be content not to impose further punishments and at the same time make it clear that the 400 sesterces he had offered them did not represent a total payment but was simply a preliminary instalment, which would be paid straight away. The men took the money but many of them were simply biding their time. Antony changed some tribunes, whom he suspected of disloyalty, before sending three of the four legions to march in detachments up the east coast towards Ariminum, which lay just inside the boundary of Decimus's province.[9]

On the other side of Italy, the citizens of Rome were alarmed at news of Octavian's approach with some of the veterans he had just recruited. Having been told that Antony was also due to return at the head of an army, many of them were inclined to believe a rumour that the consul and Caesar's heir had become reconciled once more, and were combining their forces to round up the assassins and kill them. Cicero knew better. Octavian had not only taken him into his confidence but asked his advice: should he try to intercept Antony with his unofficial army or should he go to Rome first and seek the help of Senate and People?

It was on the evening of 1 November that Octavian's treasonable letter was delivered at Cicero's door in Puteoli, distracting him from the philosophical works he was writing during his long absence from the centre of power. The young man was 'planning great things', he wrote to Atticus a day or two later:

> Plainly he sees himself making war on Antony, with himself as commander *(dux)*, so I reckon we'll be in arms within a few days. But who are we supposed to follow? Look at his name! Look at his age! And he's asking first to have secret talks with me, either at Capua or somewhere close by. How puerile, if he thinks that could be done in secret! I wrote to tell him it was neither necessary nor possible.[10]

Octavian followed up his own letter by despatching a personal emissary, Caecina of Volaterrae, to brief Cicero, and question him. The situation was growing more urgent by the day: Antony had left Brundisium and was advancing towards the capital with Julius Caesar's old and much-feared Fifth Legion, 'The Larks'. His quickest route, of course, would be westwards to Capua, where the Appian Way turned northwards to Rome, and Cicero would be uncomfortably close to his line of march if he stayed on the coast in Puteoli. He was still too afraid to go to Rome himself, and wondered if he ought not to retire to what he felt might be the safer haven of Arpinum.

He (Octavian) wanted my opinion on whether he ought to proceed to Rome with 3,000 veterans, hold Capua to block Antony's return or make his way instead to the three Macedonian legions which are marching up the east coast route and which he hopes will go over to him . . . I advised him to go back to Rome, where it seems to me he'll have the backing of the urban rabble *(plebecula urbana)* and also – if he demonstrates good faith – that of honest men as well.

Cicero ended his letter to Atticus on a note of lamentation that it should be a nineteen-year-old adventurer of dubious credentials who was seizing the initiative against Antony, rather than a seasoned republican of impeccable family. 'Oh, Brutus! Where are you? What a great opportunity you're passing up!'[11]

Cicero's advice that Octavian should go to Rome seems to have been fairly obvious, since any attempt by his irregulars – not yet drawn up in legionary formation but in loosely connected companies – to risk an immediate head-on clash with the consular forces, would be likely to end in disaster. The young man needed time and professional guidance to get an adequate grip on his army, and the *auctoritas* that the public support of senior senators would help to bestow. Cicero was not yet ready to volunteer for such a role, but in spite of his misgivings he was evidently impressed by Octavian's resourcefulness. It may be that Caecina reported back that Cicero might yet be won over with a little more effort, for Octavian had two successive letters delivered to the orator on one day, 4 November. Cicero complained

Now he wants me to come to Rome straight away, as he wants to act through the Senate. I said that wasn't possible before 1 January . . . He keeps urging me – and I prevaricate. I've no confidence in his youth and I can't see inside his head. I don't want to do anything without your friend Pansa. I dread Antony's power, and I'm not happy about leaving the coast. But I'm afraid of something sensational happening without me . . . He has strong forces (*firmas copias*) and he can side with Decimus Brutus.[12]

The tone of the brief letter was querulous at the start but much more positive by the end. Cicero was beginning to succumb.

The same pattern was repeated the very next day, in a short passage slipped in near the end of a much longer letter about other subjects. The weather was filthy, Cicero complained, and on top of that he was getting letters every day from Octavian urging him to 'save the Republic again'. That was a flattering reference to Cicero's crushing of Catiline's revolt in the year of the teenager's birth, inserted with good effect and rewarded by a genuine, if heavily qualified compliment in return.

He's acted with energy and will come to Rome with a host of soldiers, although he's still plainly a boy. He thinks the Senate will meet at once. Who will attend? And who – if he does come – will be prepared to cross Antony in such an uncertain situation? . . . The boy is incredibly popular in the towns. When he passed through Cales and spent the night at Teanum, *en route* to Samnium, there were amazing scenes of welcome and demonstrations in his favour. Would you have believed it? Because of this I'm going back to Rome sooner than I'd intended.[13]

His return, however, was not soon enough for Octavian, who sat down with his 3,000-strong detachment outside the walls of the capital on 10 November, waiting in vain for any serving magistrate to come out to meet him and bring him before a legally constituted Assembly of the People. Eventually, one of the tribunes, Tiberius Cannutius, agreed to carry out this essential task, without which Octavian's armed entry would have failed in its only remaining purpose, to drum up support for himself among the mass of citizens, because, as Cicero had prophesied, the Senate refused to go into session on his behalf.

That involved a further embarrassing delay for the troops, ironically outside the Temple of Mars, while Cannutius harangued the assembly in the Forum, explaining that Octavian, far from meaning the citizens harm, had come to save them from Antony's tyranny.[14]

Cannutius was by no means a natural supporter of Caesar's heir, but a hard-line optimate whose patron was the proconsul Publius Servilius Isauricus, yet another of the ubiquitous Servilia's distinguished sons-in-law. The tribune had already antagonized Antony by opposing him to his face at an earlier assembly the previous month. His hope was evidently much the same as Cicero's, to use Octavian and his 10,000-strong private army as part of a scratch coalition against suspected would-be dynasts such as Antony. Octavian, however, made it clear once he finally ascended the rostra – with his troops carrying concealed daggers in case of trouble – that his personal priority was to uphold the policies and memory of his adoptive father. He emphasized this pledge with a histrionic gesture of his arm towards the newly erected statue of Julius Caesar. That went down very well with the soldiery. What failed miserably was his further declaration that he and his men stood ready to defend Rome at this moment of crisis against the consul who was even now marching his army from Brundisium to deprive the People of their traditional liberty.[15]

Whatever the assembled citizens may have thought of this mixed message, it had an immediate effect on his soldiers, many of whom indicated that they had suddenly thought of important reasons why they should return home as soon as possible. It transpired that neither Octavian nor his agents had troubled to tell them they had been recruited, in the first place, to fight against Antony, and only later to come to grips with Caesar's assassins. They had supposed their young chief intended to make common cause with Antony, and pursue the same objective. Swallowing his disappointment at their response, Octavian tried to make the best of a bad job. He was in no position to insist, like Antony, on their obedience on pain of death. Instead, he said he counted them as his father's friends, not simply soldiers under military discipline, and therefore any who needed to go home on urgent business could do so.

The result was a fiasco. About 2,000 took their leave while promising to come back as soon as they were able.[16] In the event, a surprisingly large number of them did rejoin him later at Arretium, where he was to set up a temporary headquarters. But the Roman venture had been a humiliating failure. Far from rousing the city's finest to fight under his banner against Antony, with the grateful approval of the Senate, Octavian was left with barely a thousand men to march away. They represented, fortunately, more than just a fig-leaf to cover his exposure. Joined with the major part of his diminished force, they made a tolerable impression as they headed north through Etruria, recruiting more veterans and other volunteers as they went.

Octavian realized he would have done better to have entirely bypassed Rome, its pusillanimous Senate and its fickle masses. Power rather than principle was the chief object of worship there. It was a lesson he would never forget, always supposing he would live long enough to apply it. His present situation was perilous. He saw now that he had made his move prematurely and with inadequate forces for their initial task. They were enough to be a bargaining counter if Antony was prepared to tolerate a negotiated settlement, but for the present they had no taste for a fight against former comrades who had served, like themselves, in Caesar's victorious legions, especially not at a time when Italy was in danger of invasion by their arch-enemies, Brutus and Cassius.

Chastened and alarmed, but not despairing, Octavian saw his best chance as keeping out of Antony's way in the short period remaining before his consulship expired. He could still rely on Hirtius and Pansa to regularize his position in the New Year, when, as the incoming consuls, they would be in a position to incorporate his illegally raised troops, along with himself, in the wider Roman army. Cicero, above all, could use his oratory and influence to smooth his path, if he could be persuaded by fresh pledges of republican rectitude to do so. If the worst really came to the worst, he could join forces temporarily with Decimus Brutus, the cunning conspirator with whom he had shared a carriage the previous summer. He positioned himself within easy marching distance of Decimus's province while he awaited events, consoled by fresh supplies of money from his ample but mysterious sources.

Antony entered Rome without ceremony in late November, prepared to deal imperiously with anyone who got in his way. He left his cavalry outside the walls, but the infantry, armed to the teeth, mounted guard over his house around the clock as if they were in a besieged camp in hostile territory, using passwords and countersigns, and changing personnel at regular intervals.[17] He summoned the Senate to meet on 24 November to debate Octavian's rebellion and his attempts to bribe the consular army to defect. The evidence was too strong to doubt the outcome: under the menace of Antony's troops, the Senate would have little choice but to approve a motion naming Octavian a public enemy, so that every citizen's hand would, in theory, be turned against him. The prescribed punishment for such an outlaw, when caught, was to be tied naked to a cross-tree and beaten to death with heavy rods.

The young man's phenomenal luck held. The crucial Senate meeting was postponed after one of the legions which Antony had ordered to march up the east coast mutinied in Octavian's favour. This was the redoubtable Martian Legion, named after the god of war. Officers and men turned aside from the north road to march west towards Rome. Antony rode out with his cavalry to intercept them before they could reach the capital, if that was their intention. He confronted them from a vulnerable spot outside the gates of Alba. They replied to Antony's efforts to persuade them to return to their former loyalty with a shower of arrows from the walls, and the consul was forced to beat an ignominious retreat.[18] It would have taken several months to enforce their surrender by siege, and he had no time to spare.

Antony returned to Rome, apparently still intending to secure a Senate vote against Octavian. But just as he was about to enter the meeting, held at night by torchlight on the Capitol on 28 November, news came that a second legion, the Fourth, had followed the Martians' example and declared for Octavian.[19] The relative positions of the two Caesarean leaders were now reversed. It was Antony's turn to fear the collapse of his hopes. He kept his nerve, entered the Senate and confined the night's business to such matters as depriving Brutus and Cassius of the relatively unimportant provinces of Crete and Cyrene, which they had been granted as a sop, and which were now irrelevant to the unfolding strategic disaster. More positively, he saw to it that his brother, the praetor Gaius Antonius, was appointed Governor of Macedonia, with immediate orders to stop Brutus usurping the command.[20] No mention was made of any moves to disgrace Octavian.

Next day Antony reviewed what was left of his army at Tibur (Tivoli), a few miles west of the city. While he was administering an oath of allegiance to the troops on parade, many senators and knights came to assure him of their support. With breathtaking initiative he seized the opportunity to make them swear the oath too, promising not to fail in faithfulness to him.[21] Nothing could have been more ominous for the future of the republican constitution than that a serving consul, in command of an army, should have required senators to pledge their loyalty to him personally instead of to the *Senatus Populusque Romanus*.

Antony had been reduced to making up a new constitution

as he went along. Now he literally turned his back on Rome and marched his army north, having already sent envoys ahead to demand that Decimus quit his post and leave his legions behind. For the moment, Octavian could count himself safe again. But it was only the phoney war that was over. The bloodier phase of the conflict he had so recklessly provoked was about to begin.

EIGHT

CICERO PLAYS WITH FIRE

Once Cicero was convinced that Antony would not be coming back to Rome before his consular year expired, he emerged from his bolt-hole at Arpinum to surface in Rome by mid-December. That was just in time to deliver, in quick succession, two of the most powerful speeches of his career, first to an urgently attentive Senate, then to a crowded assembly in the Forum outside. He called for full support for both Octavian and Decimus against Antony, whom he named an assassin *(percussor)*, with no apparent trace of irony. The friends and relatives of the true assassins, of Julius Caesar, now sat on the senatorial benches while he solemnly demanded that Antony be crushed as a public enemy the way he, Cicero, had crushed the rebel Catiline nearly twenty years earlier.[1]

War clouds were darkening. Decimus had defiantly rejected the consul's demand to leave his post. He refused battle and shut himself up in the walled city of Mutina (modern Modena) in the Po Valley with several unreliable legions, a host of gladiators and thousands of salted carcasses of cattle and horses to see him through the winter. Antony, with four legions, several thousand raw levies and his elite bodyguard, threw up his own fortifications in a huge ring around the city, beyond bow-shot of the walls. Octavian, also with four legions of seasoned troops, plus the equivalent of a fifth legion of recruits, was resigning himself to the necessity of settling down in winter quarters at Arretium, waiting for March or April to bring fresh troops, to be raised by the incoming consuls, Hirtius and Pansa. At that juncture, the three of them planned to launch a massive attack on Antony's besieging forces, while Decimus would sally forth from the city to complete the crushing process.

Waiting in the wings, on the far side of two different Alpine ranges, were most of the legions from Gaul, plus many thousands of ancillary troops and cavalry, anxious to find out who would win. None of those soldiers wanted to fight. Neither of their senior commanders, Plancus (hesitant republican), Lepidus (aristocratic Caesarean), was prepared to intervene on one side or the other in advance of the outcome. Both could be expected to plump for whichever came out on top. At that early stage, when Cicero was addressing the Senate, it looked as if Antony had made a serious error in delaying his attack until the snows prevented him from crossing the mountain passes with all his men. Otherwise, he could have bypassed Decimus and regrouped on the other side, powerful enough to be certain of the loyalty of his nominal allies in Gaul and Spain, and therefore in overall command of an army of at least seventeen legions. As it was, he faced being heavily outnumbered in northern Italy before the spring thaw.

Winter would be far less troublesome to Hirtius and Pansa, who had well-paved Roman roads to lead them to Mutina. By the end of February it should not be difficult for them, with all central and southern Italy as their recruiting ground, to raise enough new legions so that, added to the forces of Octavian and Decimus, they would outnumber Antony's modest force by about three to one. Ventidius Balbus, an Antonian loyalist, was trying to raise more troops in northern Italy, but Decimus had been there before him, and from the perspective of those in the capital it must have seemed a fairly faint hope. With the Alps blocked, and Cassius and Brutus rapidly taking over huge swathes of the East, Antony's best chance was to pick off his opponents piecemeal, before they all combined against him.

The armchair generals in Rome would ultimately give their backing to Cicero, not because they had grown suddenly brave and patriotic, but because they had come to much the same conclusion as he had about Antony's dangerous predicament. Octavian may not have been quite so well informed. His advisers would, no doubt, have made a correct assessment of the probablilities in the immediate theatre of war, but they would not have had such easy access to the flow of information, either from official sources or from Brutus and Cassius, that was available to the optimate leaders in Rome. There was every reason why those leaders should try to conceal from Octavian the quite startling successes achieved by the two chief assassins towards the end of the year. Equally, it was not until his troops intercepted some letters from Antony that he realized that some of the officials charged with recruiting the new consular army had been deliberately going slow in Antony's interest.

For the moment the young general no longer needed to fear for his life – unless he should prove to be exceptionally unlucky in his first battle – but the prospect of untrammelled leadership in the struggle against Antony had temporarily vanished. He had at last secured support at the highest political level, now that Cicero was backing him with apparent enthusiasm, but he was probably not yet fully aware of the extent to which that support was limited. Octavian had acquiesced in his demand that he should not oppose the appointment as tribune of a leading assassin, Publius Servilius Casca, but Cicero could scarcely have expected him to comply with a further supposed requirement for him to 'make friends with the tyrannicides'.[2]

It was about this time, at the turn of the year from 44 to 43, that Octavian became engaged to be married, for strictly political reasons. His intended bride was one of Servilia's many granddaughters (also, confusingly, named Servilia). Her father, Publius Servilius Isauricus, was originally a supporter of Cato but one who had profited greatly by changing sides at the right time, having become joint consul with Caesar in 48, the year of the battle of Pharsalus. Since Caesar's assassination Isauricus had reverted quietly to the optimate camp, as a moderate who might easily swing back again in appropriate circumstances. Thus he was just about politically acceptable to Octavian as a prospective father-in-law, while at the same time his blue-blooded marital connections (Isauricus was yet another of the elder Servilia's sons-in-law) meant that the prospective bride was related to Brutus, Cassius and Lepidus.

The younger Servilia was almost certainly an under-age child at the time of her betrothal or Octavian would probably have had to marry her straight away in order to convince waverers among the *optimates* that he would repay their support, when Cicero spoke up for him in the Senate. The elder statesman excelled in hyperbole in that first public speech about his new protégé on 20 December, describing Octavian as 'a young man of incredible, virtually god-like brains and courage'.[3] In private, among his cronies, however, Cicero made no secret of the fact that his long-term agenda held only a very minor and subordinate role for Octavian, and none at all for his crusade to avenge Caesar's murder. The boy, as he said, in a joke that would come back to haunt him, should be 'praised, promoted – and pushed aside'.[4]

It must have seemed so much more splendid a prospect for Octavian in early December, just after Antony had left for the North. Pausing only to round up the consul's abandoned elephants, the young man had hurried south from Arretium to greet, and make an initial payment to, the legions that had defected to him. He also showed himself in his increased *auctoritas* to the senators, including those who had so recently sworn allegiance to Antony but were now, for the most part, finding excuses to cast it off. The preliminary Senate debate on 20 December resulted in approval for Decimus's decision to resist the consul, and praise for Octavian and his army, coupled with an implicit promise of practical support in the new consular year that was about to begin.[5]

When a supremely confident Cicero addressed the packed Forum to report on the proceedings that had just taken place in the Senate House, he claimed that because they had passed his motion honouring Octavian, it followed that they had effectively judged Antony to be a public enemy. If the brave young man, he said, had not raised an army to protect Rome, Antony would have butchered them; so let the people prepare for the struggle to regain their liberty, sustained by the hope which Octavian had inspired. 'By his zeal, by his policy and by the spending of his inheritance he has saved the state and is now protecting your liberty.'[6] The stage was thus set for active resistance to begin on 1 January, when the absent Antony and Dolabella would be replaced as consuls by the moderate Caesarians, Hirtius and Pansa, and when the principal voice in government was to be Cicero's.

Octavian's officers and men, however, were unimpressed by what they saw as senatorial equivocation and delay. They were worried that their young leader had not yet been given official rank, which they foresaw (correctly) would be essential if they were to get the exceptional rewards he had promised them. They offered to designate some of their number as lictors, carrying the fasces – those bundles of rods and axes which signified the power of a senior Roman magistrate – to put him on a level more appropriate to his new station. Octavian referred the matter to the Senate, and declined the men's further offer to back him up with a mass demonstration of their support, believing that a little modest hesitation on his part would do him more good in the long run.[7]

He was still on a learning curve. His two new legions knew what was needed. They organized a potent expression of their power in the apparently peaceful form of a public entertainment, acting out in full armour a stage-managed 'battle', as if between equally matched sides. Nobody was killed, of course, but they left the aristocrats among the onlookers in no doubt as to their ferocious effectiveness as a fighting force under their young general. The politicians picked up the gauntlet. The marathon four-day session of the Senate that began on 1 January included debate on Cicero's craftily tabled (and successful) measure to appoint Octavian to the Senate at the level of one who had already served a year as praetor. That would enable him, as a propraetor, to exercise the *imperium* of a general of that rank; but, as he and his troops were to serve in the joint consular force against Antony, he would be outranked at all times by either or both of the two new consuls and therefore subject, under military discipline, to their orders.

The ruse represented the illusion of power, not its substance. By accepting it, Octavian would rise enormously in perceived status among the general public but would in fact effectively surrender his independent command; the *optimates* knew that, in the circumstances of the moment, he could not reject it without losing all credibility as a defender of the Republic against tyranny. He would have to console himself with the thought that he was now the youngest senator in the history of Rome. The Senate, for what the gesture was worth, also voted him a gilded statue of himself in the Forum, and, more importantly, promised to pay the two legions, which he had won over from Antony, the huge terminal bonuses he had originally pledged to them out of his own resources. Cicero further sweetened the pill with flattery – 'this divine young man *(divinus adulescens)*' – but gave a hostage to fortune when he told the senators, 'I know all his inner feelings . . . I pledge my word that Gaius Caesar will always be the sort of good citizen he is today.' Significantly, Cicero was now referring to Octavian by his adopted name.[8]

Lepidus, too, won greater recognition for his services to the state, specifically for having reached a settlement with Sextus Pompeius that now brought the one-time warlord back into the republican fold, in time to throw the considerable weight of his forces into the scale against the Caesareans, whom he naturally hated as former enemies and the chief despoilers of his late father's estate. But in the case of Lepidus, as in that of

Octavian, there was a strong ulterior motive behind the Senate's apparent generosity and Cicero's over-larded praise. The orator was far from being the only optimate who suspected the loyalty of Caesar's former Master of Horse, but he had the wit to see that reproof would almost certainly be counter-productive. Instead he persuaded the senators that Lepidus, who was notoriously vain, should be granted the rare honour of having an equestrian statue of himself set up in the Forum at public expense.

The Senate also gave the order for recruitment to begin for the proposed consular army, but refused Cicero's demand to name Antony as a public enemy. They knew the temper of the ex-consul, and were not yet totally convinced that he was effectively finished. In any case, he had a number of influential partisans among the senators, not least Fufius Calenus, father-in-law of the new consul, Pansa. Calenus was protecting Antony's wife, Fulvia, and her children, by giving them shelter in his own house. Called by Pansa to speak first in the debate, he put forward the moderate suggestion that an embassy should be sent to Antony to see if a peaceful settlement might yet be reached. Everybody present remembered only too well what had resulted the last time the Senate had forced a former consul to choose between total submission or invasion across the Rubicon.

Cicero, who in his letters had frequently condemned Antony for being 'afraid of peace', now vehemently attacked those who indicated support for Calenus's proposal as being, by implication, afraid of war. He did not, however, descend to quite the level of scurrility that defaces his so-called 'Second Philippic', so scabrous in its vilification of Antony that he wisely did not deliver it as a speech but merely circulated its text among friends. In it he accuses Antony of having been 'a common prostitute' (vulgare scortum) from the outset of his career, selling himself for a fixed rate that was 'not small' until he entered a stable 'marriage' as the harlot of an older man.[9] In his 20 December speech, Cicero widened his attack to include

Fulvia, alleging that when Antony purged his legions at Brundisium by giving orders for brave men's throats to be cut, their blood was sprinkled on the mouth of his 'most cruel and avaricious wife'.[10] It seems unlikely there was a scrap of truth in either of those allegations.

In the New Year debates, Cicero saw the necessity for more truthful arguments, although he was unable to resist a few further gibes at the expense of Antony's supposed debauchery and his undoubted taste for strong drink. He took the view that sending envoys to discuss terms with his enemy would be likely to delay the full prosecution of the war, to Antony's advantage, giving him more time to starve Decimus out of Mutina before the besieging army could be destroyed or driven off. Cicero, however, was opposed by Lucius Piso, Caesar's father-in-law, whose credentials for resisting Antony's manipulation of the constitution were much stronger than his own. It was Piso, who, back in the summer, had criticized Antony to his face at a time when Cicero was in the process of escaping abroad.

Piso pointed out, to Cicero's embarrassment, the implications for public respect for the law of the contradictions involved in backing the illegally recruited private army of Octavian against the legally appointed proconsul of Gaul, who was acting in accordance with a valid vote of the People in moving to take over one of his designated provinces from its previous governor, whose office had expired. On top of all that, he said, Cicero was now trying to have the distinguished ex-consul declared a public enemy out of hand, without permitting him his legal right to a trial. Piso suggested, in response to those who claimed Antony had secured favourable votes by menaces, that Octavian should be required to hand over to the Senate the two legions which had defected from Antony; if, at the same time, Decimus was ordered to return to Rome with his besieged legions, that would leave the Senate in control of a sufficiently large army to make it possible for them to take any future decisions without fear or favour.[11]

Senators were well aware that neither of Piso's specific suggestions fell within the bounds of practical possibilities, but his more general warning against the danger of forcing Antony to make war on them against his will, purely in order to secure his personal and political survival, helped to water down Cicero's hard-line case. So did the tears of Antony's mother and wife (the outrageously maligned Fulvia), who both spent the night of 3 January going from door to senatorial door pleading his cause,[12] in advance of the crucial vote fixed for 4 January. The result was a compromise. Piso and Philippus, Octavian's stepfather, were named as two of three envoys to order Antony to submit to the Senate, raise the siege of Mutina and withdraw his forces from the contested province. That sounded firm enough, but their real mission, as Cicero saw, was to offer Antony a last chance of backing away from confrontation, without too much loss of face on either side.

Naturally, that meant postponement of the move to have him declared a public enemy. In reporting the Senate's decisions to the citizens waiting in the Forum, Cicero assured them that the proposed embassy would fail.[13] He was right, but not because Antony was obdurate. Antony demonstrated statesmanship by offering to give up his perfectly legal claim to the governorship of northern Italy, if that would avert civil war. When Piso and Philippus returned early in February – the third envoy having died on the wintry journey – they evidently thought they had negotiated an acceptable basis for settlement. Cicero was implacable. Casting himself in the role that Cato had played against Julius Caesar, he used his mastery of negative invective to wreck any chance of peace.[14] The toothless Senate passed the ultimate decree, ordering the consuls and Octavian to take whatever measures were necessary to safeguard the Republic.

Cicero thought his hour had struck at last, after two decades of comparative political failure since he had broken the back of Catiline's revolt in the year of Octavian's birth.

He, rather than the two plodding consuls, Hirtius and Pansa, now held sway in Rome as the acknowledged leader of the stern, unbending *optimates*. Among a Senate largely composed of inexperienced members – a consequence of the terrible loss of aristocratic lives during previous civil wars – Cicero stood head and shoulders above the rest, in terms of intellect, energy, articulacy, commitment and his lifetime's experience as a backroom political fixer. He saw his agreement with Octavian as a master stroke against the anti-republican tendencies of that succession of outstanding military leaders whose exploits had kept him, until now, just out of reach of the supreme recognition he craved. In fact, that bizarre alliance would prove to have precisely the opposite effect. It catapulted the teenager to an unmerited prominence that placed him in pole position to destroy the Republic rather than save it.

Antony's terms,[15] although not couched in conciliatory language, make it clear that he was trying to avoid provoking a full-scale civil war. His optimate opponents could not realistically have expected him simply to walk away from Mutina, without firm guarantees for his future safety and that of his men. The Senate was a body which invariably sought to exploit any sign of weakness, whether in an enemy or a friend. His statement to the envoys that he planned to execute Decimus, alone of the assassins, as a way of purging Rome's contaminating guilt for the murder of Julius Caesar, was partly bravado but also an acknowledgement that the relentless pursuit of all the former conspirators – Octavian's agenda – would require civil war for its completion. Antony was effectively holding out an olive branch to the other assassins, and especially to Brutus and Cassius, acknowledging their right to return to Rome to stand for the consulship, so long as he was allowed to retain his five-year command in Gaul until after they had given up the provinces that would be assigned to them after their consular year.

It was a balanced peace package, with something for

everyone except the unfortunate Decimus. The ancient world was fully familiar with the concept of the scapegoat, whereby one man might be sacrificed for the wider good of the state. Religious sensibilities were important here. The perceived moral pollution caused by such a treacherous murder as that of Caesar, who was not only the secular head of state but its chief priest, could, in contemporary theory, be cleansed only by an appropriate ritual, in which sacrifice was offered up to the gods on behalf of the whole people. The assassins might well claim that they, too, had killed Caesar for a wider good; but their idea of what constituted the good of the state was obviously not shared by the great mass of the soldiers or by many lower-class citizens. To them, Caesar was a hero, possibly even a god. There could be no genuine peace and harmony while his ghost remained unpropitiated, if not totally avenged.

Acceptance of the package would have given Rome its best chance of restoring the Republic as a legally functioning entity under the traditional rules of behaviour, which accepted fierce competition among aristocrats as both normal and desirable. While it is true that Antony's position in Gaul would have been anomalous and potentially threatening, he had always tried to work within the letter of the law even if he had sometimes violated its spirit. That might or might not have been a problem for the future. Meanwhile, assuming the soldiers were given what they were owed and could settle down to their duty or their retirement, the state would be in a position to expect a breathing space of up to five years of productive peace, instead of an immediate resumption of civil war.

Why was Cicero so determined to slam shut this window of opportunity for peace? The probable explanation is that he miscalculated the future outcome of events, allowing too little scope for human mistakes and the random operations of chance, and that he was unwilling to pay attention to the warnings of people he considered to be his intellectual inferiors. Cicero's contempt for the peace initiative was so extreme that he wrote at once to Cassius, 'Nothing could be more disgraceful or scandalous than Piso and Philippus . . . they have brought back intolerable demands.'[16] In fact, nothing could have been more crass than his comment in a later letter to Cassius in mid-February: 'If I'm not mistaken, the outcome of the whole conflict seems to rest on Decimus Brutus. If, as we are hoping, he breaks out of Mutina, it's unlikely there will be any more war.'[17]

Cicero had done his utmost to provoke outright civil war – and now he was telling his most powerful potential ally there was no real need to hurry back to Rome, because Antony's military initiative looked like being a damp squib. Coming from the man who believed he had the wisest head as well as the most eloquent tongue in Rome, such a statement appears stunning in its naivety and imprudence. Was he unable to visualize the likely scenario when Cassius would unroll the letter two or three weeks later in Syria to discover that his services would probably not be required, and might very well already be redundant? Whatever was going on in Cicero's head when he wrote the letter, Cassius, on receipt of it, did what any self-respecting Roman aristocrat could have been expected to do in the circumstances: he decided to use his newly acquired illegal power to terrorize wealthy eastern cities into handing over money to pay his troops and to enrich himself.

Cicero could not claim to have been unaware of what had been happening in the East. Throughout January the rumoured successes of Brutus and Cassius had replaced the military stalemate at Mutina as the hottest topic at fashionable Roman tables. It was the perception of a seismic shift in the balance of power that had led the Senate at its meeting in early February to back Cicero's war policy in contrast to the much more cautious approach at New Year when they voted to send envoys to Antony. The rumours received triumphant confirmation in about the second week of February when Brutus sent a despatch to Rome, reporting with cool effrontery what he had achieved, as if he had been acting all along with proconsular *imperium*.[18]

It turned out that Hortensius, the retiring Governor of Macedonia, was an admirer of Brutus. Antony, through the plebeian Assembly, had arranged for his own brother Gaius to take over the province; but when Gaius landed at Dyracchium early in January he was received not by a respectful welcoming committee but by a group of hostile legions, led by Brutus, to whom Hortensius had transferred his entire command. Hopelessly outnumbered – Antony could scarcely spare him many troops – Gaius bolted for the garrison town of Apollonia, from which Octavian had set out nine months earlier. After seeing that resistance was hopeless, the unlucky Gaius surrendered to Brutus, who by then was also in control of Illyricum and a further three legions.[19]

Cassius's success had been even more sensational, although not yet officially confirmed. On arrival in Syria, with his modest fleet, he had found six legions besieging the optimate Caecilius Bassus, who had only one legion, in the city of Apamea. With remarkable *chutzpah* he summoned the rival commanders and managed to persuade both besiegers and besieged to end their quarrel and serve the Republic under his overall command. Next, hearing that Cleopatra was sending four legions from Egypt to support Dolabella's legitimate claim to be the new proconsular Governor of Syria, Cassius marched his forces into Palestine to intercept them. Outnumbered, far from their usual base and no better informed than anyone else about events in Italy, the four legions decided not to fight the seven from Syria but to join them instead. Thus Cassius acquired an army of eleven legions – more than twice as big as either of the rival armies of Antony and Octavian – without striking a blow.[20]

From Octavian's perspective, a lesser, but significant change in the balance of power had also occurred in northern Italy. Hirtius, as consul, ordered him to hand over direct command of the two legions, the Martians and the Fifth, which had defected from Antony. It must have been a bitter experience for the young general to watch them march out of his camp. He had had no serious alternative but to comply with the order. No doubt he had time to exchange assurances of mutual support with the men, who were naturally uneasy at this turn of events, so soon after they had risked their lives, their careers and their hopes of a worthwhile gratuity to join him there.[21]

Because Decimus and his entrapped legions were suffering severely from food shortages, Octavian and Hirtius now moved their forces closer to Mutina to give renewed hope to the starving garrison. They took over Bononia (Bologna) from the Antonians, but were not yet strong enough to force a crossing of the river between themselves and the besieged city. Antony had invested Mutina so tightly that it was impossible for the potential relieving force to know whether Decimus was aware of how close they had come. Hirtius and Octavian tried to signal him from tree-tops, but when that failed they devised a more ingenious method. A message was scratched on a wafer-thin sheet of lead, which was rolled up to an inconspicuous size and given to a strong swimmer. The man swam under the surface of the river by night to deliver it; had he been detected he could have let the lead sink to the muddy bottom. It is not known how large a part Octavian played in this enterprise, but he was certainly learning his trade.[22]

Back in Rome, the Senate, jubilant to have received Brutus's despatch and scenting total victory, voted to confirm him as overall commander in Macedonia, Illyricum and Greece. A proposal for a larger embassy to Antony, with Cicero as one of its members, had recently secured some measure of agreement, but the initiative collapsed when Cicero suddenly changed his mind and refused to go. Not long afterwards, news arrived that horrified almost every senator: Dolabella, *en route* to Syria, had tortured and killed Trebonius, the Governor of Asia. Trebonius, the man who had kept Antony talking on the Ides of March, was a firm ally of Brutus and Cassius, but he had cooperated with Dolabella to the extent of feeding his army as it passed through his province. These were, after all, hungry Roman soldiers. Dolabella repaid this concession by capturing him by deception at night, whipping and racking him for two days until his neck broke, and finally cutting off his head, which his soldiers then kicked around the streets.[23]

The Senate declared Dolabella a public enemy, which gave *carte blanche* to any Roman to kill him. Some of the blame would soon rub off on Antony, who sent a letter across the river from Mutina to Octavian and Hirtius expressing his 'joy' at the death of Trebonius, while claiming that he had secured firm pledges of alliance from Lepidus and Plancus, as well as from Dolabella. Quite what Octavian made of that letter can only be conjectured, but it must have concentrated his mind on the reality of his own predicament. If it was indeed true that both Lepidus and Plancus were fully committed to Antony's support, he would have to be very careful not to be seen as the one Caesarean leader who was out of step with all the rest, now that he had lost 10,000 of his best troops and was left only with those who had already shown their unwillingness to fight Antony.

In spite of the difficulties of communication, Octavian maintained a sporadic, largely clandestine correspondence during the winter with a number of other generals. He was anxious to demonstrate friendship wherever possible, just as they were hoping to attract his support for whatever course they might choose to take, or be forced to take, when the siege ended. Hirtius sent a copy of Antony's letter to Cicero, who read it out in the Senate, interspersing Antony's brief, pertinent statements with long-winded comments of his own. It was not one of the orator's best performances: too many of Antony's points were aimed at Cicero's warmongering policy, and could not be satisfactorily refuted by his heavy sarcasm and other rhetorical flourishes.[24]

Confirmation of a sort for Antony's claim of backing from the legions in Gaul and Spain reached Rome by 20 March in the form of official dispatches from Lepidus and Plancus, urging a peaceful settlement at Mutina while there was still time. The Senate was in no mood to listen. Recent confirmation of Cassius's achievements, in addition to those of Brutus, left the *optimates* apparently holding the whip hand. Cicero fired off a waspish letter to Lepidus, advising him not to meddle in the affair.[25] Pansa had just left Rome to join Hirtius and Octavian with four newly recruited legions, so it would be only a matter of weeks before a combined consular army of more than 60,000 men, plus about 15,000 more under Decimus inside Mutina, would be positioned for a final encounter with Antony's 25,000.

Few could have doubted the probable outcome. By mid-April, just as Pansa was toiling up the last few miles of the Via Aemilia towards his rendezvous, Cicero wrote to Brutus, who was still in Macedonia, advising him to go on a punitive mission to Asia if Dolabella was still to be found there.[26] First Cassius, then Lepidus, now Brutus had been discouraged from intervening in the localized war which Cicero had persuaded the Senate to wage against its legally appointed proconsul. Can it possibly be the case that Cicero was simply 'thinking aloud' when he wrote those three letters – spanning a period of two months, from mid-February to mid-April – and had no ulterior motive? Each, to be sure, was in response to a specific situation; but, taken together as a series, however tactfully or indirectly phrased, they have one underlying message in common: 'Stay away!'

There is surely a strong possibility – to put it no higher – that Cicero was deliberately trying to keep them out, as potential rivals who would demand a share of his anticipated glory in victory. That would certainly be compatible with his well-attested craving for public acclaim. But much more than that was at stake. All three of his correspondents were professional politicians who were fully aware of the problems Antony had faced in trying to steer a middle course to avert civil war. Octavian's intervention had forced him, against his inclinations, to adopt a harder line towards the assassins than he would otherwise have wished; and Cicero's alliance with Octavian, however well intentioned, amounted to a conspiracy against a legally elected consul, and therefore treason against the Republic.

Cicero had stuck his neck out and needed to take precautions against having it chopped off. Equally, having taken such a risk, he believed he deserved a commensurate reward. If Lepidus should put the strength of his legions behind a peace plan, or if Brutus and Cassius should return to Italy too soon with overwhelming might, the outcome of the conflict now building to a climax around Mutina would be taken out of Cicero's hands. Once before in his career, he had been sent into humiliating exile for executing his political enemies without trial, even though he had been consul at the time. In the present situation he had no official position whatever, yet he was straining every nerve to encompass the deaths of three men who had – Antony, his brothers Lucius and Gaius, plus anybody else who supported them in arms.

If Servilia's sons-in-law were to combine to avert civil war by making a deal with Antony, in the same way that Antony had effectively made deals with them, then Cicero would have left alive an enemy so dangerous he would never again be able to feel secure. If Brutus, Cassius and Lepidus could be kept out of the equation, he would once more be in a position, through his command of the Senate in the aftermath of a great victory, to slaughter a new generation of political enemies without the need to put them on trial. He might even hope, as the 'saviour of his country' for a second time, to be elected in a wave of grateful patriotic fervour to the summit of a republican career, a second consulship.

The Senate, sharing much of Cicero's confidence, sent out instructions to governors and military commanders in the eastern half of the empire to take their orders from Brutus (and later from Cassius, too) until further notice.[27] The senators naturally supposed that the pair would be bringing at least some of their huge forces, conservatively estimated at 100,000 men, across the Adriatic to deliver the *coup de grâce*, should Octavian and the consuls somehow fail to defeat Antony. Brutus did, in fact, write to Cassius at some stage, suggesting that they might usefully go back to Italy together, but Cassius replied by inviting him to come East. The 'lean and hungry' assassin had already started squeezing money from cities and islands he had earmarked for contributions; and Brutus, never much of a leader in military matters, was persuaded to leave the Senate to look after itself.

It was in vain that Cicero, a month or two later, began bombarding both men with increasingly urgent and plaintive calls for help. Cassius and Brutus turned deaf ears. Did they not have it in writing from him that their intervention was of doubtful necessity? They both knew the relative strengths of the forces directly involved. Would it not be unwise of them, just because Cicero had developed cold feet, to turn Italy upside down by appearing to be invading from the East? In any case, they could not leave Dolabella on the loose in their rear. And they had the future status of their families to think of: there was all that eastern treasure still available for them to prise out of the provincials.

Rome could wait.

NINE

THE TAKEOVER OF ROME

Octavian's first direct experience of warfare was traumatic, if we can believe his early biographer, Suetonius. The teenager had to face two separate battles, a week apart. The first took place on 14 April, mainly near Forum Gallorum, on the Via Aemilia, when Antony ambushed Pansa's marching column and Hirtius came to the rescue; the second when Octavian and Hirtius launched their counter-attack outside Mutina. Suetonius quotes Antony as writing afterwards that Octavian 'fled during the first battle and reappeared next day without his horse or his cloak'. But the biographer, author of the justly famous *Lives of the Twelve Caesars*, adds: 'It is agreed by all that in the following encounter he played the part not just of a leader but of a soldier, too, shouldering the eagle in the thick of the battle after the standard bearer had been gravely wounded, and carrying it for some time.'[1]

The problem for modern biographers is that there are several different accounts of these two battles, and it is impossible to merge them into a coherent narrative which does not involve unacceptable guesswork, especially about Octavian's role and behaviour. Did he run away? Or was he, as many historians are prepared to accept, the victim of a malicious lie? We cannot rely on the unsubstantiated word of Antony; and it would be almost as unwise to accept at face value Cicero's statement to the Senate soon after the battle that the young man defended the main camp bravely and skilfully that first day, with only a handful of cohorts at his disposal. It was in Antony's interests at that stage to portray

Octavian as a coward, just it was in Cicero's to acclaim him a hero. Perhaps the historian Dio Cassius, writing some 250 years later from historical evidence that is now lost, is nearer the unvarnished truth when he says that Octavian was hailed by his troops as *Imperator* even though he had not taken part in the first day's fighting at all.[2]

Fortunately, an eyewitness account, written by a senior officer the day after the first battle,[3] has been preserved among the great treasure house of Cicero's collected correspondence. There is no reason to question its authenticity; the drawback is that the writer, Servius Sulpicius Galba, one of Caesar's assassins, does not mention what part, if any, Octavian played. Galba had ridden a hundred miles, on Hirtius's orders, to meet Pansa and his column of reinforcements in time to give him an up-to-date briefing on the state of affairs around Mutina, and to act as his guide to the rendezvous point. On the evening of 13 April, when Pansa's troops were passing through a difficult and dangerous gorge in the Appenines, the Martian legion and two praetorian cohorts (one of them Octavian's) arrived to escort them on the last leg of their journey, precisely in order to thwart any attempt by Antony to intercept and destroy the four legions of untrained recruits.

The Martians, who had been partially decimated by Antony, were thirsting for revenge against the Antonian troops whom they considered to have betrayed their cause by staying loyal to their former chief. As a result, when dawn broke, and the flash of armour and spears was seen among the reeds in marshy land on either side of the narrow road ahead, the Martians hurried forward without orders to engage the enemy in spite of the obvious ambush which had been set up to trap them. Pansa, apparently unable to recall them, ordered two of his other legions to try to catch up with them to close the gap. Antony's cavalry, however, were able to surround them first.

Galba, a former commander of the Martians, had ridden

forward to join them, but was forced to retreat, along with many others, to the temporary camp behind them, which was presumably being guarded by the other recruits held in reserve. Antony's forces attacked the camp but failed to capture it, losing numbers of men in the process. This could not, however, be the camp mentioned by Cicero as having been defended by Octavian, because that was some miles away in the opposite direction, and from it Hirtius now marched out with two experienced legions. These fresh troops fell upon the weary Antonians as they were singing premature songs of victory, and slaughtered so many that they broke and ran to hide out in the marshes. Some are said to have escaped by holding on to the tails of cavalry horses.[4] If Octavian did in fact have to defend the base camp that day, it can only have been against a secondary body of soldiers whom Antony had sent there merely as a feint to give him time to spring his ambush.

Both sides suffered heavy losses in the battle of Forum Gallorum, but if it were to continue like that, as a roughly equal struggle of attrition, Antony saw that he would inevitably run out of troops first. He withdrew all his forces, therefore, behind his lines of circumvallation around Mutina, knowing that Decimus's men were close to the point when they would have to surrender or die of starvation. On the consular side, Hirtius claimed victory as the enemy had left the field; but Pansa was carried off to Bononia with a spear wound that would eventually prove fatal. Octavian was now second in line of command.

The first news to reach Rome of this muddled clash of armies proclaimed an Antonian victory. No doubt Antony had dispatched a messenger before the arrival of Hirtius, and the horseman evidently rode so fast that nobody with the true result managed to overtake him. Panic ensued. Families fled from the city. Cicero was rumoured to be taking over its defence, perhaps as dictator.[5] He did not have to deny it for more than a few days, because messengers arrived on 20 April telling the opposite story: Antony had suffered a defeat from which it seemed impossible that he could recover. The citizens, relieved of the fear of invasion, whether from the north-west or the east, thought they knew who to thank for it. A huge crowd came to Cicero's door to take him up to the Capitol, amid tumultuous applause, to fête him as their saviour.

'I am not vain,' Cicero wrote to Brutus next day, with a pomposity and a lack of self-awareness so complete as to be almost endearing. 'I do not need to be vain. But I am moved by the unanimity of all classes in congratulating me.'[6] That same day, 21 April, without his knowledge, Hirtius and Octavian forced the Antonians out from behind their fortifications, savaged them in hand-to-hand combat within sight of Mutina's walls, and tried but failed to capture their main camp. Hirtius fell near Antony's own tent, and Octavian made a sortie to drag his body away. It was hard to say which side had suffered the heavier casualties, but the remnants of two of Antony's legions of recruits deserted him.[7]

The ex-consul called a council of war with his remaining officers. The majority were in favour of staying and fighting on, still convinced that Mutina was about to fall. Antony, reckoning up the sheer weight of numbers against him, decided to quit rather than risk total defeat. Even if he personally managed to escape, he knew that Lepidus would not help him if he became a mere fugitive. Adversity brought out the best in him. He set out at once for Gaul with all the men who could still walk, hurrying to shake off pursuit, and led them westwards to the barren mountain ranges they would have to climb to reach the Mediterranean coastal paths. Claiming no personal privileges for comfort, he ate and slept alongside his soldiers, gnawing on the same unidentifiable roots they had dug up from crevices and drinking from the same stagnant ponds.[8]

As for the mauled but victorious consular army, Octavian found himself in temporary acting command. One consul was dead, the other lay dying. Cicero had been too clever in persuading the Senate to give propraetorial rank to his protégé. It meant that in spite of his youth, his inexperience and his (so far) sadly undistinguished record as a general, he outranked every other officer in his camp who was capable of raising a sword. The fact that Pansa was still breathing on his deathbed at Bononia, and capable of coherent speech, gave Octavian the opportunity to organize a smooth transfer of power to himself, so that his temporary command could become permanent.

Mutina taught him two valuable lessons. The first was that he did not need to play the hero – always assuming that to be possible for him – in order to win the plaudits of the troops. All he needed to do was survive as a member of the winning side. The second lesson he learnt from the lips of Pansa. The dying consul called him to his bedside and explained to him what the teenager might not yet have fully worked out for himself: the rationale underlying the Senate's policy decisions, on the one hand, and the complex manoeuvrings by himself and Hirtius to try to ensure that the Caesarians rather than the *optimates* emerged on top.

The optimate majority among the aristocracy (Pansa indicated) feared Antony and Octavian so much that they were trying to destroy them one after the other, rather than risk attacking them simultaneously and so driving them into each other's arms. The senators had been delighted at the rivalry and dissension between the two, and had lulled Octavian with flattering but cheap honours while appointing him to serve under the consuls, with the deliberate intention of weakening him by taking away his two best legions. Pansa added that he and Hirtius had complied with the Senate's resolutions, not in accordance with the *optimates*' desire to destroy Antony, but following their own priority of forcing him back into alliance with Octavian, in line with the desire of those who, like themselves, owed a personal debt of honour and gratitude to Julius Caesar.

After warning the young man that officers in the newly

recruited legions were in fact spies acting on the Senate's behalf, Pansa, almost with his dying breath, formally returned to him, presumably in front of witnesses, the command of the two legions he had given up, plus any of the others he might choose to take over.[9] It is never possible to be absolutely sure that such conversations, as set down by ancient historians, actually took place, for the same reason that scepticism is advisable over their frequent 'verbatim' reports of political speeches, which are often no more than rhetorical devices to bolster the narrative. Nevertheless, this particular report, by the Greek historian Appian, rings sufficiently true in its essence that it deserves to be taken seriously, as a statement of motives and facts, even if the actual words may have been imaginatively reconstructed well after the event.

The drawn-out death agony of Pansa at Bononia also worked in Octavian's favour by thwarting any chance Decimus Brutus might otherwise have had of taking effective command of all or part of the relieving force in the Senate's name. He was undoubtedly the senior officer of the two, both as governor within his own province (as recently confirmed by the Senate, on Cicero's advice) and as consul-designate for the following year. Decimus had been unable to pursue Antony straight away. His men were not yet capable of marching far because of their weakness through hunger and lack of exercise; and he had no effective cavalry as they had eaten all their horses. That was why he hastened instead to Bononia to confer with Pansa, who was still, so far as he knew, the general in overall command. News of his death reached him on the road.

Decimus had supposed that Pansa would agree to his urgent request for Octavian's troops to be ordered to stop Antony reaching Lepidus. By the time he met Octavian, the young man was firmly in command of the entire consular army and had no intention of cooperating with one of his adoptive father's murderers. It was no longer in Octavian's interest to do so, after what Pansa had told him. He, not

Antony, and certainly not Decimus, now controlled the biggest army in Italy, amounting to eight legions – even after he had parted with some of the troops whose loyalty he suspected. In vain, Decimus pointed out that if he acted quickly with his superior forces he could cut Antony off from potential allies and any hope of getting supplies to sustain his retreating army, thereby defeating him without needing to fight.[10]

Decimus's chief fear was that if Antony succeeded in joining up with Lepidus the *optimates* might have to fight a civil war all over again, and one that would not be geographically confined to a limited region of northern Italy. It quickly became clear to him that Octavian, without disclosing too much of his intentions, was now working to a revised agenda. He saw that if Antony was to be stopped he would have to do it himself. By the time he was eventually able to set out in pursuit with his three only moderately effective legions, Antony was already two days ahead of him. In the event, Decimus, in spite of catching a distant glimpse of his quarry, ended up going the wrong way, following a false trail which Antony had left some of his cavalry to provide.

When news of Antony's apparently abject retreat from Mutina reached Rome less than a week later, euphoria reigned among the optimate senators. They had won, or so they thought. Although they happily voted state funerals for the two deceased consuls, they failed to realize the significance of their deaths for the relative positions of Octavian and Decimus. They awarded a triumph to Decimus and instructed him to take over the consular army as commander-in-chief. Octavian was ignored. Cicero tried to persuade the Senate that the young man should be granted at least an official ovation – an honour that fell far short of a triumph – but to the satisfaction, no doubt, of the absent Brutus, the motion apparently failed.[11] It was Brutus's opinion, bluntly expressed in letters to both Cicero and Atticus – and, evidently, to others among his partisans in Rome – that Octavian had already been honoured far too much, and it would be slavish and dangerous to offer him any more.[12]

The Senate's most blinkered move, however, was to renege on their earlier decision to pay those of Octavian's troops to whom he had promised large terminal bonuses in order to secure their defection from Antony. They cut the figure by half without troubling to tell the recipients their reason, which may well have been shortage of cash, owing to the drying up of the previously huge flows of tax payments from the eastern, richer half of the empire, that were now swelling the coffers of Brutus and Cassius. As a further rebuff for Octavian, they refused to pay any bonus at all to his other troops, a move apparently intended to cause dissension among the different legions that had served under him, thus supposedly weakening his authority further. The reduced bonuses were to be paid directly to the soldiers by a board of specially appointed commissioners, on which neither Octavian nor Decimus would be permitted to serve.[13]

Not only had the *optimates* factored Octavian out of the equation, they had done so even more fatally in respect of Antony. Assuming that the capture and demise of the ex-consul was simply a matter of time, they had at last plucked up enough courage in the Senate to declare him a public enemy. It did not enter their heads that their old adversary would ever be in a position to avenge that ultimate insult. In fact, Antony had been luckier and more resourceful than they gave him credit for. During the long retreat he had acquired three fresh legions, recruited by his old lieutenant, Ventidius, who had failed, indeed, to deliver them in time for them to be of any use at Mutina, but which were now doubly welcome in adversity.

Antony's dishevelled army reached the Mediterranean some 30 miles west of Genoa, on what is today the Italian Riviera. From there they passed by less arduous stages along the French Riviera until they came within sight of Caesar's foundation of Forum Julii (Frejus). Here, on the plain formed by the meandering River Argentus, they camped within a few miles of Lepidus's headquarters. Lepidus made no move to help. He knew of the disaster that had befallen his old ally, and would have turned him away if he could. He had no wish to fight against the victorious consular army if, as he expected, it would soon be backed by most of the seventeen or so legions now controlled by his brothers-in-law, Brutus and Cassius.

Antony was more than equal to the occasion. Denied a formal welcome, he was let into the camp by an old comrade through the back gate. He was alone and unarmed, dirty and unshaven. The troops crowded around him, at first in curiosity. Some of them had served under him in Gaul. Everyone knew his reputation for generalship, at that stage the highest of any living Roman, even though his Mutina campaign had been a fiasco. He spoke to them as man to man and they eagerly answered him back. Before Lepidus became aware of what was going on, hundreds of them were calling out their support, and thousands more were to follow. Lepidus put the best face he could on it as the two commanders met in the middle of the huge, cheering crowd of legionaries. They exchanged apparently friendly greetings. Before the day was out, Antony had taken over his entire force as commander-in-chief and added it to his own, graciously retaining his old rival's services as his second-in-command.[14]

As Decimus had prophesied, the civil war was back on course. He wrote to Cicero blaming Octavian for refusing to act on his suggestions. It was useless trying to get Octavian to do anything, he grumbled; the boy just wouldn't be told.[15] If Antony had gone to Lepidus for safety, so Decimus went to Plancus, Governor of Gallia Comata. His welcome was just as uncertain. Plancus, still claiming to be loyal to the Senate, distanced himself from Lepidus by moving up to the high Alpine valleys around Grenoble. Decimus, no longer strong enough to take on Antony, spent weeks toiling up mountain roads with his puzzled troops to join him. It is hard to be sure precisely what their purpose was, unless to keep as far as possible out of Antony's way should he come back to Italy in a vengeful spirit before Brutus and Cassius arrived.

As Cicero could have told them, and as they presumably found out from other sources, Brutus and Cassius were in no hurry to return from the East, where they continued to build up their forces, and to tax the provincials so mercilessly that in some areas there were cases of fathers selling their children into slavery to pay the assessments to avoid being enslaved themselves.[16] Plancus, a prolific writer of letters that were elegantly phrased but conveyed little, kept up a polite correspondence with the most influential people of his times, gradually adjusting his position to the realities of power in the Italian peninsula until the moment when he felt it safest to offer his support to Antony. Decimus was hemmed in among much larger forces, and so had to relinquish his own. Plancus permitted him to leave with a small escort, but Decimus was captured by Gallic tribesmen while trying to reach Macedonia by the land route through the Alps, and was executed by them to curry favour with Antony.[17]

Late spring had brought Octavian a long pause for reflection, if not entirely one of masterly inactivity. He stayed put in northern Italy, rebuffing attempts by the Senate to make him do what he was told, while keeping his large army in trim for any eventuality. His camp became something of a political centre, as people who thought it might pay to ingratiate themselves with the new, rising power travelled up from Rome during the long sunny days to pay their respects. Messengers came and went from Antony, from Plancus, from Cicero and many others. Pollio, the distinguished Governor of Further Spain, joined Antony's coalition with his pair of legions – not that he had much choice. In his old age he would write an acclaimed history of his era, which was extensively quarried by later historians in antiquity but, alas, has failed to survive into modern times except as scattered references in other people's works.

Octavian's interlude for assessment of the options open to him finally crystallized in his decision to stand for the consulship left vacant by the deaths of Hirtius and Pansa. Elections to replace them had not so far been held, partly owing to technical difficulties over the complex republican rules for appointing an *Interrex* (who had to be a senior patrician) as electoral returning officer and temporary head of state. The delay, which involved religious scruples as well as political tradition, was yet another chance factor that worked in Octavian's favour. He would not have been a serious contender while Antony was still in headlong retreat, with the triumphant return of Brutus and Cassius widely thought to be imminent. Now he was in a strong enough position to dictate his own terms, if he should choose to do so.

The major imponderable factors of that confused period, in the immediate aftermath of Mutina, when the Senate had believed it could fully reassert its ancient authority, had now been largely clarified. Antony and his allies in the West could now count on the support of as many as twenty-five legions, possibly more, compared to the seventeen believed to be currently available to Brutus and Cassius. Both sides were actively recruiting, so those tentative numbers would surely grow. It was now clear that the eastern legions were mostly too far distant to make it practicable for them to cross the Adriatic in sufficient force until the following year. Antony, however, was waiting only to complete the satisfactory redeployment of his forces before leading them back from Gaul.

Octavian opened his quest for the consulship with a confidential approach to Cicero for his support. The precise terms of what he was offering in return are open to speculation, but they were clearly pitched to make maximum appeal to the ambition and vanity of the elder statesman. Would he perhaps be tempted to consider joining the young general in a joint bid for consular power? As his senior colleague, Cicero could be responsible, it was said, for the ordinary day-to-day matters of government, while Octavian went about his adoptive father's business.[18] That would mean, of course, that Octavian would simultaneously foster the aggrandisement of Caesar's memory, while preparing an all-out attack on the assassins.

It was a poisoned chalice. Cicero, to his credit, rejected it. He would have loved nothing better than a second term as consul, and he had often enough in his chequered career resorted to deception and subterfuge to get his own way. This would have been a step too far. Even he, with all his rhetorical talents, would not have been able to disguise the underlying reality, that by promoting Octavian's candidature in tandem with his own he would be elevating to the summit of republican power an opportunist, who had shown his contempt for the Senate's authority by holding on illegally to an army whose very existence was now threatening the integrity of the state. Perhaps that was the moment when he finally admitted to himself that his ingenious policy of playing the two leading Caesarians off against each other had ended in disastrous failure. It can have been little consolation that, but for the random operations of chance, he ought to have won hands down.

In the middle of May, Brutus had written reprovingly to Cicero of his fear that if Octavian were to become consul he might suppose he had risen too high ever to come down – in other words, that he would make himself king, just as Caesar had hoped to do. 'I'm so afraid of that young man!' Brutus concluded,[19] reporting a rumour which had just reached him on the march that Cicero had already been elected to the consulship. That was false. Less than a month later, Cicero seemed as if he might be inclined to concede Brutus's main point, about the peril of trusting Octavian, in a letter to Brutus's cousin, Decimus – who may have lived just long enough to receive it, although no reply has survived. 'What's the use?' Cicero asked despairingly, referring to one of his earlier initiatives concerning Octavian. 'Believe me, as a man not given to undervaluing myself, when I tell you I'm right out in the cold now. The Senate was my instrument but it has come to pieces in my hand.'[20]

On 25 July Cicero again visited Servilia, at her request. This time the company was far less distinguished, and included Casca, the assassin whose appointment as tribune Octavian had refrained from opposing as an earnest of his support for the Republic. She asked two closely related questions: should her son be recalled to Italy, and, if he were, would that be in his interests? Cicero replied with the unequivocal declaration that it would greatly advance Brutus's reputation if he came back as soon as possible to help his collapsing country. He might have saved his breath. Although Servilia's response is not recorded, it is clear that she would not advise him to return if she thought it too dangerous. In reporting the conversation to Brutus in his last extant letter, Cicero acknowledged the dispiriting extent of his failure to keep Octavian on the straight and narrow path of republican virtue.[21]

By that time, Octavian had given up on him. Even if he had wanted to, Cicero could no longer hope to deliver the votes of the majority of senators. In July the much-vaunted alliance between teenager and statesman was revealed as a sham. Four hundred of his soldiers, led by centurions, entered the Senate House. They were unarmed and initially respectful, but the menace of their presence could not have been in doubt as they asked for payment in full of the gratuities they had been promised, and for their young general to be made consul. The senators were outraged at what they considered to be their effrontery, and some were courageous or foolhardy enough to show it by displays of anger. The leading centurion, Cornelius, left the chamber and returned wearing his sword. Throwing back his cloak to reveal the hilt, he patted it, saying, 'This will decide it if you don't.'[22]

The return of the deputation empty-handed to Bononia was the cue Octavian had been waiting for to launch another march on Rome, for the second time in less than a year. He had already told the men that the Senate's intention was to send them off on campaign after campaign until they were all killed, so that no further payments would need to be made. Now they believed him, and they clamoured to be led to the capital in arms to claim their just rights. Like Julius Caesar six years earlier, his heir crossed the Rubicon, but with eight legions at his back rather than only one. The Senate sent envoys to tell Octavian he could stand for the consulship *in absentia*. It was much too late for that. They also sent, more slowly, a guarded wagon train of money to buy off the troops. Octavian briefed a squadron of cavalry to ride ahead and force the wagons to turn aside, out of his line of march, in case his troops should break ranks to raid the money chests.

Just as the *optimates* thought all was lost, two legions arrived at Ostia, Rome's harbour, from Africa, whence they had been summoned, more in hope than expectation, some months earlier. There was already one legion based in the capital. For a couple of days it seemed as if they might be enough to defend Rome against the invader. While Octavian was actually interviewing the Senate's envoys on the details of their terms, news came that their previous decrees in his favour had now been withdrawn.[23] The envoys retired in confusion as Octavian broke camp and pressed ahead at redoubled speed, fearing for the safety of his mother and sister, whom he now heard were being sought as hostages for his good behaviour.

Riding ahead of the main body of his army, he entered Rome with no more than a bodyguard, having sent other cavalry forward to assure the ordinary citizens that he meant them no harm. The three legions supposedly guarding the capital went over to him, while their commander, Cornutus, fell on his sword. Great crowds of the common people ran out from their houses to cheer him. He went straight to the Temple of the Vestal Virgins, where his mother and Octavia had been kept in hiding. They embraced in relief and joy, in the heady excitement of the moment. Senators, now fearing for their own safety, flocked to assure him of their good will.

Cicero, having cautiously arranged a private meeting through intermediaries, assured him that he had personally proposed him to the Senate for the consulship. For both men it was the end of a long day. Octavian observed with laconic irony that Cicero was the last of his friends to greet him.[24]

A night of high farce followed twenty-four hours later, after a rumour that the Martian and Fourth legions, the ones which had defected from Antony the previous autumn, had defected again, this time to the side of the Senate, as they were not prepared to be led against their fatherland. The Senate met by night and dispatched a magistrate, Aquilius Crassus, to Picenum to recruit more troops. Cicero is reported to have welcomed members at the door as they entered the Senate House, but once the rumour was proved to be false he escaped in a litter.[25] Octavian laughed on being told of the incident, but as a precautionary measure he moved his army onto the large public expanse of the Campus Martius beside the city walls. Aquilius Crassus was brought before him in the slave's clothes in which he had tried to disguise himself, and received at least a temporary pardon.

Now that his hold on the city was secure, Octavian demonstrated the concern that was to become his hallmark, for staying within the letter of republican laws while violating their spirit. He helped himself to public funds to pay his troops, on the grounds that the Senate had at some stage voted such payments, even if they had later rescinded them. Then he ostentatiously moved a short distance outside the capital so that the elections could take place without apparent pressure. He and his cousin, Quintus Pedius, were voted in as consuls. They took office on 19 August, a month before his twentieth birthday. As he re-entered Rome, twelve vultures are reported to have flown above his head while he offered the traditional sacrifice to the gods, the same sign that had marked the beginning of the rule of Romulus, the legendary founder of the city.[26]

Octavian moved swiftly to consolidate his position and pave the way for the alliance he was contemplating with the other Caesarean forces now massing on the borders of Italy. He secured the ratification of his adoption by Caesar through a formal *lex curiata*, passed by the most conservative of the public assemblies. That not only put beyond further legal challenge his right to call himself Caesar, but also gave him authority of patronage over the many former slaves who had been freed by his adoptive father, some of whom were rich and would now be obliged, as Octavian's freedmen, to contribute heavily to his funds.[27]

As consul, he presided at a special court hearing to try, in their absence, all those who had conspired to assassinate Caesar, not simply the ones who had wielded daggers but those who had advance knowledge of the action, even if they had not been physically present in Rome on the Ides of March. All were judged guilty. One judge alone had the temerity to vote for acquittal; he survived for the moment, but was later proscribed to meet the same fate as the assassins. The Senate further obliged Octavian by repealing the decrees naming Antony, Lepidus, Plancus and Dolabella as public enemies. In the latter's case, however, the vote came too late: he had already committed suicide after being trapped by Cassius, whom he feared might torture him to death as he himself had tortured Trebonius.[28]

In the four months since Mutina, Octavian had played a difficult and dangerous hand with precocious skill and not a little courage. It had taken nerve to defy the Senate so openly after the flight of Antony and before his juncture with Lepidus. If Antony's forces had been wiped out, Octavian would have been left with no perceptible ally, not even Cicero. Syme acknowledges the point: 'If Brutus and Cassius came to Italy with their host of 17 legions, his 'father' Cicero would have no compunction about declaring the young man a public enemy.'[29] By that time Octavian would have served his purpose, which was to restore a republic on terms agreeable to Cicero and Brutus, but in which Caesar's heir would have no political role except in conformity to their will. Given his character and theirs, such a contradictory situation could only have been resolved by his death. Cassius, for one, would have been determined to kill him. Octavian's eight legions, however loyal, would not have been enough to save him.

It was not only Pansa but Antony himself who had warned Octavian of what he could expect, in the letter he wrote to him and Hirtius during the siege, and which Cicero later read out to the Senate. Antony had compared Cicero to a trainer of gladiators, who set two groups of men to fight each other even though they were really part of one body. 'He has been lucky to have deceived you, using the same ornaments of speech with which he gloried in having deceived Caesar.'[30] Octavian now accepted that Antony had been right in that judgment. He wrote to congratulate both Antony and Lepidus on no longer having to bear the stigma of public enemies. The two senior generals, already on the march, replied with congratulations on his election and promises of friendship and cooperation.

They needed Octavian almost as much as he needed them. As summer turned to autumn, the young consul headed north with his fully legitimized and well-paid army, now swollen to eleven legions, to take the next important step on his path to the top.

TEN

THREE TO RULE THE WORLD

Octavian was not in the mood to take chances, and neither was Antony. Their representatives agreed on an elaborate protocol, under which each was to advance with five legions to opposite sides of the River Lavinius (Lavino) near Mutina and halt to face each other some distance from the banks. After performing this time-consuming manoeuvre early on an autumn morning, with a combined total of about 50,000 men, the two principals advanced with an escort of 300 each to the bridges leading to a small island in mid-stream. Lepidus went ahead on his own while they watched him search the island for hidden weapons. After he waved his red cloak to signal that all was safe for the two others to join him, they crossed the bridges, leaving their escorts to stand guard out of earshot.

Octavian, in spite of his youth, took the central chair in recognition of his new rank as serving consul. With Lepidus and Antony sitting on either side – and, no doubt, with plenty to eat and drink – they spent the whole of the rest of the day there in conference together.[1] Next morning they resumed, still protected by their waiting armies, and another entire day passed in hard bargaining, as each of them was forced, to varying extents, to retreat from their original negotiating positions. We may be sure that Lepidus, who in some degree was present on sufferance, would have supported the arguments of his new commander-in-chief against those of Octavian. By the morning of the third day they had effectively decided the future and fate of the entire Roman world for the next five years – so far as that was practicable.

Their fundamental decision, which underpinned all the rest, was to form themselves effectively into a dictatorship of three, to rule, initially, for the next five years. They did not give it that name, of course, because the title of dictator had so recently been abolished, with anathema, by Antony himself. They announced themselves as *Tresviri Rei Publicae Constituendae*, 'Three men for sorting out the Republic'. The title was both euphemistic and ambiguous; *constituendae* in such a context could equally have meant 're-establishing' the old republic or 'establishing' a reformed and revised one. To history the three leaders are known collectively as 'The Second Triumvirate', also something of a misnomer in that they were the first of their kind – radically different from the so-called 'First Triumvirate' of Pompey, Crassus and Caesar sixteen years earlier.

Whereas the First Triumvirate had been essentially a private and unofficial alliance for manipulating the levers of government in its principals' own interests, the Second Triumvirate would actually *be* the government of the state. There would be no question of the traditional magistrates or the Senate acting against, or even speaking against, their decrees; any man who opposed them, at least initially, would risk having his head chopped off and stuck on a spike in the Forum. Many would not be given even a chance to knuckle under to their new masters, but would be hunted down as outlaws, with a price on their heads, and the death penalty extended to any who sheltered them. Cicero was to be their most prominent victim. Octavian is said to have argued against his proscription for the first two days, but to have yielded rather than see the negotiations collapse through Antony's insistence on this one point.[2]

Antony, in fact, got most of what he wanted. In terms of *realpolitik* he had more legions than anyone else in the empire, as well as the greatest reputation. He reserved for himself proconsular authority over northern Italy and most of Gaul; Lepidus was granted the whole of Spain, plus the area of Gaul nearest the Pyrenees. Octavian got the equivalent of the wooden spoon, the province of Africa (Tunisia) and the islands of Sicily, Sardinia and Corsica. He would have to fight if he wanted to set foot on them. The Governor of Africa, Quintus Cornificius, was in the process of sending two legions to Rome to bolster the Senate, and he would refuse to recognize the triumvirate. Sextus Pompeius, with the Senate's commission as admiral-in-chief in his pocket, had already taken over Sicily, and his powerful fleets would make any invasion of the other islands a hazardous enterprise.

Octavian was persuaded to give up his consulship in favour of Ventidius, who had brought the three fresh legions to Antony when his chief was at his lowest ebb and in danger of being rejected by all. No doubt Antony and Lepidus convinced the young man that, henceforth, the honoured position of consul would be subservient to that of triumvir; their primary objective would have been to nip in the bud any claim that, as the only serving consul of the three, he had superior rights or status. They also agreed on who should serve as consuls under them for the next few years. Plancus and Lepidus would share the task in the coming year; in 41 Antony's brother Lucius would have Servilius Isauricus as his colleague; in 40 it would be the turn of Pollio and Gnaeus Domitius Calvinus, who had commanded the Caesarean centre at Pharsalus.

As for the menace of Brutus and Cassius, the triumvirs agreed that Antony and Octavian should lead the bulk of their forces against them to regain the eastern half of the empire, while Lepidus remained behind in Rome to keep Italy and the West secure. The proscriptions were intended to do the major part of that job for him; nobody was to be left alive in their rear who had the capacity and motive to lead a rebellion against them in the optimate cause. Most of the original conspirators against Caesar, however, had already sought sanctuary with either Sextus in Sicily or with the growing forces of Brutus and Cassius. Many more would follow rapidly in their wake before the triumvirs could reach Rome with their lists of intended victims.

There is much scope for argument about how many people were proscribed and how many actually killed as a result. Appian claims that 300 senators and 2,000 knights were among those whose names were posted up in the Forum, but that seems an exaggeration. Livy, whose history for this period is lost except for a brief chapter-by-chapter summary, puts the number of senators at 120. Plutarch, in one biography, says 200, and in another, 300, but he does not say of what rank.[3] The tally of those mentioned by name in the various ancient sources is less than 100. It seems unlikely that Octavian, whose experience of public life had been so short, actually knew many of the men proscribed.

Greater human misery was caused by another decision of the triumvirs, to expel the inhabitants of no fewer than eighteen Italian towns in order to provide future homes for their soldiers once the projected civil war against Brutus and Cassius was over. These included such prominent regional centres as Ariminum, Beneventum, Capua, Nuceria, Rhegium and Venusia.[4] It was intended as a form of payment in kind rather than in money, because hard cash was now in short supply, and what little was available would need to be conserved for the soldiers' ordinary wages before and during the coming campaign. Many of Rome's richest individuals had gone abroad, taking care not to leave much behind for their enemies to steal. The intense recruiting drives had removed tens of thousands of young men from productive occupations, and the hostile movements of armies, in both the West and the East, had depressed trade and stifled commerce. Provincial tax revenues dropped away catastrophically, and prudent civilians buried much of their money along with any other items of gold and silver, while hoping for better times.

A further decision by the banks of the Lavinius, which would affect Octavian's private life, was prompted by a noisy demonstration on the part of the troops rather than the will of the triumvirs. The Caesarean soldiers, anxious not to have to fight each other again, wanted to ensure that Octavian and Antony did not fall out again as quickly as they had done twice before. They pressed for the pair to forge a family link. As Antony was already married to Fulvia, Octavian was the only available candidate. He agreed to give up the younger Servilia, to whom he had become betrothed the previous winter but had not yet married, and promised to wed Claudia, Fulvia's daughter by her first husband, Clodius, Cicero's old enemy. Suetonius describes her as *vixdum nubilis* – 'barely at puberty'.[5] The marriage was to be brief; and Fulvia would turn out to be a mother-in-law from hell.

It is not known whether his own mother was still alive to learn of her son's matrimonial rearrangement. Atia died while Octavian was consul, a period of only fourteen weeks from his election on 19 August to his official resignation on 27 November. It may well be that the experience of hiding from her son's enemies who wanted to take her hostage shortened her life. Octavian used his triumviral authority to arrange a public funeral for her, which would have been a focus for all shades of Caesarean opinion to unite in memory of the great man's niece. Philippus, his stepfather, survived his wife's death by several years.

Execution squads were dispatched to Rome ahead of the triumvirs to kill seventeen men named on the first proscription list. The information was not made public, so nobody in the city but the executioners and Pedius, Octavian's consular colleague, knew who they were after. Four were killed as soon as they were spotted in the street or caught at home. A dreadful night followed, as armed groups went from house to house searching for other victims. At dawn, against the triumvirs' orders, Pedius published the list of seventeen, believing wrongly that they were the only ones who would be marked for death, and he sent heralds around the city to reassure the other citizens. The task was too much for him. The following night Pedius died of strain.[6]

The first serving magistrate to be killed was the tribune Salvius, whose veto had saved Antony on 3 January from being declared a public enemy by the Senate, but who had later given his full cooperation to Cicero. Not knowing whether he would be reprieved on account of the earlier action or condemned for the later, Salvius gave a banquet for his friends in case it should be his last. An execution squad, led by a centurion, burst in during the meal. Some of the guests rose from their seats as if to intervene – or perhaps to flee – but the centurion ordered them to sit down and keep quiet. He then grabbed Salvius by the hair, pulled him partly across his own table, and cut off his head. Before carrying it away he warned the guests to stay where they were or suffer the same fate. They remained on their couches far into the night beside their host's headless corpse.[7]

The triumvirs entered Rome separately, on three successive days, each escorted by one legion and an elite praetorian cohort. Octavian, as consul, came first. After all three had arrived a token public assembly was called on 27 November by a tribune, Publius Titius, who proposed the enabling legislation to set up the triumvirate – to a Forum of citizens hemmed in by armed men. The measures were passed into law without time being given for scrutiny, much less for argument. All exits from the city were guarded as new proscription lists were displayed. Rewards of 100,000 sesterces were offered for each victim's head brought in; but if the bounty hunter were a slave he would be granted his freedom plus 40,000 sesterces.[8]

The Caesarean generals decided to take this opportunity to settle old quarrels within their families. Paulus, the brother of Lepidus, was listed along with Lucius Caesar, Antony's uncle. Plancus condemned his brother Plotius, while Pollio revenged himself on his father-in-law. Another of the victims, Thoranius, is said to have been one of Octavian's former tutors. Paulus was apparently permitted to escape, but Lucius Caesar was saved only by the intervention of Antony's own mother, Julia, who stood between the soldiers' swords and the old man when they tried to enter her house, and later rebuked her son in public where he sat in the Forum with Octavian and Lepidus, giving judgment and paying bounties. Antony grudgingly agreed to let his uncle, who had occasionally opposed him in the Senate, live on.[9]

As the proscriptions continued, men started to anticipate their fate before they were actually listed. They joined earlier fugitives in trying to escape from the capital. Like them, they hid in sewers and down wells, up chimneys and under roof-tiles. Some died sword in hand, others made no resistance. Some were informed on by their slaves, others were allegedly betrayed by their wives. There were cases of suicide by drowning in the Tiber, leaping from tall buildings and self-immolation. Hardier and more fortunate ones got clean away with the help of wife, child, brother or slave. Some wives died helping their husbands. Some slaves were even said to have dressed up as their masters and to have been killed in their place.

The widow of a man named Ligurius followed his severed head to the triumvirs' tribunal in the Forum and shouted to them that she had sheltered him and therefore ought to be executed, too. They pretended not to see or hear her, so she went away and starved herself to death.[10] An eighty-year-old senator, Statius, who had fought with the Samnites in the Social War, is reported to have been proscribed, like a number of others, not for any offence but because of his great wealth. He opened the doors of his house and invited passers-by to take away and keep whatever they could carry. When the place had been stripped bare, he shut himself inside and set fire to it, killing himself and inadvertently setting fire to his quarter of the city.[11]

At Rhegium, across the water from Sicily at the foot of Italy, a group of proscribed men were joined by local citizens, because the town was one of the eighteen earmarked to be handed over to discharged veterans. Led by a certain

Vetulinus, they killed the centurions who had been sent to find them, before crossing the Straits of Messina to join Sextus Pompey.[12] Vetulinus was outdone by Hirtius (who may or may not have been a relative of the late consul), who fled from Rome with his servants and built up a substantial force of fugitives and their supporters, with which he attacked several towns. The triumvirs had to send an army against him, but he and his men successfully avoided battle and also escaped to Sicily.[13] The most enterprising escapee was Pomponius, who dressed himself as a praetor, kitted out his slaves as lictors, talked his way onto one of the triumvirate's ships by pretending to be an official envoy to Sextus, and completed his escape in style.[14]

Cicero could easily have evaded capture. Warned that his name was listed, he left his Tusculan villa and took ship from Astura, intending to join Brutus in the East. Horribly seasick because of a storm, he put in at Caieta, further down the eastern coast near Formiae, to spend the night at a villa which he owned. Next day, as his slaves were carrying him back to the shore in a litter, he was pursued by troops under Popilius Laenas, an officer whom Cicero had successfully defended some years earlier against a charge of killing his father. Cicero's slaves were apparently ready to fight to save him, but the old philosopher told them to put down the litter, and stoically stretched out his neck. It took Laenas several blows to hack off his head. The officer also cut off his right hand, with which he had written the Philippics. Fulvia is reported to have stuck pins in his shrivelled tongue before Antony had these grisly trophies nailed to the rostra in the Forum, where Cicero had made so many great speeches.[15]

On the first day of the New Year, 42 BC, it became clear that the triumvirs would not be satisfied simply for the Senate to pass on the nod those items of legislation which they had drawn up. All the senators and all the magistrates were required to swear a solemn oath to support and maintain the decrees which Julius Caesar had made when he was dictator.

Nobody is recorded as having refused. To rub in the lesson, the triumvirs also arranged for Caesar to be officially recognized as a god. This legislative provision must surely have been inspired by Octavian, who was now able to describe himself as *divi filius* – son of a god. Antony became the first priest of Caesar's cult, whose rites would be celebrated in a temple to be built in the Forum on the site of his funeral pyre. It was later enacted that any senator who failed to celebrate Caesar's birthday in July by wearing laurel leaves would be fined a million sesterces.

In the real world, however, where soldiers needed to be paid and fed, the triumvirs were finding themselves short of money. All the property of the proscribed victims became forfeit to the state, as a matter of course, but because of the sudden over-supply at auction, coupled with general monetary tightness, the prices achieved were derisorily low. Potential bidders may also have feared for their lives should Brutus and Cassius win the coming clash of arms. In an attempt to make up the shortfall of cash, the triumvirs imposed heavy taxes on all citizens living in Italy. These men had paid no tax at all for many years, subsidized by the unfortunate provincials. Now, for example, a knight (who was required by law to possess a fortune of a certain size) was ordered to contribute a year's entire income.[16]

An unprecedented edict, announced without consultation, assessed 1,400 of the richest women in the land for taxation. Women had never been formally taxed in the history of the Republic, although they had sometimes, at moments of national crisis, taken off their jewellery to throw into collecting baskets as a patriotic gesture. Many of them were friends of the triumvirs' families, and they complained at first to Octavian's sister and Antony's mother, who interceded for them, but without success. Fulvia rebuffed them with hard words, provoking a group of them to make a public stand at the triumvirs' tribunal. Their spokeswoman, Hortensia, daughter of a well-known orator, argued that because women had no share in political rights they should not be taxed; they would gladly give their jewels, she said, to fight a foreign enemy, but not for a civil war. The triumvirs ordered the lictors to drive the women from the Forum, but the indignant uproar of the crowd made them stop. Next day the women's taxation list was officially cut by a thousand names to just 400.[17]

Much worse depredations were under way at the same time in the East, where Cassius was especially rapacious. He ordered a levy of 1,500 talents of gold on Tarsus – later to be the birthplace of St Paul. The sum was so huge that it proved impossible to raise, even after many free women and children had been sold into slavery. The local magistrates then started selling the men, too, and numbers of them committed suicide. Only when he was finally convinced that no more treasure remained to be extorted did Cassius relent and march his troops away. Later he captured and terrorized the island of Rhodes, which had threatened rebellion, as a further example to others. After this exploit he demanded the equivalent of ten years' tribute money from all the people of the once rich province of Asia.[18]

Octavian, hoping to take over the islands which had been allocated as his preliminary share of the western half of the empire, assembled a fleet to attack Sextus Pompey. He was not, however, intrepid enough to lead it in person. That task he entrusted to Salvidienus, one of the young men who had originally accompanied him from Apollonia after the Ides of March. Sextus, superior in ships and naval experience, easily defeated him, but Salvidienus survived to fight another day. Octavian went in person to the mainland towns near Sicily to drum up support against his adversary, promising the people of Rhegium and Vibo, two of the eighteen towns designated for takeover as future military colonies, that he would remove them from the list if they would help him. But he had to leave in a hurry at the urgent request of Antony, who was trying to embark the bulk of their legions at Brundisium for the much more important campaign in the East, but was being harried by another section of the republican fleet, commanded by Cassius's allies, Staius Murcus and Domitius Ahenobarbus (Shakespeare's 'Enobarb' in *Antony and Cleopatra*), son of the hard-line optimate of the same name who had died fighting against Caesar at Pharsala.[19]

The remnants of Octavian's defeated fleet, added to the few ships under Antony's control, proved sufficient to complete the task, as most of the republican vessels had been called away to try to intercept and destroy a flotilla sent from Alexandria by Cleopatra. Cassius had, in fact, been on the point of invading Egypt to punish her for supporting Dolabella – and, of course, to help himself to the country's fabulous treasures – when a message from Brutus convinced him that his first priority must be to join their two armies together in order to meet the triumvirs' threat. Cleopatra was not going to sit idly by, waiting for his return: hence, her alliance with Antony, whom she had probably met while living in Rome as Caesar's mistress. Although her flotilla came to grief in a storm, and so never reached Antony, its very dispatch towards Italy drew off a squadron of enemy ships, and so proved its value in clearing the triumvirs' way across the Adriatic.[20]

Antony had already shipped eight legions to Macedonia, which, if unsupported, would have been vulnerable to a swift attack by Brutus and Cassius, whose combined forces now totalled nineteen legions, plus many thousands of soldiers supplied by eastern monarchs and other rulers, some of whom had joined their entourage. The brief window of opportunity enabled Antony and Octavian to ferry no fewer than twenty more legions to the probable war zone. While those 100,000 men were disembarking, the original vanguard of eight legions was ordered to advance rapidly to Thrace to hold the mountain passes, through which the key west–east route, the Via Egnatia, made its meandering way. By a stroke of bad luck, Octavian was taken seriously ill and had to stay behind at Dyracchium.[21]

Cassius, now in overall command of the republicans, was unable to force his way through by the major route, and lost several days trying to find an alternative passage, with the help of local guides whom the soldiers did not trust. They ran out of water as they struggled through the parched and rocky landscape, but reached a lake in time to survive the experience. Norbanus Flaccus, commanding the vanguard opposing them, had to retreat back along the way he had come in order to avoid being outflanked and cut off from the main body of the triumviral army. He occupied the town of Amphipolis, as his last hope of holding up Cassius's advance, and Antony reached him with enough reinforcements to prevent the republicans making further progress.

Before Antony was in a position to launch a full-scale attack, however, Brutus and Cassius had time to build a virtually impregnable line of fortifications straddling the Via Egnatia, at a point where their right flank was protected by a mountain range and their left by a marsh covering many square miles down to the coast. Immediately behind them was the town of Philippi, only about ten miles from the port of Neapolis (Kavala). Although outnumbered, the republicans enjoyed both the tactical advantage of their superior position on the higher ground of the potential field of battle, and the strategic command of the seas, which enabled them to receive food and other supplies through Neapolis, from the offshore island of Thasos, their storage base.[22]

It was already autumn, and Antony's position would become untenable by the winter, when his main supply line across the Adriatic would no longer function. As a direct frontal assault was unthinkable he started to build a causeway through the marshes in the hope of mounting an attack from the side or rear. When Cassius became aware of the danger, he began to extend his defensive line to keep pace with the causeway. It was at this point that Octavian, although still so ill that he could scarcely stand without support, forced himself to travel up to the front line in a litter, fearful that if he did not at least show his face to his troops he would lose all credibility as their general. Because he would have been a liability rather than an asset on an open battlefield, he claimed the softer option of defending his camp, which was opposite Brutus's legions.

Cassius tried to avoid battle for as long as possible, but a skirmish between the men on the causeway and those building the defences against them gradually turned into a serious engagement as more and more troops were committed from each side. On the other flank, Brutus saw his chance and attacked the camp supposedly under Octavian's command. His troops broke in and slaughtered the defenders, who included 2,000 Spartans who had been recruited *en route* through Greece. Octavian, mysteriously, was nowhere to be seen. It would appear that, as in the case of the battle of Forum Gallorum near Mutina, the young man had fled.[23]

By the time he returned, having allegedly hidden in a nearby part of the bog, the first battle of Philippi was over, Brutus had returned behind his fortifications, and Cassius was dead. That was to be the second, greater mystery of that confusing and bloody October day. Antony had won the struggle beside the causeway, pushing back the republican ranks, driving many of them to headlong retreat and briefly capturing Cassius's camp. Cassius himself, temporarily isolated in the company of a few friends and unaware of Brutus's success, feared the whole battle was lost. Unable to see clearly because of his bad eyesight, he sent an aide, Titinius, at the gallop to see if a group of soldiers he could see running towards him in a cloud of dust were his own or the enemy's. Cassius saw Titinius being surrounded by the running troops and he assumed they were killing him.

Cassius called his freedman, Pindarus, to his side, and together the two men entered a tent while the rest waited outside. Not long afterwards, when Titinius returned with the news that the troops were Brutus's, and that they had embraced him as a friend, Cassius lay dead. Titinius thereupon fell on his own sword. What had happened in the tent? The ancient sources, including Plutarch, tell us that Cassius, in despair at what he believed to be his defeat, covered up his face and instructed Pindarus to kill him with his sword. Pindarus promptly obliged. But Plutarch adds that because, after his master's death, Pindarus was never seen again, some people believed he had killed Cassius without waiting for the order.[24]

That does, indeed, appear to be the most likely explanation of this bizarre incident, although the tradition of Cassius's 'suicide' has been almost universally accepted ever since, and features in Shakespeare's *Julius Caesar*. A further interesting, but usually disregarded, piece of evidence is that Cassius's head was found later to have been severed from his body. That does not fit in with the Roman tradition of a sword-thrust through the heart, whether self-inflicted or achieved with the help of an assistant. The probable reason for anyone to cut off Cassius's head would have been to take it to one of the triumvirs to claim the reward. That would perhaps provide a double motive for Pindarus, whom we may well suppose to have had little affection, if any, for a master noted even by his friends for his harsh and ruthless behaviour.

We are not told the identity of the other men outside the tent, but if they, like Pindarus, were his freedmen or slaves, they would have had every reason for pretending that Cassius had killed himself, because of the inflexible rule that if a slave killed his master, then every other slave in his household, regardless of age or sex, would also be put to death. Pindarus, admittedly, was a former slave who had been freed, but punishments of some degree could extend to freedmen as well in such circumstances. Cassius, after all, was not just any officer, but the commander-in-chief of an army of at least 100,000, mostly all still within a mile or two's radius of him. The accepted account of the assassin's death is scarcely more plausible than Octavian's excuse for failing to defend his camp – that his doctor, Marcus Artorius, had seen in a dream the young man being warned to get up from his sick-bed and leave the camp. In his memoirs (now lost) Octavian wrote that he acted on the warning by arming himself and fighting in another part of the field.[25]

By coincidence, on the day of the first battle of Philippi, a bloody naval engagement took place on the Adriatic, when the republican fleet (under Ahenobarbus and the Pompeian admiral Murcus) destroyed a large flotilla of inadequately guarded transport vessels (under Domitius Calvinus) carrying essential supplies from Italy for the triumviral army. Because autumn was now well advanced, and few other ships were available, there was no serious chance of further substantial supplies reaching Antony and Octavian that year by the same route.[26] News of the disaster reached the triumvirs soon enough, but apparently took much longer to be reported to Brutus. He had taken nominal overall command of the republican forces, but was in practice unable to exact obedience from all his varied allies, some of whom had already deserted or were planning to do so.

Brutus may well have been on the verge of what we, in modern parlance, would call a nervous breakdown. A month or two earlier, when his army along with Cassius's had been about to cross from Asia to Greece, Brutus sat alone in his tent one night, entirely wrapped up in his own thoughts in the middle of the silent camp. Suddenly he looked up as he thought he heard someone enter his tent. In front of him stood 'a strange and terrifying phantom'. Nerving himself to question it, Brutus asked what it wanted of him. 'I am your evil spirit, Brutus,' the phantom replied. And as it vanished, it added: 'You will see me again at Philippi.'

That is the story, as told in Plutarch's *Life of Brutus*.[27] There is no reason to suppose that the biographer made it up or that Brutus did not genuinely believe that he had seen a ghost. He lived in a superstitious age. It is not uncommon even today for people to report their supposed sightings of paranormal apparitions, however sceptical we may rightly be about their authenticity. In the cold light of dawn, Cassius gave Brutus the benefit of a strikingly modern-sounding analysis. Phantoms, as such, do not really exist, Cassius said; what his friend had seen was a figment of his own imagination, prompted by the great strain of the experiences he had undergone.[28] Cassius did not list those experiences, but we know, of course, that they included murdering his mother's former lover, Julius Caesar; facing possible sudden death from Lepidus's vengeful troops; being forced out of Rome by fear of mob violence; effective exile from his native land; risking his life and career by illegally taking over Roman legions abroad; and having to command soldiers in action, a job for which he seems to have been temperamentally unsuited.

On top of all that, Brutus had very recently received news of the appalling suicide of his wife; she had swallowed a live coal. The highly-strung Portia had tried to conceal her distress at parting from her husband when he had to leave Italy, but became increasingly depressed as his absence wore on and the political and military tide in Italy turned against him. Plutarch tells us that she wept, sometimes daily, before a painting of the scene from Homer's *Iliad* where the faithful Andromache says goodbye to Hector, taking from his arms their baby son, before the Trojan hero sets off for his doomed encounter with Achilles, who drags his dead body behind his chariot around the walls of Troy. Portia's death[29] was yet another unforeseen consequence of the civil war that, it might well be argued, Brutus himself had launched by his assassination of Caesar. One might also add that Cassius's perceptive analysis of Brutus's mental condition, emphasizing the difference that can exist between appearance and reality, further supports the argument that Cassius is unlikely to have confused one with the other so readily as to take his own life by a similar mistake.

Brutus continued to hold out for nearly three more weeks behind his fortifications after the death of his colleague, while Antony and Octavian tried vainly to winkle him out. To their surprise, one morning in mid-November, he suddenly deployed his legions voluntarily in the open. There could have been no military justification for such a move. By that time, apparently, he knew of the success of his fleet in denying the two triumvirs their much-needed supplies. He needed only to ignore for a comparatively short time the shouted insults and provocations of the frustrated Caesareans, and they would have been forced to withdraw in order to forage for food in the imminent winter. It is reported that he gave in to pressure from some of his own officers, who were eager to attack,[30] but it may be that the tension of waiting had become too much for him, and that he had simply snapped.

Whatever the reasoning behind his decision, the result was total disaster for the republican cause. There was a moment in the battle when Octavian's legions barely held steady under his direction, but Antony mounted a devastating attack to win the day. Brutus escaped into the mountains with the remnants of four legions, but decided, correctly, that his position was hopeless. He committed suicide, as did a number of other senior *optimates*, including Marcus Livius Drusus, father of Octavian's future wife, Livia. Some other bearers of once-famous names died fighting, like Cato's son, who killed a number of opponents that day before succumbing to weight of numbers. Proscribed men among the prisoners are said to have reviled Octavian when being led away to execution, but to have saluted Antony as a worthy winner.[31] It may be that they thought the young man a coward. They may have been right.

ELEVEN

TWILIGHT OF THE REPUBLIC

The defeat of Brutus and Cassius at Philippi is traditionally regarded as marking the end of the Roman Republic. The transition to 'Roman Empire', in the sense of a monarchical and vastly extended state, ruled by one man as its emperor, is held to have emerged more or less inevitably from the brief transitional period of the Triumvirate. That view is tenable only with the help of an over-large dose of hindsight. The years immediately after Philippi were so filled with localized civil strife and social upheaval in Italy – against a background of an almost universal desire for peace among those not directly affected by the resettlements – that a reversion to some form of oligarchic republican government was among the possible outcomes, along with division of the empire into two or more separate entities.

One reason for the tradition of Philippi as the definitive watershed is that the written sources become less plentiful after it.[1] Modern historians have tended to pass swiftly forward to the battle of Actium in 31 BC, when Antony and Cleopatra went down to catastrophic defeat. But if there was ever a genuinely popular 'Roman Revolution', in the sense of a grassroots uprising against the government in Rome, it was surely when peasant farmers and townsfolk alike rose spontaneously in most regions of Italy in 41 to try to prevent their homes and farms being seized, under Octavian's administration, by landless ex-soldiers.[2] They fought the triumviral system partly in the name of the Republic, whose restoration they championed as the most likely means of holding on to their land. Their revolution failed, and history has little time for losers.

By brute force the discharged legionaries eventually took possession of the private property that the triumvirs had allocated to them. In many cases it was achieved over the bodies of the previous owners, who had done nothing to deserve being reduced to homelessness and beggary by such ruthless expropriation. It constituted a large-scale change of ownership, whereby lower-class men took over the houses and fields of people largely of the class just above them, but also from those of their own class. It was not a revolution of the proletariat, in the Marxist sense. The proletarian soldiers were simply collecting on the contract they had made with Antony and Octavian for fighting, effectively as mercenaries, against the *optimates*.

Antony, the undoubted victor of Philippi, chose for himself the more congenial task of regulating the largely cowed and prostrate eastern half of the empire. He did not return with Octavian to Italy, but headed east immediately, hoping to raise enough money for cash gratuities for the veterans, to be paid in addition to the promised transfers of land. He took eight legions, two of which he borrowed from his young colleague, leaving the rest to be repatriated. Their numbers were now swollen by the many thousands of optimate troops who had surrendered. Antony knew how hard it would be for Octavian to control that huge agglomeration of men, who may have numbered up to 170,000, many of whom were now surplus to requirements. Feeding and clothing them for their wintry march back through the Macedonian mountain regions, and then transporting them across the Adriatic, would inevitably be a series of logistical headaches.[3]

Octavian is reported to have taken on this heavy responsibility as a matter of personal choice. That could be later propaganda to boost his reputation for caring for his veterans – and to disguise the otherwise obvious truth that his prestige, at that point, stood much lower than his colleague's.

If, however, it is true that he wanted the job, it demonstrates astonishing political maturity. The decision would nearly cost him his life on two occasions, when he had to outface outraged mobs of his own and Antony's soldiers, but the successful completion of the task would bring him a power base that was longer lasting and more reliable than that of any of his predecessors or contemporary rivals.

Before parting to go in opposite directions, the two triumvirs reshuffled their portfolios of provinces to reflect Antony's superior status, but also to upgrade Octavian at the expense of Lepidus. In addition to the eastern half of the empire, Antony took the whole of Gaul beyond the Alps, but agreed that northern Italy (Cisalpine Gaul) should cease to be a province and become part of Roman Italy, controlled directly from the capital, as originally planned by Julius Caesar. Octavian took Spain from Lepidus, who was suspected of treasonable negotiations with Sextus Pompey. It was left to the young general to decide the fate of Lepidus; if he should turn out not to be guilty, he would receive the turbulent province of Africa.[4]

On his way home, Octavian's continuing illness took a further turn for the worse. Rumours reached Rome that he had succumbed during the trek through Macedonia. He struggled on, with frequent stops, and endured a bad crossing of the Adriatic to reach Brundisium. There he stayed for some time to recuperate, feeling the need to write a reassuring letter to the Senate, many of whose members had been torn between rejoicing and panic according to whether they believed him to have died or recovered. He was returning in a spirit of mildness, he told them, like his adoptive father before him. It was true, at least for the moment, in their case. If he could secure their backing it would ease the resettlement process.[5]

He did force the reluctant Senate, whose members had mostly supported the losing side, to celebrate the battle of Philippi as a major victory for Rome; but that was scarcely too harsh an imposition on men who had been praying that

Octavian as the Augustus ('the consecrated one') wearing a breastplate showing scenes of his diplomatic triumph when the Parthians, fearing invasion, handed back legionary standards captured from earlier Roman generals. His bare feet indicate divinity – gods have no need of shoes. This statue was found at Prima Porta, Rome, in the nineteenth century. *(Vatican Museum/Bridgeman Art Library)*

Antony and Cleopatra: in literature they are a pair of star-crossed lovers as romantically doomed as Romeo and Juliet. In real life, Cleopatra was as politically ambitious as Caesar or Antony, whom she successively seduced. Richard Burton and Elizabeth Taylor are shown in a 1963 still from a film version of Shakespeare's play, based on Plutarch. *(Bettman/Corbis)*

Pompey: his misguided refusal to allow Julius Caesar a safe passage to stand for re-election as consul led to a four-year civil war. *(Ny Carlsberg Glypotek, Copenhagen/Bridgeman Art Library)*

Caesar: his assassination by aristocrats catapulted Octavian into public prominence as his heir and sworn avenger. *(Vatican Museum/Bridgeman Art Library)*

Cicero: his cynical attempt to use Octavian as a pawn in the republican power struggle backfired spectacularly. *(Uffizi, Florence/Scala Archives)*

Livia: the wife whom Octavian 'abducted' from her first husband's house when six months pregnant. As mother of Tiberius she manoeuvred to ensure his succession as emperor. *(Louvre/Bridgeman Art Library/ Peter Willi)*

Marcellus: groomed to be emperor, he died too soon. Louis XIV bought this statue for his palace at Versailles. Today it stands in the Louvre. (*Bridgeman Art Library*)

Julia: Octavian's only child was married successively, for dynastic reasons, to young Marcellus, Agrippa and Tiberius. She was exiled for immorality, in the biggest scandal of the reign. (*Pergamon Museum, Berlin/ Bridgeman Art Library/Alinari*)

The overgrown Mausoleum of Augustus, which he built for himself beside the Tiber, but which first accommodated four of his designated successors, who predeceased him. (*Richard Holland*)

Sir Lawrence Alma-Tadema (1836–1912) was one of a number of artists who, before the advent of modernism and its prejudices against 'history painting', enjoyed successful careers creating imaginative representations of classical times. His *An Audience at Agrippa*'s seeks to portray in authentic detail a typical incident of daily life in Rome when Agrippa, seen here walking down the steps in his toga, was Octavian's deputy and nominated successor. The Prima Porta statue (see Plate 1) is on the right. *(Dick Institute, Kilmarnock/Bridgeman Art Library)*

Members of the imperial family going to the sacrifice: one of the sculpted reliefs on the Altar of Augustan Peace, which stands in the district of Rome once known as the Field of Mars, where soldiers exercised. For the ancient Romans, peace was inconceivable without war, or the threat of war, to impose it. *(Bettman/Corbis)*

A Favourite Custom by Sir Lawrence Alma-Tadema (first shown at the Royal Academy, London, in 1909) is a reminder that life was not totally dominated in imperial Rome by war, politics and bloodthirsty gladiatorial games. The painting, based partly on photographs of excavated baths to ensure accuracy of detail, gives a charming impression of how pleasant and sociable life could be for upper-class women. *(Tate Gallery)*

The Forum at Rome, seen from a lower slope of the Capitol, with the Palatine Hill on the right. Most of the surviving structures date from post-Augustan Rome, but in the centre (dwarfed by the three columns of the Temple of Castor and Pollux) is the plinth of the Temple of Julius, all that remains of the building completed by Octavian in memory of his adoptive father. On the day of the photograph in November 2003, fresh flowers reposed on the altar (not visible), testimony to the emotions still stirred in modern Italy by the potent name of Caesar. *(Richard Holland)*

Julius Caesar's murderers would kill his heir as well. Octavian had a signed and sealed copy of Antony's compact in his pocket when he eventually reached Rome in the early spring of 41, and he produced it to secure the cooperation of the two new consuls, Sulpicius Isauricus and Antony's brother Lucius, as well as of Lepidus. Any cooperation was minimal and short-lived. Isauricus was understandably offended by Octavian's rejection of his daughter Servilia. The patrician Lepidus must have hated having to explain himself to a 21-year-old upstart in order to secure his reinstatement in favour. Octavian gave him the benefit of the doubt, so that he retained his position as a triumvir.

Lucius cooperated at first, along with his sister-in-law Fulvia, both of whom may have been expecting the recent marital connexion, through Fulvia's daughter, to extract from Octavian the degree of shared power they evidently believed to be their due as Antony's closest family members. They seriously underestimated the young man's character and mettle. Now he had got over his illness he had no intention of delegating any more of his dictatorial power than was absolutely necessary, and especially not to his mother-in-law, who made the further mistake of nagging him in a penetrating voice. Before long, she and Lucius began actively obstructing him, with the help of Antony's agent, Manius. So long as they kept within the law there was little Octavian could do about it without risking a disastrous split with Antony. But their opposition became so blatant and intense that he began to suspect that Antony himself was behind it.

He was probably right – at least to the extent that Antony would undoubtedly have briefed them in advance on his need for them to protect his interests while he was absent abroad. Antony, after all, must have known he was taking a considerable risk in entrusting Octavian with the command of a bigger army than his own; that may have reflected, however, his professional opinion of the young man's generalship, or lack of it. Whether he followed this up with later instructions to Lucius and Fulvia on what to do in specific circumstances is more problematical, given the difficulties of communication, but it is scarcely improbable. Certainly they claimed to be acting in his interests, although some of the senior legates Antony had placed in charge of his Gallic legions were to demonstrate serious doubts on that point.

Modern apologists for Antony, such as Syme, say it would have been against his character and principles to renege on the solemn agreement he signed with Octavian; so Syme blames it on Fulvia. 'She must force him – by discrediting, if not by destroying, the rival Caesarian leader,' he writes, 'and thus win for her absent and unsuspecting consort the sole power which he scarcely seemed to desire.'[6] In the final analysis, the evidence for or against Antony's direct involvement is inconclusive, but his motivation for wanting to rid himself of a dangerous rival is plain. Octavian had threatened his career more than once in the past, and might well do so again. Antony probably hoped that his former enemy would make such a hash of resettling the troops that he would lose all credibility.

The job Octavian had undertaken would have tested the labour of a Hercules. The country was in turmoil. Hordes of discharged veterans clamoured for the eighteen cities that had been promised as their reward for victory to be handed over to them immediately. The civic leaders, just as naturally, protested that the whole of Italy should share their burden and that those giving up their land should get financial compensation. No compromise was possible between those alienated groups of landholders and the marauding ex-soldiers. An initial phase of clubbings and broken heads developed into fights to the death in city streets and the surrounding fields and orchards.[7]

Famine ravaged the land. Not only did the soil remain untilled in many areas, with flocks and herds slaughtered for food, but around the coasts the ships of Sextus Pompey intercepted the grain fleets bound for Rome and sent raiding parties ashore to steal whatever else they could find. Evicted peasants and other small landowners made their way to the capital, often with large families in tow, to parade their undeserved destitution. Why, they demanded to know, were they being driven from their fields like cattle? The Roman crowds are said to have wept in pity for them,[8] but cash was harder to come by than ever, and they were hungry, too. Meanwhile, the senators were lobbying Octavian to be exempted from the land requisitions; and as he needed their acquiescence in the struggle to resettle his increasingly unruly soldiers he gave in to their pleas.

The Greek historian Appian, writing about these scenes of social agony and communal disintegration, commented that ordinary people now realized that the recent wars had not been waged and won for the sake of the Republic, but against themselves and for a change in the form of government. The ultimate reason for founding so many colonies of former soldiers, they now suspected, was not just to reward the soldiers for faithful past services, but to have a readily available supply of trained troops for whatever future purpose or emergency their rulers might need them.[9] That would certainly be the result for Octavian. For Rome, it marked the virtual extinction of democracy, however limited that democracy may have been.

The energetic young man toured the country trying to defuse the worst of the troubles. He knew that his speeches to hammer home the necessity of his policy would fail to satisfy the threatened land-holders, but he hoped that many might be persuaded to give up the struggle rather than be killed out of hand by soldiers determined to claim their promised reward. In fact, in many places, the soldiers were seizing more than they had been allocated, choosing the best lands and ignoring any protests, even those of Octavian. They were contemptuous of their new rulers, Appian writes, because they knew that those rulers needed them to confirm their own power at the top; equally, the men also knew they had to maintain those same rulers in power in order to guarantee that their possession of the land they were seizing from others would be permanent.[10]

In the midst of all this uproar, Antony's brother, Lucius, tried to profit by playing one side off against the other. As consul, he harangued those former legionaries who had fought under his brother's direct command, suggesting they would not be fairly treated unless Antony himself had a role in apportioning the land. Octavian knew that any serious delay in the resettlement process could only lead to more and greater violence. With the seas so unsafe for his messengers, it might take months to get a letter by a land route to Antony, wherever he might be, and receive a reply back. He defused the potentially explosive situation by agreeing, unexpectedly, to appoint Antony's own supporters as leaders of some of the colonies.[11]

Octavian had already experienced the veterans' propensity for barely controllable violence when they thought they were being mistreated. When a soldier sat in one of the rows in the theatre reserved for knights, Octavian ordered him to be removed, but a rumour spread that he had been executed. Octavian found himself suddenly surrounded by a mob of his vengeful comrades. Suetonius reports that he was saved from being killed only by the man's fortunate reappearance.[12] On another occasion, when Octavian was late for a meeting of veterans, some of them killed a centurion who had taken his general's part in the preliminary discussion, and threw the body in the Tiber. Despite being warned by friends not to go among them, Octavian took the risk. Turning away from the centurion's body, which had by then been fished out of the river, he proceeded with the division of the land, while reprimanding them for the killing. His coolness won their applause.[13]

It was against such a background that Lucius offered to champion the cause of the dispossessed farmers and small property owners. He claimed his constitutional right as consul to recruit troops without needing anyone else's permission. Promised the leadership of a serving consul, the scattered forces of resistance that were already engaged in the fight united to flock to his banner. Many of Octavian's remaining opponents among the *optimates* rushed to join them. The young triumvir suddenly found himself opposed by a new coalition of Antonians, *optimates* and desperate revolutionaries with nothing to lose.

Fulvia initially opposed Lucius's bewildering change of course from supporting the veterans to backing their opponents. She changed her mind, according to Appian, because Manius persuaded her that Antony – supposedly, at that time, sharing Cleopatra's bed in Alexandria – would not return to Italy if the country were to become peaceful again.[14] That may be no more than a reflection of the common prejudice of that era that women, in so far as they took political action at all, did so only for emotional reasons, in this case, jealousy. It is just possible that Antony had arrived in Egypt by that date, but unlikely that accurate news of his relationship with the queen would yet have reached Rome.

Antony spent most of the year 41 trying to settle problems that had arisen in the more important regions of the eastern half of the empire during the ruthless tenure of Cassius and Brutus. Chroniclers of the time made much of his (probably deserved) reputation for womanizing and drunkenness, as well as his taste for the exotic – allowing himself, for instance, to be worshipped as Dionysos (Bacchus) when he made a triumphal entry into the great Asian city of Ephesus.[15] But he did not neglect the serious part of his mission. He made an outrageous demand for ten years' tax revenues from the Asians, responding to their pleas for mercy by conceding that they need pay only the equivalent of nine years' taxation, and spread out their contributions over two years instead of one.

By contrast, those who had resisted the assassins were compensated. He ordered the liberation of the citizens of

Tarsus, who had been sold into slavery in order to meet Cassius's tax demands, and also helped Laodicea, Xanthus, Lycia and the island of Rhodes.[16] It was at Tarsus that he met Cleopatra, whom he had summoned from Egypt, not as a lover, but as a ruler whose actions during the civil war had seemed ambivalent. She evidently managed to convince him that the four legions which defected to Cassius in Palestine had been sent by her to help Dolabella, not Caesar's assassins. Her own spectacular arrival at Tarsus, being rowed up the River Cydnus arrayed as Venus and fanned by little boys dressed as cupids – to the sound of flutes and pipes, in a barge with purple sails, golden trappings and silvery oars – did her case no harm at all.[17]

But Cleopatra, having succeeded in clearing herself of suspicion, returned alone to Egypt. It was months later that Antony, clearly not yet her lover, followed – and his primary intention must surely have been to raise more money. His wife, out of touch in Rome, could scarcely yet have had evidence of his supposed infidelity. If Fulvia had a personal motive for joining forces with Lucius against Octavian it was much more likely to have been based on their sudden family rift. At some stage after his return from Philippi, Octavian divorced her daughter, Claudia. The marriage had never been consummated. He sent the girl back to her mother, *virgo intacta*. It was a slap in the face for both her and Fulvia, and a public demonstration of his rekindled hostility towards Antony.[18]

Officers among the Caesareans moved quickly to try to keep the peace. A tentative initial agreement between Octavian and Lucius lapsed because most of its provisions were not being observed. One provision that was honoured, however, was for Asinius Pollio, who was still in northern Italy as Antony's legate, to stop hindering the march to Spain by six of Octavian's legions under Salvidienus Rufus. Another legate, Ventidius, in command of more of Antony's legions, was also showing signs of cooperating with Lucius, as consul, rather than obeying Octavian, as triumvir. With the former republican fleets under Sextus Pompey and Domitius Ahenobarbus still raiding the coasts of Italy from east, west and south, it was plain that if all the opposing forces in the region were to attack Octavian simultaneously, he would be hopelessly outnumbered.

The young man had concentrated so exclusively on the task of resettlement that he had failed to maintain an adequate power base. He ought to have ensured that he had enough legions to protect himself and his inner group of supporters, both from his old enemies and the new ones he had been making daily, often by the thousand. His most elementary mistake was to have continued to insist on Salvidienus taking six legions to Spain even after Lucius had shown his hand. Perhaps pride over acquiring such a huge territory in the West had clouded his judgment. He sent messengers post-haste to order the six legions back, but it might already be too late. What Pollio had done once he could do again, by blocking Salvidienus as he attempted to return to Italy along the narrow coastal strip from Gaul.

For the moment, apart from his substantial bodyguard, Octavian had only four available legions of his own troops at Capua. He despatched one of them to Brundisium, ostensibly to defend the south-eastern port against the continuing attacks by the fleet of Ahenobarbus, but more probably to delay a potential invasion by Antony, which he must have suspected and dreaded. To match the threat of Lucius and Fulvia, he too started a recruiting drive throughout Italy, calling back to the colours some of the men he had resettled with so much difficulty. To pay them, he 'borrowed' money from the sacred stores of various temples.[19] Fulvia personally raised two legions from among her husband's veterans and placed them under the command of Plancus. She herself took refuge in Praeneste (Palestrina), east of Rome, along with numerous senators and knights. Wearing a sword, she is said to have issued orders to the troops defending the town.[20]

None of the leaders on either side had troubled to ask the professional soldiers if they wanted to fight another civil war so soon after the apparent end of the last one. Most emphatically, they did not. Caesareans of all shades, whether partisans of Antony or Octavian, were united in their desire for a respite from the slaughter and a return to normal conditions where adequate food supplies would be assured. The result was an unprecedented demonstration of military muscle in the cause of peace. Thousands of veterans tramped up to the Capitol at Rome, ignoring the Senate, the magistrates and the civilians in the Forum below them. As if they were a properly constituted Assembly of the People, they ordered that the compact signed by Antony and Octavian be read out to them.[21]

It was this document, they evidently believed, that represented their best chance of preventing war. If both sides could be made to observe its provisions there would be no adequate *casus belli*. Octavian was present as the troops voted for its ratification, but it is not clear what part, if any, he had played in organizing or inspiring their stand. Undoubtedly he approved of their vote, as it was Lucius who was threatening to breach the compact while claiming the support of his absent brother. In a further vote, which, in the context of the republican system, can only have been regarded by the senatorial aristocrats as a breathtaking usurpation of their traditional rights, the soldiers' assembly constituted itself as the arbiter between the rival claims of Octavian and Lucius.[22]

In a show of assumed legality, they inscribed the result of their votes on tablets and delivered them for safekeeping to the Vestal Virgins. Then, in their self-appointed role as members of a tribunal, they told Octavian to present himself before them on a specified date, and sent an embassy to Lucius ordering him to come, too. The venue chosen for the tribunal hearing was Gabii, near Praeneste. Octavian arrived first. To make sure Lucius was not bringing too large an army with him, he sent some cavalry on a reconnaissance mission along the road to Praeneste. There was an apparently unplanned clash of arms in which several of the consul's escort were killed. Lucius, not surprisingly, declined to come any further. In his absence, the tribunal condemned him and Fulvia as being in the wrong, but their backing for Octavian is unlikely to have made them any more willing to fight against their former comrades. Civilian landholders, however, would be a perfectly acceptable target.

Was this whole business of a military assembly and tribunal no more than an elaborate charade? Was it, in other words, cunningly designed by Octavian to drum up support for himself and perhaps delay the start of hostilities until his six legions could get back safely (which they did) from their aborted march to Spain? Much may be suspected, but nothing proved. Lucius derided the affair as a 'parliament of boots', and continued his recruiting campaign. Octavian, basking in their approbation, left Lepidus to guard the capital with two legions while he himself marched north. That was a strategic as well as a tactical error. Lucius marched south by a different route with four legions and entered Rome. Lepidus fled to Octavian, leaving behind his two legions, which promptly defected to Lucius rather than defend the city.

The consul convened the Senate and an Assembly of the People, which, of course, would have included his own soldiers. He told them, to applause, that Antony intended to resign as a member of the Triumvirate and accept the consulship instead, thus exchanging an illegal appointment for a lawful magistracy. In the meantime, he (Lucius) would punish both Octavian and Lepidus for their illegal actions as triumvirs. It was an unequivocal call for restoration of the Republic, and he was acclaimed as *Imperator* by the People. With their cheers ringing in his ears, he marched north again, now with six legions, apparently intending to join his forces with those of the Antonian legates, Ventidius and Pollio.[23]

Once more, and for the very last time, the *optimates* scented victory. Yet again they would be disappointed. Sextus Pompey, in spite of commanding large forces and enjoying control of the sea, did not stir from his base in Sicily except for piracy, even though his camp held many optimate fugitives. Antony would not return to Italy until the following year. The cause of Lucius was further dampened by the arrival in Italy of his brother's quaestor, Marcus Philippus Barbatius, who affirmed that Antony disapproved of those who were taking up arms against Octavian to the detriment of the Triumvirate. Appian indicates that Barbatius was deliberately trying to deceive his hearers because he had fallen out with Antony; but, whatever the truth of that assertion, some of those who had been supporting Lucius, in the belief that he spoke for his brother, now switched sides to Octavian.[24]

On his way back north, Lucius found himself in danger of marching not to the safety of his supposed allies, Pollio and Ventidius, but straight into the arms of Salvidienus and his six returning legions. At the same time, he became aware that a fresh batch of Octavian's troops were treading hard on his heels under the dynamic command of the triumvir's childhood friend Agrippa, who was roughly the same age as his master but would prove himself to be greatly superior as a fighting general. Unwilling to risk a battle in which his largely untrained recruits might be surrounded, Lucius fatally turned aside and camped outside the walls of Perusia.

Knowing that Plancus, Pollio and Ventidius were only a few days' march away, Lucius evidently supposed he would not need to shelter behind the barely penetrable walls of the ancient Etruscan city, which was sited on an eminence among the Umbrian mountains, about a dozen miles from Lake Trasimene and barely two miles from the upper course of the Tiber. His assumption that the three Antonian generals would fight their way past the Octavian forces to rescue him proved woefully unfounded. By the time he realized his mistake, and moved his army inside Perusia, it was too late to gather supplies to withstand a long siege. Octavian himself now came up from Rome with more re-enlisted veterans to join Agrippa and Salvidienus, and to close the trap around the incompetently led consular army.[25]

Pollio and Ventidius did not like each other, and neither of them liked Plancus. Lacking an Antony to force or cajole them into mutual cooperation, they continued to operate their respective groups of legions virtually as separate armies. They had no agreed plan, and were not minded to take their instructions from a woman, however loudly she might denounce them to her husband later. Lucius might be the serving consul, but in terms of military capacity and experience he was very much their junior. They could only guess what Antony would want them to do in the circumstances, so they naturally erred on the side of caution. Twenty miles from Perusia, sufficiently close for Lucius in his eyrie to see their fire signals, they called a halt as Agrippa and Salvidienus lined up opposite their position in battle formation but did not sound the charge.

The stand-off turned into another victory for the politicized soldiers of both sides. Octavian did not apparently bother to watch their retreat, as the 'allies' of Lucius marched away without having cast a single spear. He was too busy building concentric lines of circumvallation and contravallation around Perusia in imitation of the technique of his adoptive father. Having run his quarry to earth he did not intend to let Lucius escape to fight another day; not needing to scale the city walls, he made sure Lucius could not break out past his inner ring of defensive works, nor a potential relieving force pierce his outer ring without an army of overwhelming size. Then he sat down to wait for hunger to do its work.[26]

Pollio, meanwhile, went into winter quarters at Ravenna, Ventidius at nearby Ariminum, and Plancus further south at Spoletium. Proximity to the coast would give them the chance, if necessary, to escape by ship. They now knew for certain that their men would not fight against Caesar's heir on behalf of landowners and *optimates*, who would undoubtedly oppose their resettlement in the future when the time came for their own discharge from the army. A further eleven Antonian legions remained idle in Gaul, most of them fairly close to the Alps, under the command of Fufius Calenus, who had stoutly defended Antony's interests in the Senate when his star had appeared to be waning. Calenus may have known better than the others what Antony's true thoughts were. It was he, evidently acting on Antony's instructions, who had refused to part with two of his legions to Octavian – to replace the ones loaned to his fellow-triumvir after Philippi – in spite of the fact that such a transfer was specified in the written compact.

Lucius tried to end the stalemate by attempting a breakout on New Year's Eve, but he was driven back inside Perusia in heavy fighting. By that time Octavian had constructed no fewer than 1,500 wooden watch-towers at intervals of about 20 yards all the way around the city. Nevertheless, Lucius tried again to get through, fighting a running battle at night around the entire circumference. That failure led him to ration the remaining stocks of food more tightly than before, and to deny any provisions at all to the slaves. He also denied them the chance to escape by taking servitude among the besieging soldiers, so they should not reveal how severe was the famine inside the walls. These unfortunates tried to survive on grass and leaves. When they died they were buried *en masse* in trenches instead of disposal by the usual Roman practice of cremation, in case Octavian should guess the truth from the smell of burning bodies.[27]

The defenders gave up at the end of February, after envoys sent by Lucius were told by Octavian that he would grant a full amnesty to Antony's soldiers, but that the rest must surrender at discretion. That decision was popular with the triumvir's own troops, who embraced the starving men as they emerged to freedom. Lucius also walked free, but a number of senators and knights among his followers were put to death. Octavian ordered the execution of all members of the city council of Perusia – as a warning to others – except for one man who, as a juror in Rome, had voted for the condemnation of Caesar's assassins. The lives of the ordinary inhabitants were spared, but their city was given up to pillage by the troops, an event which was drastically curtailed after one of the residents, said to have been mentally deranged, set fire to his house with himself inside and burnt down all the other buildings.[28]

Long after the siege ended, a story went the rounds that Octavian had behaved with barbaric cruelty. Both Suetonius and Dio report as rumour that 300 knights and senators were held prisoner until the Ides of March a fortnight later so that they could be sacrificed as offerings at an altar dedicated to the divine Julius Caesar. Appian, whose account of the Perusian War is the most detailed to have survived, makes no mention of this alleged incident , although he devotes space to the treatment of various other people who surrendered. Few historians today give much credence to this tale of human sacrifice. Suetonius invites scepticism by reporting a further rumour, even less believable, that Octavian's real motive in waging war was to give any secret senatorial and knightly opponents the chance to join Lucius and thereby unmask themselves, so that he could seize their estates to pay his troops.[29]

The defeat of Lucius led to the collapse of organized resistance to the land resettlement scheme. Italian cities that had supported the former consul now declared for Octavian. Fulvia fled with her children to Brundisium, where she met a fellow fugitive in Plancus, now bereft of the two legions she had raised. They sailed together to Athens. Calenus died of natural causes and his eleven legions were taken over by Octavian. Ventidius drifted north to hold Venetia for a while, apparently with his army still intact. Pollio, in what should have been his consular year, took refuge with Ahenobarbus, and persuaded the republican admiral to throw in his lot with Antony.[30]

But the Republic itself finally and for ever perished in the flames of Perusia. Octavian decided to convert the honorary and hitherto temporary title of *Imperator* into his own first name, so that he would be known as *Imperator Caesar Divi Filius* – 'Emperor Caesar Son of a God'. Nearly half a millennium had passed since Rome expelled King Tarquin and rejected monarchy as a form of government. Never again would the *Senatus Populusque Romanus* rule its citizens and its many subject peoples except in the sanitized form to be devised later by the 22-year-old author of its downfall, who now returned to his capital as *de facto* ruler of half the empire. It had taken him four years since quitting his studies at Apollonia.

TWELVE

THE NEW MASTER OF THE WEST

Antony woke up from his dream of love with Cleopatra to discover that his other dreams, of future glory and domination, were in danger of evaporating like a Nile mist. While he had idled away the winter at the court of the Ptolemies, the Parthians had launched a major invasion of Syria, and his young rival had outmanoeuvred all his generals back home in Italy. He left Egypt and Cleopatra (pregnant with his twins) at about the time Perusia fell. Hurrying north with the firm intention of countering the Parthian threat, he turned west as details of the disaster in Italy reached him by successive messengers – as if he were the doomed protagonist of a classic Greek tragedy, in which the main action occurs off-stage. By the time he met Fulvia at Athens he knew the worst: the bungled intervention of his brother and his wife might well cost him the supremacy he had fought for.

His rage was horrible. Fulvia was already ill. She died not long after enduring his bitter reproaches; but the full depth of her despair may not have been reached until the day Antony left Greece without her, when he refused to go to see her, even to say goodbye, before resuming his voyage. Now it was his turn, like Octavian before him, to sail towards Italy's eastern coast, not knowing whether the regime in Rome would accept him or attack him. He could have been in no doubt as to Octavian's underlying hostility. Sextus Pompey had already sent envoys to him at Athens offering to help him recapture Italy. Antony's mother, Julia, came with the envoys. There had been no overt threat against her by Octavian personally, but the fact that she had felt obliged to flee from the mainland to Sextus for protection told its own story.[1]

Antony was paying the price for leaving to the discretion of others what he should have overseen himself. He was well aware before he arrived in Egypt, to renew his acquaintance with Cleopatra, that Lucius and Fulvia were making it as difficult as possible for Octavian to carry out the tasks which he himself, as the senior triumvir in terms of *auctoritas*, had approved and authorized. Octavian despatched two high-level emissaries during the summer of 41 to protest to Antony about what was being done, apparently in his name, and urging him to put a stop to it. That was scarcely an unreasonable request. One of the diplomats returned to Rome, evidently empty handed; the other, Lucius Cocceius Nerva, stayed on in Antony's entourage and accompanied him to Alexandria.[2]

It appears that both triumvirs trusted Nerva as a diplomat of the utmost discretion, but he is likely to have become Octavian's most reliable informant on Antony's policies and state of mind, although not a man to stoop to gossip about his notorious private life with the queen. Plainly, Antony ought to have told his brother, his wife and his agent, in blunt terms, not to block the resettlement programme and to show restraint. Had he done so they would surely not have gone on to provoke a civil war against his express wishes and claim it was what he wanted. That appears to suggest that even if he did not egg them on he did nothing to lead them to believe he would seriously disapprove of their blatant alliance with the *optimates*, which would inevitably lead to acts of extremism on both sides of the land dispute.

Antony may have thought he had a perfect excuse for inaction – that he was too far away from Italy to be expected to intervene effectively in what was basically a problem for Octavian and Lepidus, whose dictatorial powers as triumvirs, based ultimately on their control of a large army, should enable them to carry through any measures they chose. It is clear that he did not try to coordinate the actions of his specifically military subordinates with those of Lucius and Fulvia, or surely generals of the calibre of Ventidius and Pollio would have intervened before they got themselves into the untenable position from which it proved impracticable, although not actually impossible, to extricate them later.

By declining to accept responsibility for what was being done in his name, at a time when clear instructions from him to all his chief supporters should have been enough to hold the Caesarian party together, Antony lost all along the line when Lucius and Fulvia split it apart. They taught the soldiers to associate the name of Antony with betrayal of the resettlement scheme, just as Octavian had taught them that his senior colleague could not be trusted to punish Caesar's assassins. That lesson would be reinforced when Antony failed to provide the monetary gratuities he had promised. By contrast, Octavian had shown single-minded determination to fulfil his obligation to resettle the troops and pay them as much as he could, even though some of it had to come from his personal resources, as well as from taxes and loans. However much those ex-legionaries might admire Antony as a conquering general, few of them, from now on, would be prepared to fight for him against Caesar's heir, even if they lived in one of the nominally Antonian colonies of veterans.

Antony was not yet ready to accept that uncomfortable truth when he eventually arrived in Italian waters in the summer of 40 with a fleet of 200 ships he had constructed in Asia to ferry the advance guard of his army back home. His first apparent success was a rendezvous at sea, on the crossing from Corcyra, with the swashbuckling republican admiral Domitius Ahenobarbus, formerly his deadly enemy, whose final abandonment of the lost cause of Brutus and Cassius had been negotiated by Pollio after the fall of Perusia. The sudden appearance of their merged fleets off Brundisium caused the five Octavian cohorts guarding the city to deploy in haste to deny them access to the harbour. Whether or not they might have allowed Antony himself to drop anchor there, they could have no truck with Ahenobarbus, a public enemy with a price on his head, who had been attacking the port and the surrounding region for the past two years, cutting off food supplies and destroying or stealing the crops.

When Antony came ashore with cavalry further along the coast, the garrison shut the city gates on him to prevent his entry from the landward side.[3] That convinced him that they must be acting under Octavian's specific orders, or they would not have dared to risk offending a man who, at least in theory, enjoyed the same dictatorial powers as his rival – and had already shown his readiness to decimate recalcitrant troops. Believing that this was the opening encounter of a new civil war, sought by Octavian in revenge for the Perusian conflict, Antony landed the rest of his advance guard, sent for reinforcements from Macedonia and settled down to besiege Brundisium. He would need the port to disembark his legions quickly and safely; and now that he had command of the sea, through Sextus and Ahenobarbus, he evidently reckoned that his best course would be to secure a bridgehead from which he could launch a mass invasion.

Sextus promptly sent ships to harry the southern and eastern coastline from his secure base in Sicily, and landed soldiers to attack Thurii, the town asociated with Octavian's natural father, Gaius Octavius. Menodorus, a former slave promoted by Sextus to the command of four legions, simultaneously invaded the large and strategically important island of Sardinia, off the west coast of Italy, and defeated the outnumbered forces stationed there. Octavian, unaware for some days of Antony's arrival, sent Agrippa from Rome towards Brundisium with an army, which the general augmented *en route* by recalling to the colours some of the recently discharged veterans. At first, these men thought they were going to fight Sextus; when they realized their main target was to be Antony, some of them turned back home.[4]

In alarm, Octavian himself marched after Agrippa at the

head of other veterans, who apparently made it clear to him that their priority would be to secure a permanent and lasting reconciliation between the two warring triumvirs. By the time he arrived in the vicinity of the besieged city it was already cut off from rescue by a line of heavily manned fortifications and trenches, which Antony had swiftly constructed across the neck of the small peninsula on which it stood. A series of inconclusive skirmishes followed; Agrippa relieved Thurii and took a grip on the countryside; Antony, in a characteristically daring mission, led out 400 men and their horses surreptitiously by night and routed 1,500 opposing cavalry before they had a chance to wake up properly. Soldiers from both camps, however, fraternized with each other to such an extent that the leaders on both sides became increasingly reluctant to contemplate a large-scale battle.[5]

Antony came to realize, too late, that he had left himself no serious alternative, short of abject flight, but to stay behind his fortifications. Unless and until he could capture Brundisium and take control of its harbour, he was trapped between the city walls and Octavian's army, which was growing daily as more and more recalled veterans arrived from all over Italy. His own reinforcements from Macedonia would scarcely be able to relieve him without risking a contested landing elsewhere along the hostile coast, now evidently monitored from dawn to dusk by Agrippa's patrols. He could not begin to re-embark his army without provoking the battle he sought to avoid and could not now win. He himself might easily escape with an escort in small boats to row out to rejoin Ahenobarbus and the fleet, but much of his heavily outnumbered vanguard would have to stay behind in a hopeless cause.

News of Fulvia's death, at Sicyon, while on her way home through the Gulf of Corinth, increased Antony's depression but acted as a catalyst for peace talks to open.[6] He may have been feeling guilty, knowing that however much she had displeased him, Fulvia had acted in what she had supposed to be his real interests. He had now shown himself to be just as short-sighted as Lucius had been in becoming bottled up at Perusia. If Antony or his generals had come to Lucius's rescue the previous autumn, that struggle would have turned out very differently. As he mourned his wife's death, he had every reason to reproach himself for having abandoned them to their fate. Then, the odds would have been overwhelmingly in his favour, with the armies he had placed in Gaul and northern Italy at hand to enforce a negotiated settlement of the Perusia crisis on terms that could have left him without any credible rival.

Now, in the consequent crisis of Brundisium in the summer of 39, Antony would be the one forced to make concessions. It was at this point that his friend Nerva came into his own as a diplomat. After a private discussion with Antony, he visited Octavian, who stoutly denied having ordered his fellow-triumvir to be barred from landing in Italy. That decision, he claimed, had been taken by the Brundisium garrison without his knowledge. The young man affected to be too proud to write directly to Antony to set out his case by way of explanation, but under Nerva's tactful promptings he agreed to write instead to Antony's mother, Julia, who had accompanied her son from Greece after her temporary stay in Sicily. He told her he could not understand why she had taken it into her head to go to Sextus, when it would have been a point of honour for him (Octavian) to treat her with kindness and respect. That was probably true. And the letter addressed to Julia instead of to Antony demonstrated there was little Nerva could now teach him about diplomacy.[7]

As Nerva left Octavian's camp, some of the senior officers – undoubtedly expressing the new attitude of the bulk of the old Caesarean party – assured him that they would fight if Antony refused the hand of friendship. He did not tell them that the time for fighting on that particular field was already past. Neither their well-intended warning nor the pleading of his mother would be needed to make Antony seek the best terms he could get. To show good faith, he sent away both Sextus and Ahenobarbus, the latter elevated to the governorship of Bithynia. According to Appian, it was Octavian's soldiers who now organized the peace process, to suit their own agenda, arranging a meeting where Pollio would speak for Antony, Maecenas for Octavian, and with Nerva present as a friend of both the principals.[8]

The outcome was the Pact of Brundisium, signed in September or early October of 40, and sealed with the betrothal of Antony to his colleague's recently widowed sister, Octavia. Ironically, her husband, Marcellus, had been the consul of the year 50, whose presentation of a sword to Pompey had triggered the outbreak of civil war with Julius Caesar. His widow now took on the opposite role, of peacemaker, to nip a new civil war in the bud. Octavian and Antony embraced each other in front of their assembled armies to tumultuous cheers from soldiers who continued to look forward, perhaps with more optimism than conviction, to the prospect of an end to the cycle of bloodshed.[9]

The pact was a birthday present for Octavian, now aged twenty-three, but represented a bitter draught for Antony to swallow. The victor of Philippi was forced to give up any specific territorial claim in the western half of the empire. Rule over the whole of Gaul, which he had insisted on two years earlier as part of his spoils after the defeat of Brutus and Cassius, now passed officially to the man who had fled that battlefield and spent hours hiding in a marsh. As a sop, Antony was to have the same right as his colleague to recruit in Italy, but in practice he was never able to exercise it without hindrance, and eventually gave up trying. The boundary of their respective spheres was to be the frontier between the provinces of Illyricum and Macedonia, on the far side of the Adriatic, in what is today Albania. Everywhere east of that frontier was confirmed as Antony's; everywhere to the west became Octavian's. Lepidus was to get Africa, with six of the legions that would otherwise have been claimed by Antony.[10]

Could Antony, as some commentators imagine, have afforded to reject those terms? They gave him nothing he did not already have. And they deprived him of a vast province, formerly packed with his legions, leaving him in the end without any serious prospect of controlling events in Rome so long as Octavian remained in power there. Unless we are prepared to believe that Antony suffered a sudden brainstorm, the answer must surely be that the alternative of rejecting the terms was significantly less attractive than signing up to them. Half an empire was better than none. We can rely on Octavian's making that clear to him, although not, perhaps, in so many words. The young man might be a hopeless tactician on the field of battle – quivering with nerves, perhaps, and much too ready to cut and run – but his strategic grasp was sound and his statesmanship would become proverbial.

Control of Gaul would not have been negotiable. So long as Antony continued to hold such a strategically vital province within Octavian's power bloc, destabilizing conflicts like the Perusian War would be bound to arise. If, however, each controlled a bloc of roughly the same size, clearly separated by an unambiguous dividing line, it would be in neither man's interest to fight yet another bloody civil war while so much still needed to be done to recover from the conflicts of the recent past. The Triumvirate as a form of government had proved itself to be unworkable once its members' original aim, the defeat of Brutus and Cassius as leaders of a resurgent oligarchy, had been achieved. Rather than the three of them – or, in actual practice, the two of them – trying to rule one area in concert, it would be preferable to minimize inevitable conflicts of interest by each of them ruling one clearly defined area for long enough for genuine stability to be restored to the people. By retaining the nominally triumviral leadership of the empire as a whole, cemented by the proposed marriage between Antony and Octavia, they would be better able to guard against the possibility of a permanent split into two rival empires.

The wobbly Triumvirate was thus re-established on an intermediate-term basis of mutual interest in preserving peace between the eastern and western halves, while securing the long-term integrity of the whole by a dynastic alliance. Whoever deserves the credit for the remarkable and unprecedented Pact of Brundisium, and whatever the relative contributions of Nerva, Pollio and Maecenas may have been, its ultimate failure ought not to disguise the fact that for most of the next decade Antony did rule the eastern half, and Octavian the western half, of the Roman Empire without straying so far into each other's sphere of influence as to provoke outright war – although personality clashes were perhaps inevitable.

For the present, Octavian could congratulate himself on the series of unlooked-for events since Philippi that, thanks to his firm and intelligent responses, had elevated him to supremacy in the original heartlands of Rome and mainland Italy, plus the entire Western Empire from the Adriatic to the Atlantic. Antony would continue to appoint many of the magistrates in the capital, including a series of consuls,[11] but consular power was now subordinate to triumviral *imperium*, and he would no longer have a major role in the Caesarean party. Thanks to his older rival's impatience, Octavian had found himself enjoying a military advantage over Antony at Brundisium that he could not have predicted. Could he have used that advantage to destroy him? Possibly. Would that have served his purposes so well in the longer term? Possibly not.

Even in the short term, Octavian received a boost to his reputation among honest and war-weary citizens, who saw that he and Antony had drawn back from the brink of a potential bloodbath rather than press their respective claims of personal ambition beyond the limit of public tolerance. Antony's assent to the young man's effective takeover in the West would dishearten the regime's leading senatorial opponents, who had looked to Antony as their only credible champion, now that the optimate cause had gone down to ignominious defeat at Perusia. The *rapprochement* between the two leading triumvirs raised ordinary people's hopes that the new form of government, while stifling the competitive electoral process, might actually offer a better chance of peaceful co-existence among squabbling aristocrats than the old republican system had been able to impose.

The Roman world rejoiced at the compact and the marriage. Astrologers and other seers, who for years had been claiming that one great era of history was ending and another about to begin, seized on the nuptials of Antony and Octavia as the heaven-blessed union that marked the precise moment of transition. The poet Virgil, whose family had recently been evicted from their land to make way for returning veterans, helped to restore his fortunes by writing his *'Fourth Eclogue'* (one of a set of ten) to hail the birth of a wondrous child from this marriage of the millennium – a son who would supposedly usher in a period of universal peace and goodwill.[12] Octavia, however, brought forth not a boy saviour but a girl, Antonia, who was to become the grandmother of the future Emperor Nero.

There has never been universal agreement that the wedding of Antony and Octavia was necessarily the union to which Virgil refers in his poem. The names of other candidates as bride and groom have entered the frame for solving what was once the most contentious of all literary conundrums, eclipsing even the later quarrels over the identity of Shakespeare's Dark Lady of the Sonnets. Throughout the Middle Ages, and well into modern times, the favoured duo were the Holy Ghost and the Virgin Mary. Many later scholars plumped for Octavian himself as the epochal bridegroom and father, but that contention flies in the face of certain facts that were obvious to his contemporaries but became obscured later.

Octavian had, indeed, recently remarried. His bride was a woman at least ten years older than he – Scribonia, sister of

Lucius Scribonius Libo, who was himself aged about fifty.[13] Theirs had been a wedding of such blatant cynicism that even Virgil, as court poet, could scarcely have risen to the occasion without attracting the sort of ribaldry that would have rendered the exercise counter-productive. The young triumvir, fearing the return of a vengeful Antony at the head of a coalition of all the forces of the East, had hastily commissioned Maecenas to propose to Scribonia for him, for no better reason than that her brother, Libo, was the father-in-law of Sextus Pompey. Octavian was to be her third husband. As we have seen, this marriage of military convenience failed to stop Sextus from allying himself with Antony against him almost immediately afterwards.

Octavian obtained a divorce on the very day their first and only child, Julia, was born. He had put up with Scribonia's 'awkward disposition' (morum perversitatem) – the description is quoted by Suetonius direct from Octavian's lost memoirs – just long enough to ensure the baby's legitimacy.[14] Nevertheless, as his second wife, she was the the first with whom he had sexual relations. As for their daughter, baby Julia grew up to become a byword for marital infidelity.[15] Virgil would surely have turned in his grave had he known that people supposed his eclogue to have been about her. But we must suppose there would have been laughter in heaven at the pious supposition that he had predicted the incarnation of Jesus of Nazareth – who was born about fifteen years after the great poet died.

Although the Pact of Brundisium provided for the reinstatement of Antony's new ally Ahenobarbus, no such relief was to be made available to Sextus Pompey, who remained officially a public enemy. Having failed to conciliate him via the matrimonial connection with Scribonia's brother, Libo (whom Sextus had pointedly sent to negotiate his brief Antonian alliance) Octavian decided that the better option would be to crush him. There were two short-term objections to this policy change: Octavian had not yet built enough suitable ships for an invasion of Sicily, and Sextus was using his command of the sea to block food supplies to Italy. The famine had intensified by the time the triumvirs returned to Rome, because Sextus had been able to take over and garrison both Sardinia and Corsica while they were preoccupied at Brundisium.

The celebration of Octavia's marriage to Antony took place against a background of bread riots and soaring prices. The Senate conferred its blessing on the couple in the form of a resolution dispensing the bride from the usual minimum period for widowhood of ten months[16] – a restriction which did not apply to widowers, for physiological reasons. Antony was nearly twice Octavia's age, but the marriage seems to have been a happy one at first. She had a warm, sunny nature combined with an unflagging commitment to her role as a traditional Roman matron, who put her husband first in all things. She had two daughters by him in the few years they spent together, before the emotional tug of Cleopatra would draw him back to Egypt.

Antony seems to have done his best to swallow his disappointment and try to make friends at last with Octavian. At some stage he warned him that his old friend Salvidienus, who had accompanied him on that first voyage from Apollonia, had sought to betray him. Salvidienus, whom Octavian had promoted above all his other early associates, had apparently offered to defect to Antony at Brundisium with the eleven Gallic legions previously commanded by Calenus. It cannot have been in Antony's interest to inform on him; it may be that he thought such a revelation would convince his wary young colleague of his own genuine good faith.

The unfortunate Salvidienus was recalled to Rome. where the Senate recommended his condemnation to death,[17] the first of many to share that fate over the centuries to follow, when absolute monarchy became the norm. Such extreme punishment of a man who had been a close friend was to be unusual, however, during the course of Octavian's long career. Suetonius affirms that he could think of only one other case of its kind. He writes of Octavian, 'He was slow to make friends, but when he did so he showed the greatest constancy, rewarding their virtues and merits, and even condoning their faults – so long as they were only slight.'[18]

Antony, too, believed he had a score to settle on his return to Rome. He summoned his agent, Manius, who had supported Fulvia and Lucius in their claim that he, as triumvir, backed their armed resistance to the resettlement programme. We do not know what was said at the interview, but it ended with the agent's execution. Out in the streets, Antony had to fend off questions from some of his former soldiers, who demanded to know what had happened to the money he had promised them from his expedition to the East. On one occasion, Octavian had to intervene in order to restrain a crowd of them who had surrounded him, to prevent his coming to harm.[19]

It was perhaps at about this time, when poorer people were dying of starvation, that Octavian attended a party dressed as Apollo, the god of music, and was allegedly seen 'feasting amid new adulteries of the gods'. Presumably the other guests were were in similar fancy dress, because the occasion is reported by Suetonius as 'the dinner of the six gods and goddesses'. The day after the party there was a popular commotion, as the bitter jest passed from mouth to mouth that these so-called divinities had eaten all the available grain at their feast. Octavian was reviled as 'Apollo the Tormentor'.[20] They also criticized him for lavishing money on expensive ornaments and furnishings, and for his well-attested love of gambling,[21] albeit for quite modest stakes by the standards of the old aristocracy. It was the fun of gambling that excited him, rather than the hope of gain; in later life he often provided his friends with their stake money before they rolled the dice.

Antony, in his turn, saved Octavian from serious injury, and possibly even from death, when a crowd stoned him in the Forum during a bread riot, and he was so shocked or concussed that he simply stood still, bleeding from wounds, until his older colleague hurried him away. At that stage Antony had regained some of his popularity with the hungry masses, because it was well known that he was in favour of making a deal with Sextus, in recognition of the help he had given him only that year. But later he, too, was stoned along with Octavian. His response was to call out the soldiers and oversee what turned into a minor massacre. The dead were stripped and their bodies thrown in the Tiber.[22]

Antony advised Octavian that if he was going to make war on Sextus, he had better do so quickly. The people had already torn down the official notices of an edict proclaiming new taxes to fund the conflict: now they were threatening arson.[23] Octavian was in a quandary. Sextus had spurned his earlier effort at reconciliation, and he knew that the warlord would be right to see a further attempt on his part as a sign of weakness. He also knew there could never be peace for the trading ships in the Mediterranean so long as Sextus was at liberty; it was probably only the extreme urgency of the need to complete the resettlement scheme that had stopped Octavian making funds available earlier for building a fleet to launch against him. It was against his better judgment, therefore, that Octavian now gave way to the pressure from both the people and Antony to seek terms that would end the famine.

The meeting with Sextus proved to be one of the strangest peace conferences in recorded history.[24] Octavian and Antony were watching from the shore at the holiday resort of Baiae, towards the northern extremity of the Bay of Naples, when his flagship swept towards them, and then past them with piratical dash, to keep the rendezvous. His own personal safety was clearly uppermost in his mind; Sextus trusted nobody, especially not another Roman aristocrat. He himself had just murdered his own most senior admiral, Staius Murcus, but tried (and failed) to disguise the deed by pretending that Murcus's slaves were the culprits – and having them all crucified as proof.[25]

Under his surveillance, tree trunks were now driven into the seabed a little way off the shore at nearby Puteoli, to serve as piles to support two wooden platforms. These were close enough together for the participants not to have to shout, but separated by a space of water evidently too wide for a man to leap across. Octavian and Antony shared the platform nearest the shore, within easy range of their troops, lined up on the beach. Sextus and Libo (still, for the time being, Octavian's brother-in-law) sat on the seaward platform, not too many yards from his waiting flagship, ready to board it and vanish over the horizon at short notice.

The first session was inconclusive. Sextus wanted to join the Triumvirate as a fourth member, or possibly to replace Lepidus as the third. Octavian refused. He knew that Sextus was dangerously temperamental and had few scruples. Furthermore, Sextus hated him as the crusading heir of the man who had destroyed his father, killed his brother and disinherited their family. There could be no possibility, for Octavian, of sharing rule with him. The two sides adjourned to consult their advisers, who, in the case of Sextus, included his mother, Mucia, and wife, Julia, who had come along for the cruise. Both ladies must have been anxious to rejoin Roman society and renew acquaintance with all their former friends. They pressed him strongly to make peace.

When the conference resumed, Sextus was willing to accept what amounted to a form of Danegeld, massive bribes in return for ending the blockade and promising to stop molesting other people's ships or sheltering runaway slaves. He was confirmed in possession, for five years, of any island he already held, which included Sicily, Sardinia and Corsica, and was to be given control (by Antony) of the Peloponnese, in southern Greece, for the same period. His soldiers would be entitled to the same generous discharge terms as those of the triumvirs, so long as they were free men; slaves who had become soldiers would be freed. He would get monetary compensation for his father's former estates, and would become eligible for the consulship himself and also be permitted to choose a future consul. Sextus had to promise to remove any of his troops still on the mainland, and to resume the corn tribute from the islands to the capital.[26]

Far more important for the future of Rome was the agreement that all the exiles who had taken refuge with Sextus should not only be allowed to return to the mainland but receive compensation. The announcement of that concession by the four men on the platforms caused pandemonium among troops on both sides. Their cheering was so loud, according to Dio, that the very mountains – dominated at that spot by the slumbering peak of Vesuvius – resounded with the noise. Many of those in the boats jumped into the sea, while others on shore rushed into the waves to join them. Men who had been parted by civil war from relatives and friends now embraced each other swimming, while the crush of people celebrating on the beach became so uncontrollable that some are said to have been trampled to death.[27]

The only exceptions among those permitted to return were the few remaining assassins of Julius Caesar still alive. Those who had been proscribed would get back only one-quarter of the value of their confiscated estates, but the remainder were promised full restitution. Men bearing some of the most ancient and distinguished names in Roman society would thus soon return to their native city. Schooled by exile, they would, for the most part, show themselves prepared to resist further temptation to oppose the new Caesarean dispensation, even if they might decline initially to support it. Some would join Octavian in the task of rebuilding the shattered state. Others would offer their services to Antony and go east with him. It was, indeed, the closing of an era; but not yet the firm establishment of a new one.

The peacemakers decided to celebrate their success with a series of banquets, and they drew lots to decide who should be the first host. The honour fell to Sextus, who invited the triumvirs to dine on his flagship. Wine was flowing freely, and Antony was being ribbed by the others about his affair with Cleopatra, when Menodorus, the captor of Sardinia, whispered in his master's ear: if Sextus would just say the word, Menodorus indicated, he would cut the cables to let the ship sail away; once they were a safe distance from land, they could kill Octavian and Antony with impunity. Sextus took some minutes to consider this suggestion. Then he told Menodorus he should have acted on his own initiative, and cut the cables without telling him, thereby avoiding his having to break a solemn oath. As it was, he (Sextus) could not now order such an action, without forfeiting his honour.[28]

That story has been told and retold with relish for more than two millennia, as one of the great 'What if?' moments of history, but it begs the question of what Sextus could have hoped to gain from murdering Octavian and Antony in those circumstances. Lacking credible allies, he was in no position to profit by taking over the state against the opposed might of the predominantly Caesarean army. All he could have looked forward to was a few more months of life until an avenging armada swept him off the islands he still clung to. He would lose all the financial advantages he had gained in the negotiations, as well as his chance of participating in the new ruling dynasty through his daughter.

As was now becoming quite routine in such diplomatic encounters, a marriage was projected to bind the signatories of the Peace of Puteoli more closely together. Sextus's three-year-old daughter Pompeia, who was also the granddaughter of Octavian's temporary brother-in-law, Libo, now became betrothed to Marcellus, son of Octavia by the late consul of that name, and therefore Antony's stepson as well as Octavian's nephew. Whatever the truth of the tale of Menodorus's whisper, Antony and Octavian survived the hospitality of Sextus with nothing more damaging than a hangover. The two erstwhile cut-throats sailed off to Sicily without their potential victims, who returned to Rome to receive the gratitude of the populace for ending the famine.

There was one further consequence of that bizarre peace conference. Octavian, for the first and only time in his life, fell in love – so extravagantly that he seems to have been prepared to do anything, however outrageous, to get his hands on the young woman concerned. Her name was Livia Drusilla. She was already married, with a two-year-old son and pregnant with a second child. Her husband, now no longer a proscribed exile, bore three names that from now on would echo down the centuries: Tiberius Claudius Nero. His genes, rather than those of Octavian or Julius Caesar, would predominate in the future ruling dynasty of Rome.[29]

THIRTEEN

OCTAVIAN IN LOVE

Octavian's requited passion for the nineteen-year-old Livia showed that the law of unintended consequences that had advanced his political career was now operating in the personal sphere, too. She returned to Rome with her husband, as a direct result of the triumvirs' new deal with Sextus, before the summer was out. Less than two years earlier she had been a hunted fugitive from Octavian's soldiers, barely managing to keep one step ahead of her pursuers. Claudius Nero had somehow managed to escape from Perusia when the city fell, perhaps by pretending to be a man of lower rank. He would otherwise have faced execution as a renegade Caesarean, one of those *optimates* rounded up after the siege whose appeals for mercy to the victor were reportedly met with two words: *Moriendum esse* – 'You must die!'[1]

Claudius Nero fled first to Praeneste, then with Livia to Campania, where he tried ineffectually to foment a slave revolt. Refuge at Naples lasted only until the soldiers burst into the city. The couple made their way stealthily down to the port, to escape by ship to Sicily, but were nearly betrayed before they got on board by the sudden bawling of baby Tiberius, when an over-helpful attendant, trying to hurry things along, tried to separate the future emperor from his wet-nurse's breast. Later, after quitting Sicily for Greece, Livia again had to flee with her son, this time from Sparta, where the Claudians had supporters. She escaped the troops by running through part of a blazing forest, clutching

Tiberius to her chest, and emerged the other side with scorched hair and clothing.[2]

Nothing in her earlier life could have prepared her for such nightmare escapades. She was by natural descent a Claudian who had married another Claudian, almost certainly one of her cousins. Their clan had become notorious, even among the nobility, for overweening pride: its members could plausibly claim that their record of providing senior magistrates to serve the Republic was second to none over a period of centuries. Livia's father had been born a Claudian, but was adopted into the Livian clan by the maverick tribune, Marcus Livius Drusus, whose murder in 91 had sparked the Social War throughout Italy.[3] Her father thus took the adoptive name of M. Livius Drusus Claudianus. As an unswerving optimate, he was proscribed by the triumvirs, fought under Brutus and Cassius, and committed suicide in his tent at Philippi when the battle was lost.

Claudius Nero, however, had some claim to serious populist credentials. His father (of the same name) had spoken out against the proposed execution of Catiline's associates during the crucial Senate debate of 63. Before meeting Livia, the son had been an unsuccessful suitor for the hand of Cicero's daughter, Tullia, who married Dolabella instead. In 48 Claudius Nero became one of Caesar's quaestors, and for a while commanded the dictator's fleet during the battle of Alexandria, apparently with success. As a reward, he was sent in 46 to oversee the foundation of two Caesarean colonies at Narbo and Arelate in southern Gaul, today the thriving French towns of Narbonne and Arles. But after Caesar's assassination he changed sides, and was reckless enough to propose in the Senate that Brutus and Cassius should be rewarded for their deed.[4] That move, however, would have made him more acceptable to Livia's family, and the pair were married either in late 44 or in 43.

Livia's recent biographer, Professor Barrett, says we cannot exclude the possibility that it might have been Octavian's

unloved wife Scribonia who introduced the attractive young
mother to her own husband. There is no direct evidence, but
a tantalisingly suggestive family connection is thought to
exist. Before his suicide, Livia's father is believed to have
adopted the son of Lucius Scribonius Libo, father of
Scribonia, as his own child. If so, it would have made that
young man Livia's adoptive brother and Scribonia's nephew.
As Claudius Nero would have been facing the loss of three-
quarters of his former estate under the terms of Puteoli as a
formerly proscribed exile, nothing would have been more
natural than that Livia should use that family link to advance
her first husband's case for preferential treatment – and thus
ask Scribonia to fix up a private interview with Octavian.
Whether or not that is so, we know that Scribonia soon began
to complain about her husband's mistress, whom Professor
Barrett identifies as 'almost certainly Livia'.[5]

Much less likely is the further possibility that Livia was the
unnamed lady in one of Suetonius's more scandalous
anecdotes, whom Octavian is said to have taken into a
bedroom from his dining room beneath the eyes of her
husband. When she returned some time later, her hair was in
disorder and her ears red.[6] Suetonius got the story from
hostile comments by Antony, whose target was not Livia but
Octavian, and who may therefore have tried gallantly to put
his audience off the scent by asserting that the blushing
victim was the wife of a former consul (which Claudius Nero
was not). The story's wide circulation and continuing
popularity is attested by the later Emperor Caligula's remark,
when stealing a certain Livia Orestilla from her fiancé to
become his second wife, that he was 'following Augustus's
example'.[7] Against that may be set the verdict of a man who
actually knew her, Velleius Paterculus. In his judgment,
Octavian's Livia was 'the most eminent of Roman ladies by
birth, honesty and beauty of form'.[8]

Tacitus asserts that Octavian forcibly abducted her from
her husband, carrying her off to his house.[9] That may, of

course, have been a charade to ensure that Octavian himself bore the full responsibility, so that no hint of loose morals should attach to Livia. Claudius Nero was certainly a complaisant husband, who is said to have personally given her away at the wedding that followed her 'abduction'. A small boy wandering among the guests at dinner one evening told Livia, who was reclining beside Octavian, that she was in the wrong place – her husband, he said, pointing to Claudius Nero on the other side of the room, was occupying a different couch.[10] It is not known whether the remark was made in all innocence, or whether the child was put up to it.

Before his marriage, Octavian shaved off his beard and thereafter kept a smooth chin for the rest of his life. A Roman citizen's first shave was by tradition an important occasion, usually performed ceremoniously as a rite of passage. The hairs would be preserved in some suitable container among other heirlooms, and probably dedicated to a god or an ancestor. Octavian marked the event by putting on a festival to which all citizens were invited. Dio says that at that time Octavian was already beginning to fall in love with Livia, and the order of events in his text suggests strongly that the divorce of Scribonia on the day of their daughter Julia's birth was a direct consequence of the new romance.[11]

Octavian was sufficiently worried by the impropriety of what he was doing to take the precaution of consulting the priestly college of pontifices for advice on the appropriate timing for marriage to a woman who was already pregnant by her first husband when she obtained a divorce. The priests, who evidently knew better than to raise objections, came up with a convenient formula that would enable him, in the absence of any precedent, to marry her as soon as practicable. Livia gave birth to her second son, Drusus, in mid-January of 38. Three days later she was well enough to go through the wedding ceremony.[12] She would never have another child. In spite of Octavian's desperate political need to father a legitimate male heir, he did not divorce her, as he could so easily have done, to marry another. Although they were to have serious disagreements, especially over his plans for the succession, theirs remained a love match to the end of their lives. The later allegation that she poisoned him to allow Tiberius to take over is malicious invention.

Antony and Octavia did not attend the ceremony. They had already left Rome for Athens before winter made it too dangerous to risk crossing the Adriatic. Antony transacted much diplomatic business there at intervals over the next two years, trying to settle some of the unresolved problems of the East. There was no longer any need for him to repel the Parthian invasion of Syria, because Ventidius had already done it for him, in a brilliant campaign that would earn him a triumph back in Rome. That was to be a remarkable and unprecedented honour for a general who, as a boy, had been paraded through the streets of the capital among the chained prisoners of Pompey the Great's father, Strabo, who was officially triumphing at the conclusion of the Social War.[13]

Octavian had little time for a honeymoon before trouble flared up again with Sextus, who claimed he was being swindled over the five-year grant of the Peloponnese. Antony, he alleged, had plundered it in advance to reduce its value. Octavian defended his colleague by pointing out that under the terms of their agreement the territory had been ceded on condition that Sextus either paid the tribute money already due from its inhabitants or waited until Antony had collected it. That explanation was not enough to satisfy Sextus, who resumed the blockade, but without admitting it. Some 'pirates', who were caught in the act, confessed under torture that they had been acting on Sextus's orders. Under the curious Roman system of relative values, the confession of a slave had no legal validity unless it was obtained under torture. Octavian publicized the slaves' testimony to prepare Italy for a resumption of the war.[14]

An early success was the defection of Menodorus, formerly the would-be assassin of the triumvirs, who turned Sardinia over to Octavian along with his fleet and troops. Sextus had ordered him back to Sicily, but the admiral suspected that might be an invitation to his own death – like that of Murcius, his old colleague as admiral. Octavian invited him to dinner. This was considered a great compliment, demonstrating the value of his action; according to Suetonius, he was the only freedman to be so honoured during Octavian's career. Before he could sit down at table, however, Menodorus had to be enrolled among the list of men of free birth, but his change of masters did not long survive the series of naval disasters that Octavian was about to suffer.[15]

Before mounting an all-out attack on Sextus, Octavian had appealed to Antony for assistance, asking him to come to Brundisium on a specified date in spring. Antony came, but was not a man to be kept waiting. When Octavian failed to show up on time he sailed back to Greece, leaving a curt message warning the young man not to break the treaty with Sextus.[16] Both triumvirs were now angry with each other. Octavian protested that Antony should have waited a little longer, and may have begun to reflect on how well it would suit Antony to protect and encourage Sextus as a potential ally against him. As for Lepidus, the third triumvir had simply ignored Octavian's call for help. It was clear that if Antony were to recruit both Sextus and Lepidus to his side, Octavian could find himself, in Italy, facing enemies from three points of the compass.

The young man stepped up his ship-building programme and resolved to eliminate on his own initiative the threat posed by Sextus. Yet again, however, he proved to be a hopeless tactician at close quarters. He found himself with an unexpected advantage as his new fleet encountered by chance a significantly smaller force under Sextus. Instead of attacking at once, Octavian decided to wait for reinforcements which he knew were on the way. Sextus escaped. A day or so later, Sextus swooped down on him when the odds were reversed and destroyed up to half of his ships. A sudden storm accounted for most of the rest. Octavian managed to scramble ashore as his vessel sank under him, but he had lost the means to pursue the struggle further that year.[17]

Festina lente – 'Make haste slowly'. That proverbial saying was to become Octavian's motto.[18] Perhaps it was as he surveyed the flotsam of his wrecked fleet and mourned the loss of so many sailors slaughtered and armed men drowned, that he resolved never again to let his impatience to complete a necessary task place him in unnecessary danger. His return to Rome was marked by a resumption of bread riots, as the spectre of famine again stalked the city. This time, however, he was in no mood to compromise. He saw how absurd it was that the greatest military power in the known world could be held to ransom by an outlaw operating from an offshore island. He sacked his chief admiral and called Agrippa back from Gaul to take charge of a massive rearmament and training programme. Rome was to get a professional navy.

Agrippa had already been voted a triumph for a victory over rebels in Aquitaine, but he tactfully declined that honour on his return to Rome at the end of 38 at a time when his friend was so unpopular. Italy soon felt his firm hand and would come to recognize his organizing ability. Coastal towns were invited or coerced to contribute warships constructed according to his and Octavian's master plan. Slave-owners were told to supply the rowers, and a total of 20,000 men were to be granted their freedom for that purpose. Other slaves toiled to create a huge salt-water expanse where the crews could train, safe from storms or sudden hostile attacks. They cut channels to link lake Avernus with the nearby lake Lucrinus, north of the Bay of Naples, and then breached the narrow strip of land that had hitherto kept out the sea.

Each newly built ship was brought around the coasts to this vast harbour, where Agrippa supervised the training to his exacting standards. He devised a new form of grappling iron and tested it in mock action, firing the heavy contraption by catapult from one vessel to another. It proved much more difficult to remove quickly from rigging and sails than existing projectiles of that sort, so allowing more time for the men who had fired it to haul on the attached ropes and drag the target ship within boarding range. That, in turn, would allow Octavian's soldiers to use their superior numbers and disciplined tactics to destroy their enemy, whose ships were mostly smaller than their own new ones, which had an elaborate defensive superstructure, including towers.[19]

Maecenas had been despatched to Athens, meanwhile, charged with the difficult task of persuading Antony to relent and make a second crossing to Brundisium. Antony came in the summer of 37, with an armada of 300 ships, but by that time Octavian had become too wary to accept his help. Brundisium shut its harbour against him again. This time Antony sailed on around the heel of Italy to anchor off Tarentum in the shelter of its gulf, demonstrating that he was not prepared, a second time, simply to go away. He meant business. His messages to Octavian that his forces were big enough and ready to deal with Sextus were rebuffed with lame excuses. The ancient sources provide only limited clues as to what underlay the manoeuvrings of the two triumvirs. What was really going on?

Part of the the truth, surely, was that Octavian was afraid of the threat which Antony's presence, backed up by such a huge fleet, represented to his control of Rome. If he were to cooperate by embarking his legions on Antony's ships, would he ever get them back? Sextus would stand little chance against their combined might, but victory in such circumstances – with the forces inevitably under Antony's direct command – would bolster the older man's prestige to renewed heights. If he went on to celebrate a triumph in Rome itself, and stayed to challenge Octavian's rule, his superior *auctoritas* might well be enough to propel him once more to the summit of power. His word, not Octavian's, would then become law in the West as well as in the East.

Octavian was right in assuming that his rival had not

gone to all the trouble of asembling his armada simply to help a colleague overcome a local difficulty, but he probably misjudged Antony's immediate motives. His sister, Octavia, now set out from Tarentum, with an escort provided by her husband, on a mission to disabuse her brother of his worst suspicions. Much has been made, in both ancient and modern times, of Octavia's supposed skills as a diplomatist, and the idea of her saving the empire from civil war by her talent and her tears is undeniably attractive. But her brother had never yet been known to allow personal feelings to prejudice his hold on power, and he certainly did not do so now.

Octavia was well aware of her husband's basic intention. Antony had not given up his ambition to conquer Parthia, in the footsteps of Alexander the Great, and after two years of comparative inactivity in Athens he had placed the project at the top of his agenda. Octavian, however, had been blocking his attempts to recruit fresh troops in Italy in breach of the terms of the Pact of Brundisium. Antony wanted to make sure his army was both big enough and loyal enough for the task, and he would be able to place much more reliance on men from his own homeland than on those available in the largely Hellenistic East. He could not force Octavian to comply with his treaty obligations except at the risk of war. By removing Sextus he would be able to take over the unreliable warlord's legions and, perhaps, coerce his brother-in-law to supply more troops on loan.

Antony was fully justified in his view that Octavian could not be trusted to keep his word; in this particular case he was in breach of the letter of the agreement as well as its spirit. Octavian, however, had evidently decided that he would be a fool to allow his rival to recruit troops that might be used against him. His agents had told him that Antony had sent his freedman Callias to Africa for talks with Lepidus, possibly to propose a hostile alliance. Octavia, in her role as diplomatic go-between, denied the allegation, saying that Callias had simply been making arrangements for a possible marriage between a daughter of Antony and a son of Lepidus.

Octavian also complained that Antony had effectively left him in the lurch by refusing to wait for him to get to Brundisium the previous year. That excuse, however, ignored the fact that it was Octavian who had asked for the meeting and would have found it easier to keep the appointment; Antony, after all, would have been subject to the vagaries of the weather on his voyage from Athens, and would have been quite unable to predict the precise date of his arrival. Octavia may also have needed to rebut an allegation that her husband had come to Italy to spy on him. That, at any rate, is the motive which Dio attributes to Antony; but, even if true, it could not be applied retrospectively to excuse the earlier infringement of the pact.

The conclusion must be that the young man was determined not to share his power with anyone else once he had acquired it, whatever he may have signed up to during the course of its pursuit. That is a deeply unattractive characteristic, but only too typical of men whose chief motivation is the will to power. He is unlikely to have acknowledged it as a fault, even to himself. He may well have justified his action by reckoning he was simply giving his rival a taste of his own medicine, harking back to the aftermath of the Ides of March when Antony had promised to help him validate his adoption by Caesar, but in reality had done his utmost to block its passage through the courts.

The mediation of Octavia paid dividends for him. She wanted the two to meet, as brothers-in-law should, on terms of friendship and mutual cooperation. Her primary motive was perhaps to save her marriage, which, judging by later events, seems to have been on the verge of collapse. If, in phrasing her appeal to her brother, she let him see the weaknesses in her husband's hand, it is little wonder that Octavian changed his mind and agreed to negotiations. She got what she chiefly wanted at that particular time. She was able to return to Tarentum to give Antony the welcome news that she had persuaded her brother to come at last to meet him, and on a friendly basis.[20] To set Octavian's mind further at rest, Antony sent the unfortunate Callias to him, with his permission to 'put him to the question': in other words to torture him to confirm the innocence of his dealings with Lepidus.

Octavian saw no need to put the freedman to such inconvenience. Scenting a fresh diplomatic victory of his own, he set out at a leisurely pace with an entourage that included Maecenas and Nerva, and two newcomers to the world of high politics, the poets Horace and Virgil, useful for stamping the seal of literary approval on his regime. Antony was waiting close to the shore, on the Tarentum side of the River Taras, with his great armada in view and rows of soldiers at his back. Octavian's own massive forces were lined up on the other bank of the river, near the town of Metapontum. He passed by their ranks to face his old rival, who climbed into a small boat and rowed out alone into mid-stream. Not to be outdone in the matter of demonstrating confidence in personal safety, Octavian quickly found a similar craft on his own side and rowed out to join him.

The only dispute at that stage was which of them should go with the other. Octavian claimed the right to cross to Antony's side on the grounds that he wanted to greet his sister at Tarentum.[21] Entirely without guards, he spent that night fraternizing with both of them. The outcome was the Accord of Tarentum, under which they agreed to a five-year renewal of the Triumvirate, whose unconstitutional powers had in theory expired at the start of the year – although nobody had been foolhardy enough to mount a challenge against them in the courts. Lepidus, for the moment, would retain his anomalous position as one of the three.

That was mere legalistic form. Much more important, in terms of future relations between the two paramount chiefs of the Roman world, was Antony's trustful decision to hand over a hundred of his warships, along with twenty other vessels, in return for Octavian's promise to supply him with 20,000 troops at some unspecified date in the future. Octavia, no doubt knowing her brother much better than did Antony, persuaded him to part with a further 1,000 soldiers immediately in return for a further ten ships.[22] Ultimately, Octavian would supply only ten per cent of the troops he had promised – and after a delay of nearly two years.

Octavia and her husband set out together for the East, but she only reached Corcyra, on the far side of the Adriatic, before being sent back to her brother at Rome. Antony claimed, with some initial degree of plausibility, that he was acting for her own safety and that of their daughter and unborn child, who would be in danger if they accompanied him on the Parthian expedition. He placed them formally in Octavian's care. The next news of Antony was that he had met Cleopatra at Antioch, ostensibly having summoned her as a subordinate ruler in his part of the empire, but in fact to resume his adulterous relationship with her.[23] It was the effective end of Octavia's marriage, although the official divorce would not come for five years; until then, she would live in Rome as his faithful wife, assiduously looking after his interests.

Her brother now had the unfinished business of Sextus to deal with. Even with the added benefit of Antony's 130 ships, Octavian still did not consider his naval preparations enough to mount an immediate invasion of Sicily. It was not until 1 July 36 that he launched a massive three-pronged attack, with Lepidus, Agrippa and Statilius Taurus as his admirals, who would also have to double as generals. Even in modern times, when ships move under their own power, elaborate combined operations at sea have shown a built-in tendency to go wrong. In days when oars and sails provided the forward thrust, and the art of weather forecasting depended on an examination of birds' entrails, it would have been a rare triumph of hope over experience for much to go right.

Octavian himself set out from the Bay of Naples after performing a complex lustration ceremony to propitiate Neptune, whose son Sextus now claimed to be. Lepidus set sail from the province of Africa, with the advantage that his designated landing zone was at the opposite end of Sicily to where almost all the enemy forces were concentrated to guard the Straits of Messana, which separated the island from the Italian mainland. Taurus started from Tarentum, and must have moved very slowly, perhaps against the prevailing westerly wind, because when a storm burst over the area on 3 July he had not yet engaged the enemy, and had time to turn back and run for shelter.

The commander-in-chief was not so lucky. The storm wrecked Octavian's section of the fleet so comprehensively that it could no longer play any part in the operation, as originally devised. Many of his beached warships were capable of repair, but the process would take a full month, even with every available worker hard at the task. Octavian sent Maecenas post-haste to Rome to quell a rumour that Sextus, in his new green cloak as the sea-god's son, was about to take over the city. He himself went on a tour of the many colonies of veterans around the Italian peninsula, hoping to boost morale at the same time as he recruited fresh troops to replace those who had drowned. He was able to assure them that Lepidus, at least, had reached the south-west of the island, formed a bridgehead and was rapidly landing a substantial force.[24]

By the time Octavian's repaired ships were ready to resume the offensive in early August, Lepidus had built up his force to twelve legions, although he, too, had lost many drowned in a second storm. Agrippa now engaged Sextus's main naval force off Mylae, on the north coast, to give Octavian an opportunity to ferry four legions across the Straits of Messana to what he assumed would be comparative safety. He managed to get three of them across before part of the enemy fleet came up and began a furious engagement that ended with yet another defeat for Octavian, who had to scramble ashore on the mainland with only his armour-bearer for escort.

The experience was probably just as chastening as when he hid in a marsh at the first battle of Philippi to avoid getting killed. What may have made it worse was that he was the man in overall command of the operation, and there was no Antony to retrieve the situation. For a while he appears to have believed that all was lost, and is reported to have briefly considered suicide – unlikely though that may be. He must have reasoned that the appearance of Sextus's fleet, or a large part of it, indicated that Agrippa had been defeated off Mylae, with ominous implications for the future. In fact Agrippa, after seeing off Sextus, had gone ashore in force and captured an important enemy base at Tyndaris. News of that success did not reach Octavian until after he was rescued from his enforced isolation by troops under Valerius Messala Corvinus, a man whom he and his fellow-triumvirs had once proscribed.[25]

Far from being on the brink of defeat, Octavian was shortly to achieve total victory. Sextus was losing so many bases to land forces under Agrippa and Lepidus that he decided to risk everything by offering a major battle at sea while he could still provision his ships from the island. Agrippa welcomed the challenge, which Octavian wisely left to him to take up rather than accepting it himself. The battle of Naulochus, fought in September 36, ended in disaster for Sextus, whose ships were more manoeuvrable than Agrippa's floating towers but outnumbered and vulnerable to the new grappling hooks. When most of his fleet had been reduced to wrecked or burning hulks, Sextus sailed east with what vessels remained, leaving behind eight legions of his irregulars, to offer his services to Antony. He might have continued to flourish for a while had he not, typically, also offered to fight for the Parthians. His end came when one of Antony's legates captured and executed him.[26]

There were two final twists to the Sicilian campaign before

Octavian could celebrate victory. Lepidus accepted the surrender of the fortified city of Messana along with Sextus's abandoned troops. That boosted the total under his direct command to no fewer than twenty legions (about 100,000 men). The disregarded 'third triumvir' decided his hour had struck at last. When Octavian arrived on the scene, Lepidus ordered him to leave the island immediately. No doubt Lepidus had decided to do some empire-building on his own account, by adding Sicily to his existing province of Africa. It seems to have been an opportunistic rather than premeditated action, and there is no evidence that he had consulted Antony.

Octavian was in a difficult position. Many of his own troops had mutinied as Sextus departed, demanding cash rewards for their services as well as discharge settlements for those who had been fighting for their young general from as far back as Mutina. But what Lepidus thought would be decided by a simple calculation of military odds was turned by Octavian into a struggle for the hearts and minds of all the soldiers, whether in the third triumvir's camp or his own. That was his forte. If he could persuade legions to defect from Antony, as he had done early in his career, he could do so in the case of Lepidus, who had never been popular with his men. The trained partisans of Octavian went to work, and in just a few days almost all Lepidus's troops changed sides.

When the young victor next entered the rival camp Lepidus begged for mercy. His life was spared but his career was finished. Stripped of his title of triumvir, he was sent under escort to Italy, where he lived out his remaining years in obscurity, not quite a prisoner but under close supervision.[27] The disgraced patrician may have owed his survival to the fact that he was *Pontifex Maximus*, an office which, though highly politicized, was nevertheless sacred and was bestowed for life; Octavian would wait until Lepidus died naturally before taking it over. He was merciless, however, to the 30,000 runaway slaves in Sextus's surrendered army. The peace of Puteoli had provided for their freedom on discharge, but Sextus had broken the treaty and Octavian no doubt felt justified in disregarding that provision. Those slaves whose former masters could be traced were returned to them for punishment. He ordered the remaining 6,000 to be crucified.[28]

On his return to Rome, Octavian was feted as a conquering hero. The privation which the citizens had suffered so long seems to have been forgotten as food was now plentiful in the capital once more. The young deliverer seized the opportunity to increase his prestige further by having the sacrosanctity of a tribune of the People attached to his person, although it would be some years before he would acquire the actual powers of a tribune. For what the protection was worth, it now became an offence against the state religion to cause him physical harm. He also secured the right to wear a laurel wreath, like Julius Caesar before him, an honour that would demonstrate in public, for all to see, his unique position as the chosen son of a god.[29]

Octavian evidently felt in need of such cosmetic boosts to his reputation, chiefly perhaps because of Antony's activities in the East. His rival had spent the winter with Cleopatra in Antioch, preparing for his long-delayed invasion of Parthia. The queen had brought the twins he had fathered on her at Alexandria four years earlier, and persuaded him to acknowledge legitimate paternity in public. That was disturbing to Octavian because of its dynastic implications, as well as representing an insult to his sister. The twins, Alexander Helios and Cleopatra Selene – their second names mean respectively 'sun' and 'moon' – could not be recognized as legitimate in the Roman courts, because marriage between a citizen and a foreigner was *ultra vires*, but that would not prevent recognition by the dependent eastern monarchs; nor would it necessarily stop Antony providing for them in his will.

It is not clear whether Antony and Cleopatra went through a form of marriage at that stage, or perhaps postponed the ceremony until their return to Alexandria a year or more later. What is certain is that the queen received a stupendous 'wedding present' at Antioch in the form of selected tracts of the Roman Empire for her to rule over. These included the central region of Syria, along with its main city Damascus; part of the Palestinian coast; Cyrenaica, whose capital Cyrene was some 500 miles west of Alexandria along the North African littoral; and the island of Cyprus. Antony refused her repeated requests to take Judaea from Herod the Great, but he compensated her with the lucrative bitumen monopoly centred on the shores of the Dead Sea, and also the balsam groves of Jericho.[30]

Egypt was already the richest single country in Rome's recognized sphere of influence, and it was only Cleopatra's astute manipulation of Julius Caesar and Antony as her successive lovers that had stopped its being incorporated within the Roman Empire. Antony's territorial gifts amounted almost to a reassembly of the former Egyptian Empire of her celebrated ancestor, Ptolemy II Philadelphus (308–246 BC), son of the founder of the dynasty, Ptolemy I Soter, who had been one of Alexander the Great's generals. All the Ptolemies, of course, were of Macedonian/Greek descent, including Cleopatra. It was Ptolemy I who had introduced the religious cult of Alexander to Egypt, and it was Antony who was about to follow in Alexander's footsteps by proposing to lead a largely European army into the heartlands of the former Persian Empire, now ruled by the Parthians.

The name of Alexander Helios given to Antony's son by Cleopatra was far from coincidental. The queen regarded herself as a new incarnation of the goddess Isis, daughter of the Sun-god Re. She would have known of Virgil's prophecy – albeit made with due allowance for Western poetic licence – of a boy saviour to be fathered by Antony.[31] Virgil, to be sure, was referring to Octavia as the lawful wife and mother, but she had produced two girls instead of a little Antonius. Was it not more plausible, to Eastern minds, that the wondrous child should be the offspring of Antony and Cleopatra?

Octavian, brooding at Rome over the news from Syrian Antioch, had every reason for apprehension over the possible future career of four-year-old 'Alexander the Sun', coming from such parents. Even more alarming would be any move by Antony to promote the career of Cleopatra's eldest boy, Caesarion, now about eleven years old and universally assumed by contemporaries to be the son of Julius Caesar. Octavian's entire career depended on his being Caesar's adoptive son and heir. The last thing he could tolerate would be a supposedly legitimized rival son of royal birth, especially at a time when he had just heard that Antony's messengers were hailing a victory by their master over the Parthians.

FOURTEEN

THE MENACE FROM THE EAST

Antony did win a battle, against a combined force of Medes and Parthians, but he nevertheless contrived to lose the war. Once again, the man with the reputation of being the greatest fighting general of the post-Caesarean era had trapped himself and his long-suffering legions. A series of elementary mistakes, bred of overconfidence and compounded by impatience, led to a situation where he had no choice but to retreat over mountain passes in winter, with scarcely any food, inadequate clothing in the snowstorms and a hostile army hanging on his flanks and rear. Napoleon, that keen student of Roman military campaigns, must surely have thought of this Antonian disaster when leading the similar retreat from Moscow some eighteen-and-a-half centuries later. At least Napoleon plundered his enemy's capital first and gave his men a breathing space. Antony did not even make it past the Parthian frontier.

Cleopatra, who had a much firmer grasp of the realities of power than her lover would ever show, had been deeply sceptical of the value of invading Parthia. The risks of Antony's plan were too great to justify the supposed rewards. He would have to march a thousand miles through mainly difficult and unfamiliar terrain simply to reach his preliminary objective, the fortified Median town of Phraaspa, of which he may have known little more than the name and its position, some 130 miles west of the Caspian Sea. He knew nothing at all of the combined strength of the forces he would be attacking, whereas they knew about his in detail. He

229

could not maintain adequate lines of communication over such a huge distance, so there was no serious possibility of either supplies or reinforcements reaching him if anything should go wrong, so he would need to conserve his military strength and live off the country as he passed through it. With the heedless arrogance of a Roman aristocrat, he no doubt thought, 'If Alexander the Great could do it – and with a much smaller army – so can I.'

Cleopatra was not yet in a position to influence his policy excessively. If he really wanted to build up his personal power, she could think of better targets, closer to home, ruled by petty monarchs who were her natural enemies. In his position, her own strategy would clearly have been to use the legions to impose direct, personal rule over all the territories of the eastern Mediterranean before looking any further afield. But Antony was seeking glory, largely for its own sake. In Cleopatra's world, glory was a by-product of power. In any case, she cared nothing for the honour and glory of Rome, where she had found herself despised by patricians and plebeians alike as being no more than Caesar's mistress, in danger of being cast aside whenever he should tire of her. This was a woman who, in her own country, exercised the power of life and death over all her millions of subjects, was worshipped as a goddess, and whose predecessors ruled a great nation at a time when Roman consuls were farmers struggling to run a small city state – when they could be spared from the plough.

She accompanied Antony on the first stage of his journey, from Antioch, beside the Mediterranean, to his main assembly point at Zeugma on the Euphrates. Parthia lay on the far side of the river, but he knew better than to cross it. That had been the fatal error of Crassus, to march across the open Mesopotamian plain (of modern Iraq) where his infantry, lacking any cover, had been slaughtered like cattle by mounted Parthian archers. Antony had a bigger army than that of Crassus, bigger, even, than any Caesar had

commanded. Too big, in fact, to hide. He paraded it before
Cleopatra, and, inevitably, before the hostile eyes of Parthian
sympathizers and spies, who would need only a basic ability
to count heads, before slipping across the Euphrates with
their intelligence reports.[1]

The core of his expeditionary force was composed of
sixteen Roman legions, screened by 10,000 of his own
dependable cavalry. His new but untried ally, Artavasdes,
King of Armenia, supplied 13,000 men, of whom nearly half
were mounted. A further 14,000 light-armed auxiliary troops
came from dependent princes. That made a total of well over
100,000 men, but probably rather fewer than 120,000.
Cleopatra waved them goodbye, knowing that if Antony were
to be killed on this utterly unnecessary venture, her future
prospects would be worse than if she had never met him. She
had not completely burnt her boats, however, as neither
Octavian or his sister – nor, for that matter, Cleopatra herself
– could be sure he would not return from Parthia to the arms
of his wife Octavia.

It was probably no later than April or May of 36 when
Antony left Zeugma to resume his long journey. The army
headed north at first, in roughly the opposite direction to
Parthia, but by keeping to the right bank of the Euphrates the
marching columns gradually veered east as they wound their
slow way up towards the increasingly mountainous areas of
the great river's sources. They turned south to cross the
hostile territory of Media to reach Phraaspa, not far from the
Parthian border. By then it would have been late summer,
roughly about the time Octavian was being shipwrecked in
the Straits of Messana. Antony's weary men surrounded
Phraaspa and waited for their siege engines to arrive with the
rearguard. His master plan now stood revealed. He would
capture the town during the autumn, spend the winter there
and cross into Parthia in the spring.

The Medes and the Parthians, however, had not been
waiting tamely to be conquered. Once they knew he would

not invade by the great plain of the Tigris and Euphrates, they did not simply lose interest in his movements, as he had apparently hoped. They monitored from a distance, and possibly from within his own ranks, the direction and progress of his highly visible army. They saw their chance when he split his forces, leaving only two legions and Artavasdes's contingent to guard the wagon train, so that he could press ahead faster with the bulk of his troops. The Armenian king, evidently tipped off in advance of an enemy attack, rode home with his squadrons, leaving the rearguard without protective cavalry. The heavily outnumbered Roman infantry were killed or captured, their precious supply wagons driven off and all their irreplaceable siege engines destroyed.[2]

Antony, of course, hurried back, but was too late to rescue either his rearguard or himself. He won a battle in the sense that he drove the enemy from the field, but his infantry were unable to follow up their initial success because of the greater mobility and firepower, from a distance, of his opponents, who included 50,000 mounted archers. Loss of the siege engines in a countryside short of wood and iron should have prompted Antony to immediate retreat. He was too proud and too obstinate to accept such humiliation straight away. His efforts to continue the siege by heaping up mounds, and using what wood he could find to try to bridge the gap between the mounds and the walls, proved a predictable failure. When he sent out units to forage for food, the archers rode back to pick them off. The Medes made a sortie in strength from the town, temporarily drove away the besiegers and demolished their works. Antony's response was to decimate the survivors of that attack – as if he had not already squandered the lives of so many of his men.[3]

It was not until the Parthian king, Phraates, suggested negotiations that Antony forced himself to face up to his predicament. He asked for the return of prisoners and battle-standards, which the king contemptuously refused, offering no more than his guarantee of a peaceful withdrawal. The fortified town had been given enough warning to stockpile provisions before the Romans arrived. Autumn was now far advanced. Antony, dangerously short of food, materials and winter clothing, decided that the king's offer was better than nothing. Phraates had reached the throne by murdering his elderly father, and was therefore hardly a man whose word could be relied on. So it was to prove.

The diminished Roman army struck camp, and would have marched straight into a massive ambush if they had taken the same route by which they came in. One of their guides pointed out the trap to Antony and led them by a more difficult but safer route. Nevertheless, after a nightmare retreat of twenty-seven days, the army arrived back in Armenia with 28,000 fewer fighting men than Antony had led out in the spring. That does not count either the deaths of camp followers, who would mostly have been slaves, or the Armenian deserters under Artavasdes. Half of those 28,000 died from disease and hunger. A further 8,000 soldiers were to die in the snows as the retreat continued through Armenia, unhindered now by pursuing enemies. The contemporary historian, Velleius Paterculus, a supporter of Octavian, wrote: 'Antony called his retreat a victory because he got through alive.'[4] It was not totally unfair comment.

The general did not stay with the remnants of his scarecrow army for the final stage of their march to the lowlands beside the Mediterranean. He pressed ahead to make sure messengers were being sent as quickly as possible to Alexandria. By the waters of Sidon he sat down in temporary headquarters and began to drown his sorrows in drink, mourning the loss of a third of his comrades. Between intervals of drunkenness he would suddenly jump up from the table and run to the shore, hoping to see Cleopatra's sails. When the queen eventually arrived, later in the New Year, she was pregnant with another of his children. She brought ample supplies of warm clothing for the men but not enough money to pay them. That was perhaps as far as she dared to go in demonstrating her disapproval of what her lover had done. Antony made up the difference in pay out of his own personal funds.[5]

Octavia, the wronged wife, also set out with comforts for the troops, but not until spring made the seas safer. She transported 2,000 reinforcements for his depleted army, 18,000 short of the number that her brother had promised him. Her little fleet got as far as Athens, where she waited to hear where she ought to sail next to meet her husband, or to discover, preferably, whether he would come to meet her. His letter, when it came, was no more than an abrupt order to send the laden ships on to him but to go back to Rome herself. It must have been a bitter moment. Perhaps she knew by then that Antony had returned with Cleopatra to Alexandria. She would never see him again; their younger daughter would never see him at all.

Octavia's voyage represented a spirited attempt to save her marriage by showing she was as capable as Cleopatra of helping him when the going got tough. It did her no good, except with the Romans to whom she now returned in dejection. Her brother told her to leave Antony's house. She refused.[6] Her reputation as the noblest, most self-sacrificing of wives would grow and grow while Antony's prestige plunged. It does not seem to have occurred to the ancient chroniclers that she might actually have preferred the relative independence of life with her children under Antony's roof to the prospect of sharing her brother's abstemious household with Livia, especially during his long absences.

From the moment of the rebuff to his sister, the hostility of Octavian towards Antony was unrelenting. Although he was not yet in a position to go to war, he would take every opportunity to denigrate him in the eyes of other citizens as a man for whom Rome and its values were no longer good enough. The undoubted personal insult to Octavia and himself became, through his mastery of public relations, an insult to every Roman citizen. Without needing to tell a direct lie about his fellow-triumvir, he set about manipulating public opinion through playing on Roman prejudices towards the allegedly effete and immoral East. He did not invent stories to sustain the hostile propaganda, but he shamelessly embroidered them as they came to hand, like a modern spin-doctor, to cast Antony as being in thrall to an evil foreign queen. Within six years he would so transform public perceptions of his old rival as to be able to lead an army out from Rome on what became a virtual crusade to rid the world of the supposed threat to Western civilization posed by Cleopatra and Antony, in that order.

How could Antony have been quite so brutally dismissive in his letter to Octavia? It is not difficult to detect the influence of Cleopatra. She was much more intelligent than the man she had chosen for her consort, and like so many women in that position would have found it expedient not to make too obvious a disclosure of the fact. After the bloody fiasco of Parthia, when he could not but admit having made serious mistakes, she would have taken her chance to convince him that his true enemy was not the King of Parthia or the turncoat Artavasdes, but his obvious Roman rival Octavian. Fearing that it might cease to be true if he were to give her up and return to his Roman wife, Cleopatra was naturally hoping to persuade him to divorce Octavia officially under Roman law.

That is not quite how the ancient sources explain the case. Dio, for instance, writing (in Greek) some 250 years later, believes firmly that witchcraft was involved, and says so more than once. 'He became even more enslaved by the passion *(eroti)* and the spells *(gonteia)* of Cleopatra.'[7] That seemed logical enough, in an age of gross superstition. How else, after all, was a puzzled historian to explain how a Roman proconsul of such status could bring himself to go shopping with Cleopatra in the market-place at Alexandria, she being carried lounging in a chair while he trailed along beside her among her train of eunuchs?

Proof positive for Dio, of the queen's sinister powers over dark forces, was the way Antony obediently posed with her for portraits and statues. In some of them he represented Osiris to her Isis, or Dionysos to her Selene, the Greek moon-goddess who was also, like Isis, a daughter of the Sun.[8] Everyone knew it was Isis who brought Osiris back to life after his betrayal and dismemberment, reconstructing him from his scattered bodily parts, with the exception, according to one account, of his penis. In another version she revivifies the vital organ and conceives the god Horus. One can imagine what Roman wits might have made of those stories. As for Dionysos, that deity could be effeminate as well as masculine, according to mood, and was prone to wallow in drink, sometimes with disastrous consequences for others. The moralist Seneca was to write a century later, 'What ruined Mark Antony, a great man of high ability, and drove him to foreign ways and non-Roman vices? What but love of drink no less than love of Cleopatra!'[9]

Plutarch, just as superstitious as Dio but more psychologically astute, says that Cleopatra saw the immediate danger of Octavia's voyage to Athens and took measures to thwart her. If husband and wife were allowed to meet, Octavia might be able, by loving attention and daily contact, to win Antony back. The queen went on a crash diet to regain her former slimness (presumably, after her new baby was born), and deployed a coquettish mixture of smiles, tears and pretended swooning to convince him of the undying nature of her love. She had already planted a fortune teller among his gaggle of attendants, whose role was to tell him that his inner soul, or genius, normally so dominating and robust, was inclined to fade in the presence of Octavian's: ergo, he should keep as far away from his brother-in-law as possible.

Cleopatra now followed up these measures of psychological warfare by instructing her closest servants to tell him, as if in confidence, how extremely devoted she was to him, whereas Octavia had consented to marry him only because her brother had told her to. Under this pressure, Plutarch affirms, Antony came to believe that, if he left her, Cleopatra would surely kill herself. In fact, she may very well have been trying, also, to stop him risking his own life again. The King of Media, who had fought against him the previous year, had suggested an alliance, claiming he had fallen out with his former ally, the King of Parthia: would Antony like to join him at Phraaspe to renew his Parthian campaign? It might or might not have been true. Antony was apparently keen to go. It would seem that Cleopatra managed, if only temporarily, to din some common sense into him. At any rate, he consented to stay with her for the rest of 35.[10]

That same year, perhaps as a deliberate contrast to Antony's grandiose schemes of conquest, Octavian launched a limited but carefully planned assault against the barbarian tribes of Illyricum, across the Adriatic. There was little glory to be won and no prospect of serious loot, but the task of restraining these primitive warriors had become urgent. Some practised piracy from the many offshore islands of the Dalmatian coast, while others preyed on travellers when not fighting among themselves. Within little more than two years, by the autumn of 33, Octavian had rooted out the pirates and made a start on securing a land route by which soldiers and businessmen could travel from Italy via the frontier fort of Aquileia and the town of Tergeste (Trieste) to Greece, Macedonia and the East.

Octavian managed to improve his reputation among the troops through being wounded twice in action. The first occasion was when he was struck on the right knee by a stone from a sling; the second, more serious, occurred when he tried to step from a siege tower on to the walls of a fort, and the gangway collapsed under him and several others. He injured both arms and one of his legs in the fall. When he recovered he left Illyricum to march across North Italy and into Gaul, with the avowed intention, according to Dio, of invading Britain. There is no way of establishing the truth of that unlikely assertion. In the event, he turned round and marched back to Illyricum to put down a sudden uprising by the Dalmatians, whom he had so recently conquered. For the first time he ordered the decimation of some of his own troops for deserting their posts.[11]

Antony, meanwhile, after his fallow year recovering from the mauling he had undergone at the hands of the Parthians and Medes, made strenuous efforts during 34 to rebuild his *auctoritas*. By means of deception (Cleopatra's influence again?) he captured and deposed Artavasdes, whom he blamed for the disaster in Media, and took over Armenia as a Roman province. That won him senatorial plaudits back in Rome, but it would take the Parthians only about two years to recapture the country and put their own candidate on the Armenian throne. Antony tried to make the most of his victory by holding a triumphal procession, not in Rome but in Egypt, with Artavasdes paraded in silver chains before Cleopatra, while she sat in state among huge crowds.[12] His triumph, however, turned into a public relations disaster in Italy, as rumours spread that he was proposing to move the capital from Rome to Alexandria.

Those rumours continued to gain credence, both from Octavian's exploitation of them for his own propaganda purposes, and from Cleopatra's sensational demonstration of her increasing hold over Antony through the ceremony that has become known as the Donations of Alexandria. The queen, dressed in the sacred robes of Isis, sat beside Antony, each of them on matching golden thrones, on a platform shared with their three children and Caesarion, seated on commensurately smaller thrones. Antony, who by now had almost certainly married her bigamously, formally declared her to be 'Queen of Kings' and her eldest son, Ptolemy Caesar ('Caesarion'), to be 'King of Kings', both mother and son being jointly the sovereign rulers of Egypt and Cyprus.

Then it was the turn of the younger children. Alexander Helios, now aged about six, was allocated Parthia, Media and

Armenia, even though the first two had not been conquered. His twin sister, Cleopatra Selene, who had recently been betrothed to a son of the King of Media, received Libya and Cyrenaica, both in northern Africa. Tiny Ptolemy Philadelphus, now perhaps just old enough to walk without a helping hand, was pronounced monarch of all the kingdoms between the Hellespont and the Euphrates. The existing rulers of those countries would not be replaced, but would be required to acknowledge the royal children of Egypt as their overlords. In turn, those three children would have to recognize their mother and Caesarion as their own overlords.[13]

Plainly, this was all the product of Cleopatra's fertile brain. Antony, of course, was ultimately everybody's overlord in the East, through the naked power of the legions, but his precise role in the control and apportionment of particular realms was left to the imagination of the audience. The important point, from Octavian's perspective back in Rome, was that there could no longer be any doubt about his rival's dynastic ambitions, as defined for him by his queen. By so ordering the ceremony and making the donations, Antony revealed himself to the eastern half of the empire as no longer just a Roman general holding a temporary command that might be withdrawn, but as a Hellenistic 'divine monarch', enjoying absolute sway for life, and with succession of his regal power passing to descendants of his and Cleopatra's blood.

The breach with the Octavians, brother and sister, was made inevitable by his further declaration that Caesarion was the legitimate son of Julius Caesar, and therefore, by implication, Caesar's true heir.[14] It is hard to think of anything Antony might have said that Octavian would have found more damaging to his personal interests. Yet there was no apparent advantage to Antony in making such a statement from a public platform. Any advantage could be expected to accrue only to Caesarion and his mother. Octavian's entire career was based on his unique position as Caesar's adoptive son and heir. Antony, with Cleopatra's encouragement as a rival wife, was perceived to be raising up a prince with a closer claim than he to be Caesar's son. Octavian could not tolerate that implicit threat to his power. War was now on the horizon, and it would be a fight to the death. Whether Antony intended such an outcome is perhaps open to doubt.

Early in 33 Octavian formally reported to the Senate the details of the Donations of Alexandria as part of a denunciation of Antony's allegedly un-Roman behaviour. A sharp riposte was not long delayed. Antony complained in writing about his rival's various breaches of good faith, not only over access to recruiting but also over his refusal to provide land on discharge for Antony's veterans while giving large quantities of it to his own. He also pointed out that Octavian had acted unilaterally, and therefore illegally under the triumviral form of government, in degrading Lepidus without his consent. He had received none of the fruits of the reconquest of Sicily, for which he had provided ships; and Octavian had kept all the surrendered legions of Lepidus and Sextus for himself instead of sharing them.

Those charges were undeniable. Octavian, by now a master of political invective, did not trouble to do so. Instead he made a blistering attack on Antony and his queen. It may have been at this time that Cleopatra's alleged boast that she would one day dispense justice from the Capitol in Rome was given its first airing. The truth of the charge scarcely mattered in the context of this mendacious war of words. Octavian's reply to Antony's justified complaint over land settlements was sufficient indication that sarcasm and cheap point-scoring had replaced the truth. Antony's veterans, he declared, had no genuine entitlement to Italian lands; they ought to be settled in the eastern countries which their leader claimed to have conquered – such as Media and Parthia. As for division of the spoils, he would be willing to divide Sicily with him if Antony would give him half of Armenia.[15]

The private correspondence of the two leaders was even less restrained. In reply to reproaches over his churlish treatment of Octavia and his relations with Cleopatra, Antony resorted to the language of the barrack-room. 'What's come over you?' he demanded. 'So what, if I *am* fucking the queen? Have I only just started on her – or isn't it nine years now? As for you, do you only fuck Drusilla [Livia]? Good for you, when you read this letter, if you don't fuck Tertulla or Terentilla or Rufilla or Salvia Titisenia or the whole lot of them. Does it really matter where – or in whom – you have your erection.'[16] Perhaps it was in response to this sexual innuendo that Octavian decided the time had come to extend the sacrosanctity of a tribune to both Livia and Octavia.

More positively, Octavian was now using his control of the capital to appeal directly to the citizens as a ruler who had their domestic interests at heart. He and his close associates at the head of the reconstituted Caesarian party began to use the national wealth or the profits from their military campaigns to improve daily life in Rome. Food for citizens was already subsidized. Agrippa, taking a step down in the *cursus honorum* by becoming aedile for 33, initiated a massive programme of public works, mending the neglected roads, cleaning out the sewers and, most beneficial of all, improving and expanding the supply of good drinking water. He restored the crumbling Aqua Marcia, which dated back to 144 BC, and built the first new aqueduct in the city for more than ninety years, named the Aqua Julia in honour of Octavian's adoptive clan.

Millions of man-hours must have been saved once that water flowed directly to the many parts of Rome that before had been totally dry, obviating the need for the inhabitants to carry laden containers excessively long distances on a daily basis. Agrippa and Octavian eventually added two more new aqueducts, making up for nearly a century of neglect by the optimate oligarchy, whose priorities did not include subsidized water for those too poor to live in the well-served districts. With typical forethought and efficiency, they also set up a permanent inspection service to ensure regular maintenance in the future.

A further example of the change of attitudes under Octavian's administration was that Agrippa did not merely order slave-gangs with shovels into the sewers, he went down with them in person and, where possible, sailed underground through the tunnels of the *Cloaca Maxima* to their outflow into the Tiber. Agrippa also marked his appointment by allowing free use of the public baths throughout his year of office, for both men and women, and provided them with free olive oil – it served as a cleansing agent before the discovery of soap.[17] His wealthy colleague Maecenas created a large public park, for any citizen and his family to walk in, on the on the site of a long-abandoned burial ground on the Esquiline Hill.

Octavian himself restored the extensive complex dominated by the Theatre of Pompey, in spite of the fact that it was where Caesar had been assassinated beside the statue of his eponymous adversary. Domitius Calvinus, twice a consul, in 53 and 40, who had later led a legionary army in Spain against rebellious tribes, poured some of the profits of his successful campaigns into restoring the fire-damaged Regia, one of the oldest and most revered buildings in Rome, where the state archives of the *Pontifex Maximus* were stored. Situated at the eastern end of the Forum, the Regia had been rebuilt once before, in stone, in the seventh century BC, to replace Bronze Age dwellings. Calvinus helped to promote a trend by reconstructing it in marble.[18]

The busy year of 33 was also the year of eight consuls, a quite unprecedented number. Octavian took up the office on January 1 and resigned it after just one day in order to promote a succession of his supporters for short periods to the coveted rank that would continue to be regarded as conferring nobility on the families of its holders. If he was going to risk provoking Antony to civil war he would need all the proconsular support he could get. He had already devalued to some extent the office of praetor, no fewer than sixty-seven of whom had been appointed in just one year, although it is not known how many of them may have been Antony's candidates.

Octavian was granted power by the Senate to create new patricians, who were urgently required – after the extinction of a number of ancient families during the wars – to fill vacancies among the various priestly orders of the state, because only the most aristocratic of men were deemed to enjoy the innate gift of interpreting the will of the gods. He chose them, of course, from families which he had reason to believe would be prepared to back his regime. At roughly the same time Agrippa ordered and oversaw the expulsion from Rome of astrologers and magicians. Octavian did not want to run the risk of unlicensed fortune-tellers predicting a future Antonian victory.[19]

The Triumvirate (according to most modern calculations) was due to end on 31 December 33. Octavian had no intention of renewing it as that would mean a fresh accommodation with his rival, whom he now hated and hoped to destroy. For the first time in more than ten years he held no official office, although he was still protected, in legal theory, by the sacrosanctity, but not the power, of the tribunate. He was about to demonstrate, in case anybody had forgotten, that his power rested on his command of the legions, not on any office of state, however exalted. Antony continued to call himself a triumvir, as if he alone had the power to say when he should quit; but at the same time he played to the optimate gallery by offering to give up that now defunct title, with a view to restoring the Republic, if Octavian would cooperate.

Both the new consuls for 32 were Antonian partisans: Gaius Sosius, who had placed Herod on the throne of Judaea after capturing Jerusalem in 37, and Domitius Ahenobarbus, now Antony's effective second-in-command. Octavian deliberately stayed away from the first meeting of the Senate to be held under their aegis. The general and the admiral carried a dispatch from their commander-in-chief, but did not read it out for fear it would harm Antony by its request for senatorial ratification of his recent acts, including the Donations of Alexandria. He and Cleopatra were currently wintering at Ephesus, in the province of Asia, along with his fleet and his reconstituted army, which had marched there in November, ostensibly in preparation for a renewed assault on Parthia.

By this time, Octavian was not alone in suspecting that those many legions were just as likely to be turned against himself. That fear gained wider credence when Sosius praised Antony to the Senate, attacked the record of Octavian and attempted to move a resolution against him. The precise terms are not known, but it seems to have been intended as some sort of censure motion. A tribune's veto prevented it from being put to the vote, no doubt to the relief of the vast majority of senators, who had no wish to risk showing hostility to one side or the other. Octavian's absence from the session and his temporary lack of an official position had encouraged some of his leading opponents to declare themselves, possibly as he had intended they should.

Octavian now struck back with a show of armed strength so menacing and effective that it amounted to a *coup d'état*. He returned to Rome with his army at his back, as he had done twice before, earlier in his career. The difference this time was that he now exercised direct and unfettered control over all the forces of the West – and nobody doubted his capacity to use them to overturn the state in his own interests and those of his party. Some of those soldiers stuck close to him when he entered the Senate House at its next meeting, to occupy the former triumviral position between the two consuls. His chief party loyalists among the senators crowded the benches nearest to him, concealing daggers under their togas.

Dio reports that his speech lasted a long time and was phrased moderately, although containing many accusations against both Antony and Sosius. That mention of moderation does not quite fit in with what happened after his peroration, in which he said he would bring documentary evidence to the next sitting of the Senate to prove his charges. Neither of the consuls dared to reply. Nor did anyone else. A profound silence reigned as the 29-year-old Octavian surveyed the ranks of his elders, evidently with a stony eye. Satisfied, no doubt, at the effect he had made, he stalked from the chamber with his military guards.[20]

Sosius and Ahenobarbus fled the city, and were promptly replaced as consuls. A substantial number of senators followed them to Antony at Ephesus, but a large majority, out of a total of more than a thousand, stayed in Rome. Octavian made no move to stop the exodus, announcing that whoever wanted to leave could do so. Other senatorial figures took the reverse option of leaving Antony to rejoin his rival while there was still time. Antony himself, filled with outrage, took the long meditated step of divorcing Octavia, and sent agents to his own home in the capital to turn her out. She left, in tears, with her own children and another of his by Fulvia, saying she did not want her brother and her ex-husband to go to war because of a quarrel over her.[21]

Among the deserters from Antony's senior ranks were Munatius Plancus, survivor of the Perusian war, and his son-in-law Marcus Titius, the recent executioner of Sextus Pompey. These two brought Octavian priceless information, not just of Antony's military dispositions – many others could provide such routine intelligence – but of the fact that he had made a deeply compromising will, and had left it in Rome. The Vestal Virgins, the will's custodians, refused to hand it over, but they sufficiently compromised their honour by indicating that if he wanted it he would have to come in person to get it. When he broke the seals he saw that it repeated the controversial assertion of Caesarion's parentage and confirmed the bequests to his children in line with the Donations of Alexandria. So much was already in the public domain. The new and damning revelation was of Antony's wish to be buried beside Cleopatra in her Alexandrian mausoleum (still under construction) even if he should die in the heart of Rome.

Octavian read the terms of the will, line by line, to an outraged Senate. The effect on public opinion was electric. Antony's own words seemed to confirm the truth of what Octavian had been suggesting: that his rival had gone native in the East. He not only preferred Cleopatra to Octavia, he evidently preferred Egypt to Rome.[22] As the news spread outwards across Italy and the West, a sea-change occurred in people's attitudes to the crisis. Now they were prepared to believe that Cleopatra's malign influence was behind a grand alliance of the East, assembled under Antony's banner, with the aim of sacking Rome and transferring the seat of imperial power to Alexandria.[23] More than that: they were ready, individually and collectively, to put up their hands and swear an oath of personal fealty to Octavian, as their champion against the Egyptian menace.

'The whole of Italy swore allegiance to me of their own free will,' he would write, with undiminished pride, some forty-five years later, near the very end of his long career, in his own *Res Gestae* ('My Exploits'), that extended epitaph, designed for inscription on marble as a permanent reminder to posterity. 'They chose me to be their leader in the victorious war of Actium. The provinces of Spain, Gaul, Africa, Sicily and Sardinia took the same oath. Those who served as soldiers under my standards included more than 700 senators.'[24]

We can be certain that the Caesarian party, now wholly behind Octavian, played a major role in ensuring the success of that massive vote of confidence in their leader represented by the swearing of the oath. Those provincials who had hitherto considered Rome a distant, anonymous power ruling their lives now had an individual effectively offering to be their patron by asking them as individuals to swear their personal allegiance to him. They would use that relationship in future years to claim his protection when it was needed –

none more dramatically than an old soldier, up on a charge, who called on the Princeps to defend him in court, on the grounds that he had never refused his help when asked to risk his life in battle. Octavian immediately took on the role of defence counsel.

The Senate deprived Antony of 'all authority', including his designated consulship for the following year. But it was upon Cleopatra alone that they and Octavian declared war. To ensure that it would be a *bellum iustum* ('a just war'), Octavian went through the prescribed ritual as a priest of the *fetiales*, whose twenty members existed for that purpose. Originally, a *fetialis* would enter enemy territory, announce the *casus belli* and call on Jupiter to acknowledge the justice of their cause. This would be followed by a cooling-off period of thirty-three days, during which the enemy could sue for peace or otherwise give satisfaction. After that interval, the *fetialis* would return to the border and cast a spear to penetrate enemy soil.

That ceremony had long been adapted to contemporary conditions, but its essentials remained intact. An open area representing enemy territory had been marked out in front of the Temple of Bellona, just outside the walls of Rome. Into this symbolic earth Octavian, in front of the assembled population, flung his spear.[25] The ancient rules had been followed, and the gods propitiated. The coming war would be as just as Octavian could bring himself to make it.

FIFTEEN

SUICIDE ON THE NILE

The motives and character of the adversaries were probably more significant for the outcome of the war than the question of who had the bigger army or navy. Octavian may have had little or no direct knowledge of Cleopatra but he knew his man. Antony plainly cherished an image of himself as a hard-fighting, hard-drinking, soldier-aristocrat, bestriding a world of lesser men. His response to Octavian's casting of the symbolic spear was predictable: he snatched it up in justifiable anger to hurl it back. He did not pause to reflect that their respective military forces were so evenly balanced that whoever was first to launch an all-out assault on the other would be taking the greater risk of defeat.

Octavian had been more cautious. His desire not to lose the war took precedence over any thoughts he might otherwise have entertained of winning it quickly. His primary objective was to hold fast to the power he had already won, hoping to increase it at his rival's expense if a clear opportunity arose. By persuading the Senate and People of Rome to declare war solely on Cleopatra and Egypt, he ensured that any move by Antony to support her would be interpreted as an attack on the Fatherland, not just on Octavian personally. That would automatically make Antony a public enemy, with all the disadvantages and dangers that entailed. His property would become liable for immediate seizure by the state; and any citizen, including the many thousands in his own army, would have the theoretical right and duty to kill him on sight.

Antony also had a strategic disadvantage to consider. Octavian did not need to deal a knock-out blow by sending an armada all the way to Egypt; he had the less risky option of defeating his enemy piecemeal, starting with those areas closest to Italy, such as Greece and Macedonia. Antony's most secure power base was with Cleopatra in Alexandria, so whatever part of the West he might choose to attack from there would be even further away from him than Parthia. While it might be easier to find an unopposed landing place in Spain or southern Gaul, that would mean his having to operate simultaneously from opposite ends of the Mediterranean. Italy, in any case, was no longer so vulnerable to a land invasion now that the narrow routes from both the north-west and north-east were permanently garrisoned in depth. Realistically, invasion of Italy by sea would appear to be his best option, even though Antony had tried that once before and nearly come to grief.

Antony's relationship with Cleopatra inhibited him from taking that course straight away. As chief paymaster of his army and fleet, she insisted on keeping close to him during the campaign, partly to protect her own political interests, which differed significantly from his, but chiefly, perhaps, because of her fear that, left to his own devices, he might be tempted to agree a peace settlement which involved Octavia. So well had Octavian done his work of demonizing Cleopatra in the eyes of the Roman public, that her physical presence would make it difficult, if not impossible, for Antony to invade mainland Italy without uniting the entire Western half of the empire against him. His solution to this dilemma seems to have been to try to lure Octavian abroad in order to engage and destroy him, whether on land or sea, before setting foot on Italian soil.

His first important move after giving the order at Ephesus to mobilize and strengthen his fleet was to call together those senators who had fled from Rome, and to form them into a rival Senate under their two serving consuls, Ahenobarbus and Sosius. That enabled him to reassert his original status as a no-nonsense Roman general, setting aside for the duration of the campaign his alternative persona as Hellenistic divine monarch. Cleopatra demonstrated her financial clout by giving him the immense sum of 20,000 gold talents[1] – ransom enough for a whole boatload of kings, but only a fraction of the treasure of the pharaohs. Herod, who wanted his balsam groves and bitumen back, advised Antony in a confidential aside to take the money and kill her.[2]

Antony was evidently determined not to make the same mistake of over-hastiness that had cost him so much against Parthia. He moved in measured stages towards his ultimate objective, hoping to provoke a response before reaching it. In April he set up fresh headquarters on the island of Samos, where his constantly growing fleet could be more conveniently berthed. In May he moved on to Athens, where a deputation of his Italian clients pleaded in vain for him to send Cleopatra back to Egypt. More and more ships joined him, fresh from the makers' yards, as the summer of 32 wasted away with no sign of activity from Octavian.

The new vessels were bigger even than the redesigned war-galleys which Agrippa had used with such effect to defeat Sextus Pompey. Some had eight or ten banks of oars, the upper ones so far above the water-line that rowing them needed more coordination of muscle-power than was entirely practicable. Their excessive height and weight, protected as they were by great baulks of timber reinforced with iron to withstand ramming, meant they displaced too much water to be other than slow, ponderous and hard to steer. Experience would soon prove that Agrippa had achieved a superior balance between speed and strength in the vital matter of ship design.[3]

Early in autumn, Antony led his armada, now 500-strong, around the rocky coast of the Peloponnese to the Ionian Sea, within striking distance of Tarentum and Brundisium, while some of his legions took the shorter land route. The population of Italy must have been trembling with apprehension, but Octavian's navy did not risk intervening at that stage. Antony put his fall-back plan into operation. Keeping north of the wide opening of the Gulf of Corinth, he took over the strategically important island of Leucas, just off the coast of Epirus, where it commanded the cramped entrance, formed by two narrow and opposing peninsulas, to the Gulf of Ambracia, which was virtually an inner sea.

The small town of Actium stood on the southernmost peninsula, and Antony fortified its jutting headland before introducing his ships into the protective oval of the gulf, where they would be largely immune from bad weather. At that stage, Octavian's rather smaller fleet came out of its ports to assess the situation, but sailed back home before Antony could deploy his slower vessels to engage them.[4] Cheated of a decisive battle, on either land or sea, Antony retired with Cleopatra to Patrae on the northern shore of the Peloponnese, to while away the winter. His many thousands of sailors were left to endure the primitive conditions of the Ambracian Gulf, which was stagnant and swampy in parts, and where sources of drinking water were limited and poor. When he returned in the spring it would be to find so many of them dead from 'disease' (presumably dysentery or malaria) that there would not be enough of them left to man all the ships.[5]

Octavian, meanwhile, had been struggling to contend with riots and arson in Rome because of popular resentment at the high taxes he was imposing to finance the war. Soldiers no longer came cheap, as they had done under the former regime. All citizens now had to pay a quarter of their annual income, while freedmen were milked, in addition, of one-eighth of their capital.[6] It was the freedmen who were suspected of starting the rash of fires. In spite of the unrest, however, Octavian was more firmly entrenched than ever, thanks to the nationwide oath of allegiance. And Antony's slow advance had exposed his strategy to detailed scrutiny by Octavian's war council, who had the lull of the winter months to prepare a response that would take maximum advantage of the enemy's obvious weak points.

Antony's troops, now in their winter quarters, were strung out along the whole of the western coast of the Peloponnese to its southerly extremity at Methone. The land could not support them indefinitely, so food would have to be brought in from abroad. In spite of the weather risks, therefore, grain ships set out from Egypt as early in the spring as they dared. Agrippa, too, decided to risk the storms. He captured Methone in a surprise attack by sea, put in a strong garrison and positioned part of his fleet there, effectively cutting off half of the enemy's supplies. Octavian himself crossed to the island of Corcyra (Corfu), from where he landed an army on the mainland coast, only two miles away. Then he marched rapidly south to take over and fortify the northern peninsula at the mouth of the Ambracian Gulf.[7]

Antony had made a mistake that was ultimately to prove fatal. By the time he reached the gulf from Patrae, Octavian had already built a large fort, along with a pair of high walls leading from it down to the sea, from where he could be provisioned and reinforced in relative safety. Next, Agrippa successfully stormed the island of Leucas, which dominated access to the gulf from the south, and was thus able to blockade the invasion fleet. Its big vessels could only get out of the gulf a few at a time, and were evidently vulnerable to concerted attack by his lighter, faster ships, especially in shallow coastal waters. Antony crossed in force from the south to besiege Octavian, but was unable either to outflank him or to breach his ramparts,[8] presumably because it proved impossible to carry big enough siege engines up the headland.

Agrippa added insult to injury by capturing Patrae, where Antony had wintered, after a sea battle. He sailed on eastwards past Delphi and took Corinth, which Antony had evidently failed to garrison adequately, even though the carriage of supplies across its isthmus was his last major supply route. As summer reached its height, Antony, dangerously short of food and plagued by malarial mosquitoes, gave up the siege and withdrew to his original camp on the southern peninsula. Local Greeks (including Plutarch's grandfather) were forced to bring in what supplies they could carry on their backs over mountain passes. Others, including under-age boys, were press-ganged into manning the oars of the bottled-up fleet.[9]

The trickle of desertions from his under-employed army began to reach alarming proportions. Eastern princes, including Herod, withdrew their contingents, hoping to be able to make a deal with Octavian. Even Domitius Ahenobarbus, now stricken with fever, left without a word. Antony sent his baggage after him, in recognition of his previous outstanding services and to demonstrate his own magnanimity, an empty gesture, since the fever proved to be terminal.[10] In any case, his army, of nineteen legions plus auxiliaries, now lacked a plausible offensive role in circumstances where Octavian was successfully exploiting the terrain itself as a means of defence, and had no intention of risking a land battle in open country.

Until Antony could extricate himself and his army, it would remain tactically almost as useless to him as his monstrous fleet, whose limitations, in terms of both mobility and command, Agrippa had so cruelly exposed. Thus, for the second time in five years, Antony had led a massive force to invade a distant country, in this case Italy, but had failed even to reach it. For the second time he had trapped himself in a situation of his own making from which the obvious solution was a fighting retreat, but where he had hung on hoping for better things until humiliation became inevitable. And it was the fourth time, counting back to Mutina and Brundisium, when he had started a major siege he could not finish, and would have to seek a way out. Perhaps Octavian, by comparison, was not quite such a poor soldier after all.

With autumn approaching, Antony called a council of war. Dio says it was to decide whether to stay and fight it out on the spot, or leave and resume the struggle elsewhere. The only serious question by that time, however, was whether Antony should retreat by sea or by land. If he marched away at the head of his legions he would be risking the loss of his disaffected fleet, and therefore his ability in the short term to invade Italy; but at least he would be fairly sure of keeping his army intact. Cleopatra, however, wanted to escape by sea, taking her sixty remaining ships and her war-chest. That way they could save a proportion of the fleet and still retain control of the legions. Her view prevailed over that of Antony's senior general, Canidius Crassus, who advised him to abandon the fleet and regroup the army in Macedonia.[11]

Cleopatra's advice was perfectly logical but it left out of account the effect their sudden departure by ship would have on the legions left waiting on the shore, not to mention the effect on those fighting with the fleet. Although he would have been much safer leading the army himself, Antony ordered Canidius to march east with it once the fighting at sea was over. In order to leave nothing behind for Octavian to seize, he also ordered the burning of the many surplus vessels that would not be able to participate because they still lacked crews. Octavian thus had a grandstand view from his fort of all that destructive activity within the gulf, making it plain that when the enemy fleet finally came out it would not be intending to return.

In such a context, the accounts of the battle of Actium in the ancient sources do not make much sense, especially not the traditional description of Cleopatra suddenly panicking in the middle of the conflict, and deciding unilaterally to hoist her sails for home.[12] That perhaps owes more to anti-Egyptian or anti-feminist prejudice than to rational analysis. The hazardous loading of her treasure, which might so easily sink to the bottom or be captured in battle, puts it beyond argument that, at the very least, both she and Antony envisaged a scenario in which her squadron would be protected by the rest of the fleet, presumably until such time as she and her cargo could get clear away. No doubt they still retained some hope of winning the sea battle that they could no longer avoid, but their basic objective must have been to break the blockade so that their forces could reunite in a more favourable spot further east. A second winter in the unhealthy gulf was unthinkable.

Antony had by now probably abandoned any prospect of an imminent invasion of Italy. It would be stretching the facts too far to assume that he had already lost the Battle of Actium before it began. But if, as seemed only too likely, he should fail to defeat Agrippa on the open sea, he would be able to confirm the orders for his waiting army to march back through Macedonia, possibly as far as Asia, while he and Cleopatra, by prearranged signal, made good their own escape by sailing back around the Peloponnese. Cleopatra could then return to Alexandria while Antony moved to redeploy his forces, probably transferring legions from other provinces to counter any thrust from Octavian.

On the morning of 2 September Agrippa was waiting for them as they emerged from the gulf. They sat on their oars until Cleopatra's squadron had taken up its rearguard position, supposedly to stop desertions by any of the 20,000 troops, mostly auxiliaries and including archers, on board the forward ships. Antony, on the extreme right in his flagship, engaged the left of Agrippa's line, but his forces were evidently outnumbered by men who had already demonstrated their superior seamanship and fighting quality. When a gap eventually opened up in the battle line, the queen gave a signal and passed through it with her entire squadron. It may well be the case that she acted earlier than was absolutely necessary, but the alternative would have been to risk closure of the gap. Antony abandoned his flagship for an unencumbered, faster galley to follow her lead – betraying, as Plutarch says, the men who were still fighting and dying for his cause. He was followed by about forty of his own ships, to add to the queen's sixty. He transferred to her flagship and spent the first few days of the voyage sitting alone in the prow, apparently too depressed for conversation.[13]

Octavian, in charge of the right of Agrippa's temporarily breached line, must have been as thunderstruck as everybody else by Antony's departure, if not by Cleopatra's. Perhaps it was only after his and Cleopatra's sails vanished over the southern horizon that he could have been totally assured that Antony had abandoned his army and was not coming back. Even then, he would have known only that he had won the immediate battle, not that he had actually won the war. The Antonian fleet soon surrendered once his men were convinced that their chief had left them to their fate. The squadron immediately opposite Octavian struck its colours quickly enough for its commander, Sosius, the former consul who had attacked him in the Senate at the beginning of 32, to secure a full pardon. As for Canidius, he tried repeatedly to make the legions follow the orders of their commander-in-chief to march back east, but was lucky to escape with his life when they mutinied.[14]

The troops had had enough of Antony. To risk losing one army after a fruitless siege, as at Mutina, could be put down to misfortune. To risk a second, as at Brundisium, was carelessness. The third and fourth such fiascos, at Phraaspa and Actium, were evidence of serial incompetence, made worse by the perception that he had now left them in the lurch to save his own skin. The nineteen legions held out for a few days after the battle, but only to secure better terms for themselves by negotiation. The war was effectively over. Octavian's messengers carried news of his victory so quickly around the empire that by the time Antony arrived off Cyrenaica, on the North African coast, intending to take command of the four legions he had posted there, his former subordinate general, Pinarius Scalpus, ordered him not to land.[15] His other main military reserve, the legions stationed in Syria, also declared for Octavian.

Back in Italy the announcement of the victory meant

'drinking and dancing' for everyone, according to Horace, in a celebratory ode that heaps abuse on Cleopatra:

> Before this day it would have been a sin
> To tap the vintage from the family store,
> While the mad queen with her perverted power
> Plotted destruction to Rome's Capitol –
> She and her foul and pestilential crew![16]

Horace adds that 'scarcely one ship' of the enemy fleet escaped being set on fire, a brazen lie on the part of the regime (which supported him as a court poet), seeking to give the impression that the muddled anticlimax of Actium had been a titanic struggle by the heroic Octavian against the forces of evil, represented by the *fatale monstrum* (fatal prodigy) of the East, Cleopatra.[17]

Once he knew that total victory was certain, Octavian did not trouble to pursue the losers immediately. That could wait upon his leisure as unchallenged master of the whole Roman Empire. More urgent was the need to organize the discharge of the tens of thousands of surplus soldiers left on his hands – a danger to themselves and others so long as they continued to congregate in arms. He was also moved to feed the starving millions of Greece, who had suffered blockade and the seizure of their harvest. Having set in motion the necessary administrative wheels to accomplish those objectives, Octavian did not return to Italy but moved further east, to Athens, where he visited the Orphic cult site of Eleusis and may have become an initiate of the so-called 'mysteries' there.[18]

We must not assume that this was merely a touristic visit to satisfy idle curiosity. As a man who evidently believed himself to be in some important way associated with Apollo, he may well have been a genuine seeker after enlightenment. It is unlikely to have been entirely a coincidence that an ancient temple dedicated to Apollo dominated the peninsula of

Actium, and that as soon as practicable after the battle he presented himself at Eleusis, where the supposed writings of Apollo's legendary son Orpheus were cherished. Initiates hoped for a numinous experience that would reveal to them secrets of life and death, and of life after death. Whether Octavian underwent such an experience, or thought he did, is not recorded.

He had not intended to go back to Italy before settling the problems of postwar governance that had now arisen in the East, but a mutiny among the troops forced his return from Samos. The voyage, in midwinter, might well have cost him his life. His ship ran into two successive storms that swept the deck clear of rigging and spars before limping into Brundisium. He calmed the soldiers with promises of gratuities and land settlements to be financed from the annexation of Egypt, where Antony, in a ferocious sulk, had gone to live a hermit-like existence in an isolated hut on the Alexandrian shore. Antony, in fact, returned to the palace before too long to carouse with Cleopatra, but he had plainly given up hope of a come-back.

Octavian was saved from having to deal personally with an assassination plot against himself, because Maecenas had uncovered it at an early stage in Rome. The leader was Marcus Lepidus, son of the disgraced former triumvir of the same name. The young man's good looks, we are told, were 'better than his brains'. Marcus had married the same Servilia to whom Octavian himself had been briefly betrothed in 43, before he had been obliged to cast her off in favour of Antony's stepdaughter, Claudia. When Marcus was executed, the brave Servilia committed suicide, in line with the traditions of her family.[19]

After no more than a month in Italy, Octavian sailed east again, and removed from power a number of the petty princelings whom Antony had appointed, but he did not dismiss any of the leading potentates of the region. Their kingdoms were earmarked to become part of the empire, but the victorious general had more urgent priorities for the present than to commit resources to wholesale incorporation. They would be absorbed one at a time later. Herod was allowed to retain his territories in return for submission and a stiff contribution to the war's expenses. Antony and Cleopatra jointly sent envoys to Octavian, but with varying proposals. She offered to abdicate in favour of her children; he, according to two different accounts, asked to be allowed to live privately, in either Alexandria or Athens – or, alternatively, he is reported to have offered to kill himself if Cleopatra would be spared. Octavian gave an encouraging reply to the queen, but he did not deign to answer his defeated enemy.[20]

By the summer of 30, Octavian had marched down through the Levant from Syria to reach the Egyptian border, while Cornelius Gallus, commanding the legions of Africa and Cyrenaica, entered the country from the west to complete a giant pincer movement. Antony thereupon challenged Octavian to personal combat to prevent a clash of armies; Octavian replied that he could think of other ways for Antony to die. On 31 July his vanguard arrived at the outskirts of Alexandria, only to be promptly scattered by a cavalry assault led by Antony. It proved to be his last gasp. Next day, all Antony's remaining troops surrendered, along with the fleet. He returned to the city to be told that Cleopatra had committed suicide. Delaying no longer, he stabbed himself in the belly with his sword.[21]

As all the world knows, Cleopatra had not in fact killed herself, but had pretended to do so, before taking refuge on an upper floor of her mausoleum near the Temple of Isis. She had collected together all her richest and most beautiful treasures – gold and silver and ivory, with emeralds, pearls and other gems – and placed them on a pyre of firewood and tow, prepared to set them alight at need or, more likely, use them as bargaining counters. Antony, unable to walk, was carried to a spot beneath her window, from where she and her maids, Iras and Charmian, hoisted him up painfully to their level by ropes. She tore off her dress to spread over him, and lacerated her naked breasts with her own nails. Antony asked for wine, and drank a little before dying in her arms.[22]

Someone carried to the victor the sword with which Antony stabbed himself, still with his blood on the blade. Octavian is said to have wept over it.[23] Meanwhile, two of his officers had been trying to negotiate with Cleopatra though a grille in a door on the ground floor of the mausoleum. One of them, Proculeius, climbed to an upper window while his colleague kept her talking. Proculeius got inside in time to stop her stabbing herself. She was removed to the palace and kept under guard in a chamber where Octavian went to see her. Plutarch says she had deliberately abandoned her extravagant way of life, and was lying on a plain pallet, wearing only a tunic, when the conquerer entered.

The scene is presented as a case of West meeting East. Octavian apparently held aloof while Cleopatra, springing up with a wild expression on her face, cast herself at his feet. Her voice trembled as she tried to justify her actions as having been forced on her by Antony. Her hair was untidy, her eyes sunken and her breasts still bore the marks of her nails; but (Plutarch affirms) she had not entirely lost her legendary charm, nor even her confidence, which both continued to show themselves through the mobility of her features. Octavian advised her to sit down – and then proceeded by logical exposition to reject her excuses, point by point.

Cleopatra changed her tactics and begged for mercy for herself and her children. She produced a list of what she claimed were all her most precious possessions, only to have her words denied by her steward, Seleucus, who said she had hidden some. While Octavian watched in some amusement, she grabbed Seleucus by the hair and punched him in the face. She excused herself, after Octavian finally intervened to part them, by saying she had held back a few items to give to Livia and Octavia in the hope that they would intercede with him on her behalf. He replied that she would be free to do anything of that sort, and added that in more important matters he would treat her with more generosity than she had a right to expect.[24]

After he had left her, she was told by a young aristocrat, Cornelius Dolabella, who had apparently fallen under her spell, that Octavian planned to send her and her children away within three days – presumably by ship to Rome – while he marched back via Syria. Cleopatra suspected, probably correctly, that he intended to make her walk as a prisoner behind his chariot during his triumphal parade in front of the Roman mob. That would have been too degrading to bear. Death, for her, would be preferable. She was granted permission to pour libations for Antony at his tomb. Clasping the urn containing his ashes, she told Iras and Charmian that the grief she was suffering at her own downfall was as nothing compared with the few days she had had to live on without him.

She went from the tomb to the palace, where she closed the doors of her suite on herself and her two maids. She had a bath and a sumptuous meal before dressing as if for a state occasion.[25] 'Give me my robe, put on my crown,' Shakespeare makes her say, evidently working with the Elizabethan translation of Plutarch, by Sir Thomas North, open in front of him. 'I have immortal longings in me.'[26] She had already arranged for an Egyptian peasant to call with a basket of figs, in which was concealed a deadly asp. The snake was sacred to the Sun; its bite would deify her. Plutarch's description of her embracing the asp inspired Shakespeare to create what is surely the most poignant image in the play:

> . . . Peace! Peace!
> Dost thou not see my baby at my breast,
> That sucks the nurse asleep.[27]

When Octavian's men forced the doors they found her lying lifeless on a golden bed, with Iras dying at her feet.

Charmian, still just able to stand, was trying to rearrange the royal diadem on her mistress's head. A guard demanded of her if her action was well done. North's translation has her reply, before falling dead: 'Very well, and meet for a princess descended from the race of so many noble kings.' Shakespeare is not abashed to repeat it almost word for word:

> It is well done, and fitting for a princess
> Descended of so many royal kings.[28]

At that point Cleopatra and her faithful maids pass into legend, where we can no longer follow them. Octavian, moved by the nobility of her spirit and her end, ordered a funeral of appropriately regal magnificence for her to be laid to rest beside Antony. Aged only thirty-nine, she had reigned as queen for twenty-two years. Octavian killed both Caesarion, her son by Julius Caesar, and Antyllus, Antony's eldest son by Fulvia. Each of them had been enrolled by Antony in his army, so legally they were enemy soldiers. Either of them, left alive, might have provided a focus for future rebellion. The rest of the children he spared.[29] He was apparently hoping to make a name for himself for clemency.

SIXTEEN

THE TRANSFORMATION OF THE STATE

After quitting Alexandria, Octavian spent as little time in the East as he could safely contrive. It was not just cynical propaganda that he had projected against Cleopatra, as representing a sinister Oriental threat to Roman civilization. He believed the basic truth of what he had been saying, even if some of his actual charges were exaggerated for rhetorical effect. Egypt and some of the Asian countries may have had advanced civilizations for thousands of years, but Octavian held that the values of the more recent Western societies were infinitely superior, especially those of Rome and Greece. He visited the pyramids and inspected the mummified remains of Alexander the Great, but when asked if he would like to view the tombs of the pharaohs, he retorted: 'I came to see a king – not corpses!'[1]

He took over Egypt as his personal domain, along with all its treasures, and so became regarded by the inhabitants as their absentee pharaoh; he governed the ancient land through a prefect who reported to him personally, not to the Senate. Senators, in fact, were not allowed to set foot there without his express permission, which seems to have been rarely requested once it became clear that simply asking would arouse suspicion about their motives. The country was too valuable for him to risk its falling into the hands of a leading Roman politician in charge of an army. The succession of prefects who would rule there in his place would never be of a higher rank than that of knight.

The effects of Antony's 'Donations of Alexandria' were, of

course, nullified. Cyrene and Cyprus reverted to being provinces of the empire. Herod eventually got his balsam groves back, along with most of Palestine, previously under Cleopatra's rule. He also attracted the secretarial and diplomatic services of Nicolaus of Damascus, who had been tutor to her children, and would become Octavian's biographer. Octavian himself marched back through the Levant to Syria and the province of Asia, where he restored some works of art which Antony had looted. He had the satisfaction of executing Caesar's last surviving assassin, the otherwise unknown Cassius of Parma. But he gave a surprisingly friendly interview to the ambassadors of King Phraates of Parthia. It was a sign of future intent.

After wintering on the Greek island of Samos, where Antony had based himself less than three years earlier, Octavian travelled home to Italy via Corinth and the sea route past Actium. Taken ill at Brundisium, he convalesced in Campania, where Virgil read him the *Georgics*, that series of pastoral poems imbued with a love of the Italian countryside and its rustic ways that Octavian so obviously shared.[2] Thus fortified emotionally after his uncongenial year in the East, he entered Rome to a welcome fit for a semi-divine hero. By decrees of the Senate, his name was henceforth to be chanted in priestly litanies as the saviour of his native land, and libations were ordered to be poured to him at all banquets as if he were indeed a god.

For the first time since the founding of the Republic, the magistrates walked behind his triumphal chariot, instead of in front of it, when he celebrated his victories of Illyricum, Actium and Alexandria on three successive days in mid-August, the month that was now to be named after him.[3] Cleopatra's three children by Antony – Alexander Helios, Cleopatra Selene and little Ptolemy Philadelphus – had to march in the parade. Octavia was bringing them up as if they were her own, according to the ancient sources, although it is disturbing that we never hear anything further of the two boys. The girl, however, would grow up to marry King Juba II of Mauretania.

A few days after his triple triumph, Octavian continued to repay some of his immense debt to Caesar by dedicating the Temple of Divus Julius and inaugurating the new Senate House, called the Curia Julia, which Caesar himself had begun to build about fifteen years earlier in the new Forum that bore his name. Later, Octavian dedicated a huge new Temple of Apollo on the Palatine Hill near his home, witnessing to the role he believed the god had played in helping him beat the alien Cleopatra. The Senate had already voted to close the doors of the Temple of Janus to signify that Rome was everywhere at peace. That was not strictly true – a few tribes were still causing problems in both Gaul and Spain – but it was a fitting farewell to the series of bloody civil wars that had begun twenty years before, when Caesar crossed the Rubicon. Octavian cemented his popularity with the ordinary citizens of the capital by giving them cash donations out of his war-booty, and forgiving all arrears of unpaid taxes. Under the flood of imported wealth, local interest rates plunged by two-thirds.[4]

Confident of ultimate victory, Octavian had not waited for the demise of Antony and Cleopatra before considering the means and the manner by which he would rule the huge empire which had now fallen whole into his hands. In the century between the killing of Tiberius Gracchus and the defeat of Antony, the Roman Republic had degenerated from a system of elective annual magistracies, effectively controlled by a Senate of elders, to a murderous political arena dominated by rival warlords. Marius and Sulla, Pompey and Caesar, Antony and Octavian had successively adapted the constitution on an *ad hoc* basis to serve their particular needs of the moment. So far, only Sulla had gone on to try to create a permanent settlement, but his solution of turning the clock back in favour of a discredited minority of aristocrats doomed it to failure.

Caesar had been in the best position to impose a genuinely new settlement to reflect the changed needs of empire, but his planned invasion of Parthia at the time of his assassination showed he had not understood that the situation demanded peaceful consolidation of his regime, not risky adventurism. Antony, who perhaps had more in common with the attitudes of Pompey than with those of Caesar, emerged initially as a conciliator but ultimately proved a more divisive leader than any of them. Who can doubt that, if he had won the civil war, he would have treated both Rome and her empire as existing chiefly to feed his craving for personal glory – and would have led an even bigger army against Parthia to wipe out the stain of his earlier humiliation?

A different set of priorities was motivating Octavian as he contemplated the opportunities that Fortune and his own efforts had placed before him. Unlike Antony, whom he must surely have marked down as a shallow, vain, posturing, self-indulgent loser, who was, to cap it all, a reckless and incompetent general, Caesar's heir knew his business. Not for him the puerile fantasy of outdoing Alexander the Great as an intrepid conqueror of far-off kingdoms. He would make Parthia respect and fear him without the need for war. And he would, even so, eclipse Alexander's record by ruling a mightier empire with a firm but ultimately benign hand, as the true benefactor of his people.

To achieve that goal he was concerned to apply cosmetic, as well as radical, surgery to the ravaged body of the Republic, so as to disguise his own absolute power, based as it was on direct military force. He was to write in the *Res Gestae* at the end of his life:

In my sixth and seventh consulships [28–27 BC], after I had extinguished civil war, and by universal consent had power over all things, I transferred the Republic from my power into the control of the Senate and People of Rome. For this meritorious service I was named *Augustus* by the Senate's decree, and the door-posts of my home were publicly wreathed in laurel, and a civic crown (of oak leaves) was fixed above my door. A golden shield, placed in the Curia Julia (Senate House), was given to me by the Senate and People of Rome for my courage, my clemency, my justice and my piety, as stated in the inscription upon it. After that time I excelled in authority all other men, even though I had no greater power than the rest, who were my colleagues in the magistracy.[5]

That remarkable statement, which will probably strike the modern reader as boastful in the extreme, cannot be taken at face value. It is possible to construct a lawyer's argument to justify it in terms of legal technicalities, but its central claim is based on a lie so gross and outrageous as to baffle adequate description. Octavian did not transfer the Republic from his power. He continued to cling to that as tenaciously as ever. What he effectively did was allow some of the senators to share part of the work that was necessary to keep the empire in existence, and which he could not do all by himself. No senator of whom he seriously disapproved got the chance to do even that.

It is at this point in his career that we can detect, between the lines of the sources, the reality of Octavian in his mature role as the Godfather of Rome, grave and upright in public, affable but also sinister in private, manipulating men by a mixture of promises and implicit threats, in order to make things happen the way he wants them to happen. Along with the power of the army, which he can use to to kill anyone he chooses, he has great tact and patience, as well as genuine *auctoritas*. He knows the psychology of ambitious men and will take pains to try to win them to his side. Now that he has no conceivable rival he can afford to bide his time, select those who, in private face-to-face interviews, give satisfactory answers to his probing questions – or put a permanent blight on their careers (or worse) if they do not.

Few of the senators will have been under any illusions

about the limits of their freedom to stray from the path being mapped out for them. One by one, they will have looked into his eyes – more like those of a horse than a human, according to one source[6] – and made their decision either to accept his terms and be accorded the traditional respect appropriate to a magistrate, or reject them and dwindle in status, ultimately to disappear from the public record. Octavian knew that careful selection from among the many available candidates would produce enough for Rome's requirements, and he seems to have had a talent for picking the right type of man, who would serve him and the state well.

But what he was doing would have been judged to be criminal if he had genuinely restored the Republic and its laws. It was criminality, however, that had served him so well from the beginning of his career; it was what enabled him to destroy the Republic in the first place. Now that he had become the one who effectively made and interpreted the laws, and could not be brought before a court, he was in a position to rebuff, with every sign of indignation, any suggestion that he was other than *primus inter pares* ('first among equals'), or that his real power was unconstitutional and illegal. Without the full support of the army, however, he would long ago have been swept aside – demoted, disgraced, pauperized, exiled, perhaps even strangled in prison or flogged to death as a public enemy.

So his claim that his power was no greater than that of other magistrates of similar rank was just as bogus as his claim to have transferred the Republic from his own power into the control of the Senate and People. Had he wished to do so, he could have posted up new proscription lists in the Forum and waited at his leisure while underlings did the dirty work of execution for him. None of his other 'colleagues in the magistracy' had that power. But Octavian wanted no more political killing if he could avoid it. He had set his sights on a higher goal, and he would spend the rest of his Principate trying to achieve it.

He had every right to be proud of what he had recently done, whether illegal or not, to justify the uprecedented honours heaped on him by the senior representatives of a grateful nation, including the descriptive name of Augustus, which can be translated as 'consecrated one' or 'illustrious one', and which is connected with the taking of auguries. His restraint in using his frightening power, combined with his diplomacy in ultimately winning the approval of many of those who once considered themselves to be his natural enemies, would convert his merely military victories into a lasting peace that would embrace all sections of society, including a majority even of the aristocracy.

The verdict of an involved contemporary, Velleius Paterculus (admittedly a partisan), is not too far removed from the truth in this rare burst of eloquence from his usually plodding pen:

> After twenty years the civil war was ended, foreign conflicts buried, peace recalled, the fury of arms stilled, the rule of law restored along with the authority of the courts and the majesty of the Senate . . . Husbandry returned to the fields, respect to religion, security to mankind, with each man safe in the possession of his property. Existing laws were usefully amended, and new laws introduced for the health of society. The Senate was reformed without harshness but not without severity. The leading men – those who triumphed and held the highest positions – were urged on by the Princeps to ornament the city.[7]

Octavian's motto of 'make haste slowly' was never to be used to greater effect than in this phase of his career when his primary aim was to win the confidence of his people as a whole. His first purely political task was the updating of the Senate's membership rolls. Its importance was made obvious to everyone by the appointment of both Octavian himself and his chief lieutenant Agrippa as consuls for successive years

(28 and 27), with the added function of censors. The pre-Actium Senate had numbered more than a thousand members, of whom as many as 300 may have deserted to Antony. That estimate depends on subtracting from the overall total the 'more than 700' mentioned in the *Res Gestae* as having joined in the war on Octavian's side; the actual strength of the defectors may have been well below 300. The truly surprising aspect of the revision of membership, however, is that the two consuls do not seem to have discriminated, at that stage, specifically against surviving Antonians.

Even if that were only partly true – the evidence is not conclusive – it would be a fact of the highest importance for gauging the breadth of Octavian's appeal since Actium, and his confidence in apparently gambling his political future on the Senate's response to his policy and programme. He and Agrippa produced a list of about 200 names of men they considered to be no longer suitable to serve as senators, but the criteria for excising them appears to have been such non-political grounds as failure to meet the financial requirements or a bad moral reputation. No known supporter of Antony is named as having been expelled.[8]

Even after identifying the candidates for expulsion, the consuls were anxious not to seem too heavy-handed. They devoted much time to attempts to persuade the prodigals to leave gracefully with their reputations still reasonably intact. It was only after they had secured the resignations of about fifty of them that they moved reluctantly to expel the obdurate 150 or so who were still trying to cling on. Using the powers he had been voted earlier, Octavian created a number of new patricians from among the upper ranks of the plebeian aristocracy, but in their case it would beggar belief if he did not use that right of patronage to reward his own most faithful followers. The outcome was a Senate of about 800 members, still too large for efficiency but a first step in the shrinkage Octavian was determined to apply.

He and Agrippa also carried out in 28 the first census for over forty years. They and their teams of monitors throughout the empire produced a final list of 4,063,000 citizens. That was four times as many as were recorded during the previous census in 69, which, admittedly, was never fully completed but is believed to have covered the great majority of eligible names.[9] The huge increase no doubt reflected in part the numbers who had acquired citizenship through service in the legions or manumission from slavery, in addition to the patronage of rival dynasts eager to secure loyal support in Italy and the provinces. As the entire population of the city of Rome, including its many ineligible women, children and slaves, is usually estimated to have been much less than a million at this period, the outcome of the census puts into perspective the supposed democratic value of a citizen's vote, when each one, to be valid, had to be cast in person in the capital itself, often at short notice, in an area that could cope with only a few thousand people at a time.

If the old optimate oligarchy had been unrepresentative of citizen opinion before, it was even less representative now. And if Octavian no longer felt an urgent need to expel former enemies from the Senate, that would indicate it was not only the soldiers who had become disillusioned with Antony, but the mass of those four million citizens, for whom Octavian represented their best – perhaps their only – chance of peace. They would demonstrate again and again during the next forty years their desire and determination that only he should reign, whatever he might choose to call himself. In fact he chose to be known as *Princeps* – a word without threatening overtones, familiar for centuries in its plural form, *principes*, as designating the most senior members of the Senate. In Octavian's case, however, the title of Princeps meant much more than simply 'the First Senator'. His powers were just as extensive as those exercised by Caesar, but he was to respond to insistent public demands that he should declare himself dictator by tearing open his clothing, baring his chest and declaring that he would sooner be stabbed to death than accept any such title.[10]

That, of course, was a piece of street theatre to impress the groundlings. His true position, when he returned to Rome as ultimate victor in the civil war, was as the head of a political party which had grown to mass proportions under his leadership. From its first appearance as a single-issue splinter group of the Caesarian faction, campaigning for vengeance against the assassins, it had absorbed all its early rivals, multiplied its support many times over by championing traditional Roman ways against the alleged cultural and military menace of the East, and was now reaching out to the very people who had tried originally to crush it underfoot. Octavian could not, even had he wanted to, draw back from the path of sovereign rule on which he was set, without wrecking the careers and risking the lives of all those many individuals who had worked so devotedly for him and his cause for up to fifteen years.

Genuine restoration of the Roman Republic would have reawakened the ghosts of Cato and Cassius, Brutus and Cicero, to enter the souls of their lineal descendants, provoking them to seize once more as their birthright the lion's share of imperial riches, squash the upwardly mobile middle classes back down into their old inferior places, deny public help to the poor and use their monopoly of the courts to hound the Caesareans to destruction. Octavian and his inner circle of advisers had worked out a sophisticated plan of campaign,[11] of which an essential preliminary step was, paradoxically, to repeal all the emergency measures he himself had taken, during the period of the Triumvirate and later, which infringed republican law. That cleared the decks sufficiently for him to deliver his master-stroke at a meeting of the reformed Senate on 13 January 27, his offer to 'restore control of the Republic to the Senate and People of Rome'.

It was certainly a dramatic moment. But a substantial section of the senatorial audience not only knew what was coming but had evidently been coached in advance for the roles which their reformed Caesarean party expected them to play. The slight figure of the 35-year-old Octavian – no doubt wearing the thick-soled sandals he favoured for public occasions to project his height above his own modest 5ft 6in – rose to speak at the magistrates' bench in the middle of the long rectangular chamber of the crowded Curia Julia. Calmly, he announced that he was relinquishing, there and then, all his power over the Republic and empire except what limited amount he was temporarily entitled to as one of the two legally appointed consuls for that year.[12]

While those not in the secret wondered if they could believe their ears, and sat in shock trying to digest the implications of his words, a volley of protests began to sweep around the benches of his chief supporters, and swelled to a roar. Did he no longer care for the safety of Rome? How could he abandon them after he had done so much, over such a long period, to save the nation from its enemies? The gods themselves would surely be angry if he were to give up now! Like any twentieth-century dictator in a one-party state, pretending a principled aversion to the naked power he intended to maintain and increase, Octavian protested in his turn the seriousness and finality of his decision.

Little by little, in response to the apparently heart-rending pleas of members of his tame supporting cast, he allowed himself to yield in part to the unremitting pressure. Neutral senators no doubt began to realize that unless they joined in the clamour for him to relent they risked being identified as hard-line opponents of his regime.[13] By the time Octavian agreed to reconsider his position the Senate's vote could no longer be in doubt. He agreed to retain responsibility for those provinces alone where peace, in spite of the closure of Janus's Temple, could not be guaranteed to continue unbroken. He named Gaul, Spain, Syria, Egypt, Cilicia and Cyprus. It was no coincidence that most of the legions were based in those countries.

The remainder of the provinces, with only a handful of legions among them – in such frontier areas as Illyricum, Macedonia and Africa – he handed over to the Senate's jurisdiction. They were free, he said, to appoint governors drawn by lot from among their senior members, exactly as in the pre-triumviral period, to serve for one year each. His provinces, however, would be grouped together as one overall proconsular command, for ten years, not under governors but under legates whom he would appoint, and who would report directly to him.[14] There was a republican precedent for such a system, which the Senate had voted to Pompey during his years as commander-in-chief of Spain, when he had remained in Italy, just outside the city limits of Rome, while his own appointees led the Spanish legions.

Octavian's concession of control over the less-endangered provinces was more apparent than real. Unlike Pompey, he would be able to remain inside the capital itself because of his *imperium* as a serving consul, which would also give him a theoretical right, in an emergency, to take over any troops stationed there or even in provinces under the nominal command of senatorial governors. Those were legal niceties: no one doubted that he could take over any legions he needed, whatever his precise constitutional position. His new punctiliousness over following legal forms, however, helped to restore credibility to the entire legal system of courts and judges and the rule of law. He wanted to demonstrate that he did not consider himself above the law. But like the consummate politician he was, he used his new ten-year proconsular *imperium* to dismiss the existing governors of the 'military provinces' and replace them mostly with officers who were not members of the Senate. By purging most of the army of its overtly political generals, cast in the aristocratic independent mould, he made it almost impossible for any potential rival from that background to mount a serious military challenge.

Nevertheless, the Senate gladly took over responsibility for choosing the limited number of governors permitted by

Octavian's gesture. It was the first time since the formation of the Triumvirate fifteen years earlier that they had been able to carry out such a task unhindered. Octavian, true for the time being to the letter of his agreement, did not interfere, beyond stipulating that no senatorial governor should wear military uniform or carry a sword. He had already vetted every single member of the Senate for suitability, and such was the mood of the wider electorate that no candidate for a magistracy could currently win election without his acquiescence, if not necessarily his *imprimatur*. Dio dates the effective establishment of Octavian's monarchy from this period.[15]

Octavian no doubt returned that night in fine spirits to his new home on the Palatine to announce to Livia and Octavia the completion of a good day's work. He was now beyond reach of legal challenge. The chief source of his power, direct control of the army, had been confirmed almost in its entirety by the highest constitutional body in the empire. For his former ally, Cicero, the Senate had been both a source of power and a means to power. Under Octavian it had become a stage where his own personal, military-based power achieved social acceptance and demonstrated its respectability as an arm of civil authority.

The Senate also voted to double the pay of his recently reconstituted Praetorian Guard, which he had posted at strategic points, chiefly around central Italy and in Rome itself, to be on instant call if he should suddenly need the backing of its elite personnel against any opposition, even opposition by the Senate itself. With the brand-new name of Imperator Caesar Augustus, his original identity of plain Gaius Octavius had receded further than ever into what must have been fast becoming a scarcely imaginable past. Coupled with the dawn chorus of prayers for his health and long life that now ascended from a thousand-and-one shrines and temples around the Empire, these new honours, reinforced powers and intensified personal security had raised him to an apparently superhuman sphere of existence.[16]

It would be a mistake, however, to suppose that Octavian's only motive in staging the charade before the Senate was to enhance his own power. During the years of struggle he had come to take seriously, as a standard to aim for, an idealized view of his country's past, which was to reach its fullest expression in the works of Virgil and of the historian Livy (Titus Livius), who benefited from his patronage. In Livy's perspective it was taken as axiomatic that, in former times, a true Roman served the state for the benefit of the state, not for the benefit of himself and his immediate family. His history of early Rome is replete with examples, such as the legendary exploit of Horatius, who is said to have held back an entire Etruscan army with the help of only two comrades while the bridge over the Tiber behind them was dismantled to save the city;[17] Horatius acted for no material reward but because he could imagine no nobler death than one in defence of Rome.

The same thought was expressed by Livy's contemporary, the poet Horace (Quintus Horatius Flaccus), in the best-known line of Latin poetry to be found untranslated in a twentieth-century English poem:

Dulce et decorum est pro patria mori![18]

Horace, who had fought on the losing side at Philippi and been pardoned by Octavian, wrote of the sweetness of dying for one's country as an incentive to Roman youth to man the legions; Wilfred Owen, sick of the horrific sights of death in the trenches of the First World War, wrenched it from its context to make an explosive ending to a poem *against* war.[19] Horace, however, was less concerned to glorify militarism than to draw attention to the need for each generation of his countrymen to be ready and able to defend their homeland. That would scarcely be possible, according to Augustan thinking, unless they were brought up from boyhood to be hardy and virtuous like their peasant ancestors. What would happen if the present generation of parents were to be so corrupted by luxury and idleness as to sink into decadence?

> Not from such parents did the young men rise
> Who stained the waves with bold Phoenician blood
> And slew great Hannibal – Antiochus
> And Pyrrhus, too – but from a manly line
> Of soldiers: peasant boys trained up to break
> The stubborn earth with spades, and chop the wood
> To carry home at their stern mother's call.[20]

We must make allowance for the fact that Horace, according to his own testimony, was forced by 'audacious poverty' to write poetry,[21] and became rich under the patronage of both Octavian and Maecenas, who set him up in a country estate, which often featured in his work as if it were a simple peasant's holding. There he praised rural life and simple pleasures. His home, he writes, is not constructed of marble beams quarried in Africa, nor does the interior decoration run to panels of gold and ivory; his 'Sabine farm' is enough for him, along with a flask of wine in the evening – and a pretty girl.[22]

The taste and talent of Horace – 'genius' is hardly too strong a word – was too refined to permit himself to stoop to mere sycophantic adulation of the regime. There are a few examples of over-lavish praise in his earlier work, as for example when he looks rather too eagerly into the future and sees 'Augustus as a living god' when he shall add Britain and Parthia to the Empire[23] (acquisitions which Octavian did not even attempt to make). As he grew in stature as a poet he achieved his best effects through indirect statement, and he had a masterly knack for putting a sting in the tail of compliments bestowed on his two great patrons, finely calculated to avoid reprisals. More often than not, he, rather than either of them, is the real hero of his poems.

Horace and Virgil are the two great luminaries among the

poets encouraged by Maecenas to hymn the regime, but not the only ones whose works have survived. Sextus Propertius, for instance, is still admired for his love lyrics 'to Cynthia', but he also tried his hand at verse describing the new townscape of Rome, as a building boom began to transform the capital after Actium. Architectural rather than literary historians, however, are those chiefly in his debt for such efforts as his account of Octavian's new Temple of Apollo, with its Hellenistic statuary.[24] He made a stab at complementing Livy's project to recreate the spirit of a heroic past, as in these unremarkable lines on the she-wolf said to have suckled Romulus and Remus:

> O wolf of Mars, you best of nursing dams:
> From your sustaining milk what wall sprang up
> That I shall try to build in pious verse![25]

It was Virgil, above all, who was to awaken the sensibilities of Latin-speakers to the extent of the revolution in attitudes to both past and present which Octavian was in the process of launching. Although the *Aeneid* is nominally a Trojan soldier's odyssey, and was composed in conscious emulation of Homer's epics, Virgil's Aeneas is a new kind of hero for a new age. At key moments, the story turns on the thought processes of its protagonist, instead of conventionally heroic action; his pious sense of duty prompts him to take decisions that will fulfil his true destiny, rather than lead him to turn aside for personal advantage – as when he sacrifices happiness with Dido, who would have made him King of Carthage, by sailing away while she falls on a sword on top of her funeral pyre.

In other words, Aeneas is not like the typical Roman aristocrat of the late Republic, or, for that matter, the typical Homeric hero, competing with his peers for personal supremacy and glory. The honour he is chiefly concerned with is the honour of his nation, what little is left of it. Like Moses in the wilderness, he is leading the survivors of a chosen race to a promised land, whose nature and significance is only gradually disclosed to him by signs and prophecies. That land will one day witness the birth of Rome. In the fullness of time it will come to be ruled by a descendant of Aeneas, of the Julian house of the Caesars. Allowing for poetic licence in the matter of ancestry, that new hero turns out to be none other than Octavian.[26]

Virgil would spend the last twelve years of his life writing and rewriting various parts of his masterpiece, not necessarily in chronological order. At times he became so despairing of completing it adequately that he asked on his deathbed for it to be burnt – a request fortunately ignored. Meanwhile, in the real world, his master would make great strides in his own epic task of transforming the state. Without altering the terminology of republican forms of government by magistrates, Octavian would seek to impose a set of unwritten rules whereby ascent of the political ladder depended to a much greater extent than before on an individual's commitment to genuine public service.

Government and politics would still be the preserve of those who already had a sufficient stake in society, typically in the form of family property, but it would be barred to anyone suspected of aiming for purely personal enrichment or indulging in extravagant display. That necessarily involved curbs on certain notions that had come to be associated with aristocratic *libertas* – those freedoms which had too often found expression in unbridled ambition or the systematic sharing out of lucrative commands among the tightest practicable circle of an exploitative elite. That did not mean a head-on attack against the aristocracy. On the contrary, he saw it as vital to his own success to attract the support of members of the most prestigious families, especially patricians. He was prepared to give financial subsidies to those among them who were eager to cooperate, but who, because of the wars, were no longer rich enough to qualify for senatorial posts.

Octavian, of course, favoured initially his own partisans. He had risen to supreme power on the back of a political movement that drew its main support from soldiers and other less well-off citizens, and he needed to reward those who had risked everything to help him. But it was now becoming urgent to broaden the base of his political appeal – to reach out to those many others, especially among the aristocracy, who had opposed him in line with their traditional interests and family loyalties, but whose education and upbringing were designed to fit them for public office. Failure to win them over would have meant he could never have become a genuinely national leader, rooted in the context of the achievements of Rome's heroic past.

Since the defeat of Antony and Cleopatra he had made it clear that his policy was to slash military expenditure and concentrate instead on efficient civil administration. Only those army units would be retained which were essential for protecting and policing the Empire, and for pushing out the existing frontiers, in carefully selected areas, to such naturally defensive borders as the banks of the Danube. He was currently in the process of completing the settlement of 120,000 discharged veterans in small, strategically sited colonies, of which there would ultimately be twenty-eight in Italy, with others in such major provinces as Gaul, Spain, Greece, Asia, Syria and Africa. The army of nearly seventy legions, which he had become responsible for in the aftermath of Actium, was being reduced steadily to fewer than thirty, leaving much less scope for over-ambitious generals to go marauding on their own initiative.

It did not take too long for moderate *optimates*, however disgruntled they might once have been, to get the message that, violence having failed them, the only way they would be able to resume something of their traditional grip on the fruits of empire would be by falling in with the overall tenor of Octavian's programme They would not, of course, be permitted such gross forms of exploitation as had too often prevailed during the late Republic, but the opportunities on offer would nevertheless boost the status, and to a reasonable extent the wealth, of those willing to demonstrate their loyalty to Octavian's regime and ease the day-to-day burdens of administration.

Syme is surely wrong to assert that Octavian could not rule without the help of 'an oligarchy'.[27] It is plain that those aristocrats who now began to step forward to serve as working magistrates were no longer oligarchs holding sway over government, but subordinate politicians who had recognized that if they wanted a share in power they must take it on Octavian's terms or not at all – and that they would lose it if they crossed him. One of the basic aims of his Principate was precisely to prevent the re-emergence of an oligarchy. Behind the façade of republican forms he was gradually transforming himself into an absolute monarch in everything but name, with real power concentrated within his 'palace' (a name derived from the Palatine Hill where Octavian had his house, but where future emperors would build veritable palaces).

So far as may be judged from the behaviour of voters, the middle class had largely joined the lower class of citizens in awarding him their enthusiastic public support. They were unaware that, when it suited him, Octavian would take away their votes, just as he had cut the *optimates* off at the knees. That day was well over the horizon. For the extended honeymoon period that he would continue to enjoy during a period of several years, the voters would not be inclined to support candidates of whom he disapproved. Even if they had, he would doubtless have found other means of clipping their wings. His *auctoritas*, as distinct from his legal powers, had become so immense that many men would have leapt to carry out his wishes, legal or not, if he merely made them known.

The *Comitia Centuriata* was still weighted heavily in favour of rich property owners, but they could no longer be relied on to vote for members of distinguished families regardless of their political attitudes. After all, they had their property to think of. Octavian was paying good money to settle the latest crop of veterans, but the treasure of the Ptolemies, which enabled him to do so, was an unrepeatable phenomenon. The electors must have seen that a resumption of old-style aristocratic rivalry would lead to the recruitment of fresh mass armies, further mass slaughter and an eventual mass resettlement, probably without compensation, on the voters' land.

The process of decision-making and legislation was becoming more professional but also more secretive. Octavian might have the final word on all really important issues, but he could not be expected to show the sort of instant familiarity with the details of all areas of government that would enable him to make appropriate decisions without undue delay. His inner group of advisers who monitored complex issues of diplomacy, finance and other major policy areas joined him in confidential discussions behind closed doors. In addition he formed a Senate committee, composed of the consuls, other representative magistrates and fifteen senators chosen at intervals by lot, to make preliminary decisions about the order and nature of business to be debated by the Senate.[28] That committee would develop into the official *Concilium Principis*, a sort of privy council; but all the most important decisions would already have been taken by the secretive inner group of party loyalists, including prominent members of his own family. Lacking transparency, their decisions must have been hard to predict, and were not necessarily even disclosed. Their power would grow as that of the Senate waned.

Potential aristocratic recruits to Octavian's side would have paid particular attention to two early examples of behaviour the Princeps would not want them to emulate. The first concerned the apparently praiseworthy activities of Marcus Licinius Crassus, grandson of the billionaire colleague of Caesar and Pompey in the First Triumvirate. On Octavian's orders, young Crassus led a legionary army against a Germanic tribe, the Bastarnae, who were migrating through the Balkans and causing havoc near the north-east frontier of Macedonia. Crassus not only defeated them in 29 and turned them back, but he personally killed their tribal chief in battle with his own hands.[29]

That should have entitled him to the extraordinarily rare honour of being permitted to dedicate the spoils of battle *(spolia opima)* at the Temple of Jupiter Feretrius, supposedly built by Romulus himself, who is credited with the first of only three such exploits in the history of the city state since its legendary foundation in the middle of the eighth century BC. The second occasion was in the late fifth century and the third in 222 BC, when the consul Marcus Claudius Marcellus – hailed as 'The Sword of Rome' during his later campaigns against Hannibal – killed a Gallic chief in single combat in front of their two armies.

It is not difficult to imagine the anticipation that must have been aroused in a militaristic society like Rome's at the prospect of the triumphant return of such a heroic and successful general as Crassus had proved himself to be. The Senate did, indeed, award him a triumph. But Octavian, fearing that the right of *spolia opima* would raise him too high in public estimation, discovered a dubious technicality to justify denying him that honour.[30] No doubt many people thought it a mean-spirited action by the Princeps, but it made clear to others that he would not tolerate anyone's receiving a more illustrious honour than himself, in case such a person should be tempted to use it for political advantage and thus threaten the stability of the regime.

The second example was provided by Cornelius Gallus, the equestrian general whom Octavian had appointed as his first Prefect of Egypt. Details of his alleged misbehaviour are sparse, but it would seem that after some minor military successes he had statues of himself produced and put on display in the public squares of important towns in the province. In addition he caused an account of his exploits, whatever those may have been, to be carved on an ancient Egyptian monument. Recalled to Rome in disgrace, Gallus was brought before the Senate, which voted for his exile and the confiscation of all his property.[31] The message was even clearer than that provided by the example of Crassus – especially when Gallus, in despair, committed suicide.

The Princeps would brook no rival for public adulation. His own statues were to be the ones that from now on would dominate public squares, not just in Egypt but throughout the empire. Was Octavian becoming a megalomaniac?

SEVENTEEN

THE SUMMIT OF POWER

The mystery of Octavian's character – in particular, those apparent contradictions between the ruthless blood-letting of his early career and the benevolent restraint of his maturity – would remain a mystery if his public activities were all we had to judge him by. There exists another resource that we have not yet examined in detail. This consists of anecdotes from everyday life that naturally build up around any prominent figure who mixes on a basis of daily familiarity among a range of literate and observant contemporaries. These are often the sort of stories two servants might swap over an illicit glass of the master's best wine, or a society hostess whisper in a confidante's ear, along with an admonition never to say who told her.

Some are probably no more than the merest tittle-tattle, others downright lies – such as the claim that Livia procured a succession of innocent young virgins for her husband to deflower, even in his declining years.[1] Much more plausible is the impression conveyed by Livia's response to a friend who asked how she managed to sustain such influence over him: she did it, she replied, by being sexually faithful to him, doing willingly whatever pleased him, not interfering in matters that were his concern, and pretending not to notice women who attracted his attention.[2] On the other hand, we would be wise to take with an outsize pinch of salt that claim of non-interference by a woman who was to become notorious for her political intrigues.

While it would be vain to suppose that we can really

understand Octavian by peering across the time-chasm of two millennia that separates our age from his, a careful sifting of these often unattributed anecdotes ought to save us from pinning inappropriate modern labels on him, whether of a cold-hearted revolutionary, a po-faced tyrant or a god-like sage. In many ways he comes across as suprisingly ordinary. He is devoted to watching his favourite sports, especially boxing, and he likes playing games with children.[3] He gets irritated when teenagers behave differently from the way he used to behave when he was their age. If he spots pompous but important people approaching his door, he is not above inventing an excuse to rush upstairs to his 'den' and shut himself in until they have gone.[4]

Those are not the sort of things that tend to attract the interest of academic historians seeking clues to the causes of the rise and fall of empires. Luckily for those of us who suspect that the more important of such causes include what goes on in the hearts and mind of outstanding individuals, Suetonius formed a collection of marginal snippets a century after the great man's death. His are by no means the only ones to survive, but they are funny, touching, occasionally scabrous, and expressed with such economy and verve that his book has never been out of print since printing was invented. A less well-known compilation is to be found in the *Saturnalia* of Macrobius, a neo-Platonist of non-Italian origin who flourished about the year 400; as his sources included the works of Plutarch, it is not impossible that he may have read Plutarch's lost life of Augustus – if such a biography ever existed.

It was Macrobius who preserved for us such gems as Octavian's opinion of Herod the Great: 'I'd sooner be his pig than his son!'[5] His was also the story of the man from out of town who was brought to the attention of the Princeps because he looked so uncannily like him. 'Was your mother ever in Rome?' Octavian asked him. 'No,' came the swift reply, 'but my father was!'[6] That classic one-liner sits a trifle uneasily, however, with Macrobius's assertion that Augustus loved a good joke so long as it did not threaten his dignity.[7] Perhaps the fact that his mother lived largely at Velitrae helped.

A far better-attested story, from which Octavian emerges with credit, is told in various forms by Seneca and Dio; it concerns the wealthy Publius Vedius Pollio, a freedman's son, whom the Princeps had raised to the rank of knight. At dinner one evening at Vedius's sumptuous villa, a slave boy accidentally broke a crystal goblet. His master ordered him to be fed to the giant lampreys in his fish pond. The boy rushed to kneel at Octavian's feet, pleading not for his life but for a better way to die. The Princeps asked to see the rest of the set of goblets. When they were brought, he held them up while Vedius watched, only to drop them one by one to smash on the tiled floor. The boy survived.[8] Vedius, who died in 15 BC, left the villa to Octavian in his will.

Perhaps the best corrective to Syme's view of Octavian as a revolutionary is to be found in the long series of anecdotes recorded by Suetonius that reveal his old-fashioned conservatism. His wife, his sister and his daughter were all required to learn how to spin thread, weave it into cloth, and make the fabric into clothes for him to wear. He slept in a low, simple bed with plain coverings. Suetonius was able to inspect some of his old furnishings and vouches for their extreme plainness, many of them 'scarcely good enough for a private person's residence'.[9] As Princeps, he sponsored laws to enforce the stricter morality of an earlier age, and had Stephanio, a popular actor, whipped through three theatres for having a Roman matron dress up in men's clothes, sporting a page-boy haircut, to wait on him.[10]

He made it an offence for men to enter the Forum wearing anything but a formal toga.[11] He forbade women to watch athletics contests, in which, of course, the all-male athletes wore little or nothing. If they wanted to watch gladiatorial combats, women had to retreat to the upper tiers of seats, as far removed from the blood and guts as practicable.[12] At table, Octavian was temperate and abstemious. He ate simple food and little of it, and he mixed his wine with plenty of water, so as not to get drunk.[13] In response to a popular demonstration against the high price of wine, he reminded the protesters that Agrippa's aqueducts would slake their thirst.[14] When he moved, after Actium, to a different house further up the Palatine Hill, it was 'no less moderate' than the one he vacated.[15] Macrobius deserves the last offering on this subject: he reports him as saying of Cato that anyone who opposed change was a patriot.[16]

It is possible to argue, of course, that all these examples amount to no more than a careful façade erected by Octavian to conceal his true opinions. If that were true, he must have been remarkably consistent in his concealment over a period of more than half a century, because he gave every indication of being a young fogey before he could be convincingly accused of being an old fogey. It could equally be argued that his whole career amounted to a restoration of the *status quo* as he knew it during the period of Julius Caesar's perpetual dictatorship, before the revolutionary events of the Ides of March swept it away.

Octavian's agreeable manners in company are well attested. Although his frequent dinner parties were invariably formal *(cena recta)*, with the guests reclining on couches at tables, he went to some trouble to try to draw shy or reticent diners into the conversation.[17] His morning receptions were open to ordinary plebeians as well as to the socially distinguished, and he evidently hoped they would speak plainly and naturally to him, just as he would try to be affable in reply – always depending, of course, on what they might be asking him to do for them. He exchanged social calls with many of his friends, and once paid a special visit to sympathize with a senator, Gallus Cerrinius, who had gone blind, and persuaded him not to fulfil his intention of starving himself to death.[18]

He made no serious effort to stop the fine old Roman custom of attacking over-mighty politicians by leaving written lampoons about where he and others might find them, although he did what he could to refute publicly any charges against him.[19] He was able to make a joke against himself: when a friend asked him what had happened to a tragedy about the Greek hero Ajax, which he had been writing by dictation in his bath, Octavian replied that Ajax had 'fallen on his sponge' *(in spongiam incubuisse)*.[20] During the course of his career he composed a number of works, including philosophical essays, a collection of epigrams and a handful of poems, none of which have survived. Also lost is his autobiography, covering his life up to the age of about forty-eight.

Like so many other perfectly intelligent men of his time, Octavian was superstitious to a fault. A rational, semi-scientific explanation of the universe was available at that era in the form of a long poem by Lucretius, *'De Rerum Natura'* ('On the Nature of Things'); but Lucretius was doubly damned as an Epicurean and an atheist, while Octavian's whole career was founded on reverence for the state religion and the sacred duty imposed by the gods on a son to avenge the murder of his father. Octavian believed it was a bad omen for the whole of the day if he should inadvertently put his left shoe on his right foot in the morning, whereas light rain at the start of a journey promised a happy return. He respected foreign cults that had been established in Rome for generations, but was contemptuous of the rest – late in his life he was to praise one of his grandsons for *not* saying prayers at Jerusalem when visiting Judaea.[21]

He was afraid of thunder – which in that era was believed to be deliberately aimed at people by angry gods – and used to go to an underground room when a storm broke, carrying a sealskin with him because of the prevalent theory that seals were never struck by lightning. In response to a dream, he would stand once a year in the street, presumably very briefly, holding out his open palm to beg alms,[22] a fairly clear indication from his unconscious mind of underlying uncertainty about whether his prosperity would continue for ever. One can imagine the rush of sycophantic volunteers to help him out.

Octavian was considered a lenient as well as a conscientious judge when he sat in court,[23] and he forbade 'no quarter' fights by gladiators where the loser was denied the right to appeal for mercy to the crowd.[24] On the other hand he is said to have had a man stabbed to death on the spot, when he was still a triumvir, for taking notes of a speech he was making, claiming that the man was a spy.[25] His sensitivity on this point led him later to ban publication of reports of meetings of the Senate; he alone must control what the general public were allowed to know of state affairs.[26] He became cross if people addressed him as *Dominus* ('Master'), as that was the word typically used by slaves. To minimize fuss, he often entered and left towns by night so that the local magistrates would not have to turn out to give him a formal greeting or send-off.[27]

Is it possible to draw any firm conclusions from that miscellaneous assortment of glimpses of the Princeps going about his daily life? In spite of the shakiness of some of the evidence, it would surely be wrong to ignore the portrait that emerges, however hazily, of a deeply conventional man. He always seems keen to do what equally conservative people might be expected to consider appropriate. There is often a traditional precedent to be detected behind his actions. He wants to be in control of virtually anything and everything, and so is impatient with those who step even slightly out of line. He wants people to acknowledge his power and authority, but preferably if he does not have to parade it except on great state occasions – when nothing less would be appropriate. In sum, he is a conscientious ruler who worries about his job; and there is a hint of underlying insecurity, which can sometimes make him cruel.

It is now possible to state with some confidence, therefore, that in planning his constitutional coup[28] of 13 January 27, Octavian was not trying to be innovative, let alone revolutionary. Nor was he attempting, directly, to placate those *optimates* whose concept of *libertas* had led them to hail the assassination of his adoptive father as a noble act. That would simply be a useful by-product of his major objective, which was to remove any reason for other conservative Romans (like himself!) to suspect it might be their duty to try to take away from him the power he had illegally won. He had publicly offered to give back that power. The Senate, in line with the overwhelming wishes of the People, had refused to accept it. That, he evidently considered, got him off the hook.

The more focused power, which the Senate returned to him, thus became as fully legitimate as his personal *auctoritas*. It was a legalistic, even an artificial, solution to a problem that Julius Caesar had not recognized as existing. As an aristocrat who had been forced to risk his life, against his inclination, to win supreme power, Caesar saw no necessity to tone down his behaviour in front of those he had defeated and 'forgiven'. Octavian, son of a small-town *novus homo*, grandson of a *petit-bourgeois* money-lender, knew better. At a stroke he relieved the consciences of fellow conservatives, who ought already to have been his natural supporters, by making himself their fully legitimated national leader instead of demanding the dictatorship.

Monarch he may have been, but the last thing he wanted was to be surrounded by fawning courtiers. The very thought would have turned his stomach. It was control he wanted. One searches in vain for an adequate pre-modern substitute for the pejorative label control-freak. The evidence suggests that although he was obviously motivated by the will to power, it was not the sort of insatiable lust that turns a man into a monster. He feared being without power; he was corrupted by it, at least in part – but not, *pace* Lord Acton, corrupted absolutely. On the contrary, the achievement of legitimacy for his regime seems to have calmed his nerves and turned him into a model citizen, in the sense of one who was eager to show how much he respected the law, and would now make sure that everybody else kept it.

Absolute power, in the wrong hands, is the most dangerous phenomenon in the world. Octavian was aware of that. He could not bring himself to delegate any of his except under conditions of the strictest subordination to himself. The first quality he looked for was loyalty; it had to be total, but even that would not be enough. To be entrusted with any of his power, to handle it properly, a loyal subordinate also needed to be strong and capable. Agrippa is the outstanding example of such a man – and he knew his own worth. If Agrippa had been born an aristocrat, Octavian might not have risked using his services. Young Crassus, a capable patrician general, was never again permitted to lead an army once his official triumph was over. Octavian wanted to support the patrician order for sound traditional reasons, and subsidized some who had fallen on hard times, but his backing rarely translated into the offer of a top post. Patricians served a sufficiently important decorative purpose merely by existing.

All things considered, it seems right to acquit Octavian of the charge of incipient megalomania. Even had he not been the control-freak he evidently was, he would have had every reason for distancing himself from such a paltry show-off as Cornelius Gallus. Almost certainly he did not intend to encompass the death of his former Prefect of Egypt, and claimed as much after the suicide. He had not perhaps yet learnt that anyone hauled before the Senate on his *fiat* would stand very little chance of survival. Dismissal and exile would surely have been enough to make the point that the days were now over when command of a rich province allowed its temporary holder to ape the prerogatives of a king.

As for the constitutional settlement of 27, its true test would be the durability of his regime when he himself was no longer in Rome to manage it. Octavian must have felt the need, in any case, to resume close contact with some of his legions in the field, whose continuing loyalty was vital to his personal future as well as to his ambitious plans for development and consolidation of the Empire. He went to Gaul that summer, leaving Agrippa, as his fellow-consul, in nominal charge of the capital. The province was now largely peaceful, and news of serious revolts by the Cantabrian and Asturian tribes of north-west Spain led Octavian to march on through Gaul to suppress them, in what would prove to be the last military campaign he would directly command in person.

His elder stepson, Tiberius (the future emperor), and his nephew Marcellus, son of Octavia by her first husband, are believed to have travelled with him, but it is not known if either of them played a part in the fighting in 26, when a Cantabrian army was defeated. Octavian was taken seriously ill[29] (although not wounded), and retired to Tarraco (Tarragon) on the Mediterranean coast, leaving the subsequent victory over the Asturians to his legates. None of those battles were ultimately decisive, and it was not until the year 19 that the two tribes were finally crushed, by Agrippa. Information is sparse about the two and a half years of Octavian's absence from Rome. We do not know even whether Livia was with him at any time, although it seems likely that she would have visited him during his illness. If so, she would not have been pleased to learn of his plans for young Marcellus to marry his only daughter Julia.

The wedding took place in Rome in 25, when Marcellus was about seventeen years old and Julia just fourteen. Agrippa presided at the ceremony because her father was still unfit to travel.[30] The match was of obvious dynastic significance; any offspring would be direct descendants of the Princeps, whose hopes that Livia would present him with a son and heir must by now have been waning. Octavian had a further surprise up his sleeve the following year, after returning to Rome and giving 400 sesterces to each of 250,000 citizens, probably as sweeteners. Marcellus, still only eighteen, was elected aedile, a move that alerted every politician in the empire to the likelihood that the Princeps was grooming him to be his successor.

Marcellus would become the youngest man, by a wide

margin, ever to hold the aedileship, an office which hitherto had been open only to those who had already served a year as quaestor. As a further mark of favour, he was to be given a seat in the Senate among the praetors. During the Republic, wealthier aristocrats used to compete to be aedile, because the holder of the office was traditionally expected to organize and pay for public games – the bigger and more expensive they were, the greater the future popularity of the ex-aedile when he later came to stand for consul. Julius Caesar himself had taken that route. The same path to the consulship was clearly mapped out for Marcellus, who was granted the privilege of qualifying as a consular candidate ten years before the officially permitted date. Octavian issued instructions to the other magistrates to rein back expenditure on popular spectacles; nobody must be allowed to compete with Marcellus.

Livia's elder son Tiberius, who was also eighteen years old in 24 BC, was elected to serve as quaestor during Marcellus's year as aedile – a great honour, but clearly inferior to the one which Octavian had conferred on his nephew. In addition, Tiberius would be permitted to stand for the consulship only five years, rather than ten years, before the legal date. The preferred order of seniority could not have been laid out more clearly.[31] Rumour circulated that not only Tiberius and Livia were affronted by such blatant favouritism shown to Octavia's son. Agrippa, too, must have suspected that his old friend planned to ditch him as his likely successor. Historians have been tempted to speculate on the possibility of a clash behind closed doors, with the Princeps forced to defend himself against a united attack by his three closest allies, Agrippa, Maecenas and Livia. They would have been speaking, also, for the entire former ruling class. The notion of a potential teenage Princeps was absurd.

Octavian's policy was put to the test early in 23 when he suffered a near-fatal illness. Both 23 and 22 were plague years. The nature of his affliction is uncertain, but as it was serious enough to make him and others despair of his life, it could well have been the plague. Octavian, thinking he was on his death-bed, handed his signet ring to Agrippa rather than to Marcellus.[32] He had clearly wanted his young son-in-law to succeed him, in the fullness of time, but he was obliged to recognize that an immediate transfer of power would have been premature. His own power ultimately rested on his supreme *auctoritas*, which had won him control of the legions. That intangible asset would die with him.

Even had he made Marcellus his heir, the young man could not have matched the advantage he himself had enjoyed as Caesar's avenging 'son' in the aftermath of the assassination. There would be no great cause for Marcellus to espouse except that dictated by his own ambition. Unless his life's work was to count for nothing, Octavian had to give his blessing to Agrippa, whose *auctoritas* with the army was second only to his own. The alternative would have been to risk presenting the surviving old-style republicans with their first major opportunity to turn the clock back since Brutus and Cassius died at Philippi nearly nineteen years earlier. Worse still would have been the re-emergence of rival warlords at the head of rampaging legions.

Although at the supposed point of extinction, Octavian was still sufficiently braced for duty to go through the republican motions of handing to his latest consular colleague, Cornelius Piso, a list of the military dispositions of the legions and a statement of the latest accounts from the Treasury. If he should die as Princeps – not yet a hereditary title – Piso would automatically become titular head of state, as Mark Antony had done on the death of Caesar, in the equally non-hereditary office of dictator; but Octavian was presumably confident that the troops would continue to take their orders from Agrippa, whatever the constitutional rules might lay down, once they had identified the Princeps's signet ring, carved in the shape of a sphinx, on his finger.

Octavian recovered, after a prescribed regimen of cold

baths. But it was not quite the same man who rose from the sick-bed as he who had lain down on it. The prospect of his own imminent demise had concentrated his mind on unfinished business. Monopolizing one of the two consulships, year after year, was fine so long as he stayed alive, but useless to a successor once he was dead. The office of consul belonged to the People. It did not belong to the holder. He could not hand it on or bequeath it in his will. To circumvent that difficulty, he and his designated successor would both have had to serve together simultaneously, as permanent consuls. Such a practice, however, would destroy the carefully stage-managed illusion he had created of a restored Republic.

The Princeps, in the face of death, had seen a solution which would keep that illusion intact. On 1 July 23, only six months into his ninth successive term as consul, he shocked the nation by resigning from that particular post.[33] He had to leave town to do it, or he might have been held to have forfeited his proconsular *imperium* at the same time. He also wanted to avoid disturbances in the capital, in case the plebs should riot in his support if they believed the resignation had been forced on him by senatorial enemies. It would not have been wise to publicize his ulterior motive in advance, or the Senate would surely have been much less ready to humour his strange request to swap the higher status of a serving consul for the much lower status of a notional tribune. To facilitate his return to Rome, they voted to waive the local territorial restriction on his existing proconsular *imperium*.

Most voters would have been at least as puzzled as the senators at what, on the face of it, seemed to be a step down in rank. The powers of an elected tribune of the People were weighted on the negative side, comprising such rights as a veto against legislative measures and a privileged capacity to protect ordinary plebeians against any unfairness inflicted by magistrates. Consuls and praetors enjoyed priority over tribunes when it came to summoning the Senate or initiating debates, but from Octavian's new perspective the *tribunicia potestas* had two outstanding advantages that continuous tenure of the consulship lacked.

First, it would bind him more closely than ever to the mass of citizens, as their official protector, in line with his and Caesar's own roots among the *populares*. Secondly, he alone had the *de facto* power that would enable him to nominate another person to be invested with the *tribunicia potestas* during his own lifetime. Such an individual would be immediately recognized as his chosen successor without his having to announce it officially and thereby break the republican mould. To emphasize its importance, Octavian would reckon all the future years of the Principate from the date he received the award. Every soldier should thus know whom to serve in the event of the Princeps's sudden death. Theoretically, the Principate would survive and the Senate would remain subservient.

Back in front of the Senate and People, after his brief excusion from Rome, Octavian had the double satisfaction of being granted for life the tribune's powers he sought, plus a special grant of overriding proconsular authority *(maius imperium)* in compensation for relinquishing his hold on the consulship.[34] The *maius imperium* ('superior power') had an unchallengeable precedent: the pre-Triumvirate Senate had awarded it to Brutus and Cassius in the East. It would enable him to give direct orders, whenever he wished, to all other proconsuls in any of the senatorial provinces as well as in his own. In addition, a right to summon the Senate at any time, and to place before it whatever business he chose, was added to his powers as a tribune. Octavian now had everything he needed for legal control over the whole empire, plus the best conceivable chance to organize a peaceful succession for a member of his own family. He was emperor in all but name, and the gradual acceptance of his *praenomen* Imperator as descriptive of the Princeps's true power in the state, would, in the end, give him that title, too, if only by posterity retrospectively.

Why did the senators vote so readily for their own supersession? Apart from their healthy respect for Octavian's military muscle, it was surely because his resignation as consul had freed both of those coveted annual posts for their occupation. In future, twice as many of them as before would be able to add the ennobling honour of the consulship to their *curricula vitae*. They may also have thought they detected weakness in the Princeps in the aftermath of his illness, and assumed, too readily, that his new preference for the less important tribunate was an indication that he might be getting ready to retire into private life, following the example of the former dictator Sulla. Neither they nor Octavian were to know that barely sixty years later the consulship would be so little valued by Livia's great-grandson, the Emperor Gaius (Caligula), that he would threaten to appoint his favourite racehorse to the post.

To pacify the indignant Agrippa, Octavian now arranged for a five-year grant of *maius imperium proconsularis* for him, too, but confined it to a limited area of the East, which had suffered some neglect during the Princeps's long absence in Spain. Agrippa is said to have gone off in a huff, although another school of thought holds that he used the controversy over Marcellus to extort from his chief this extra boost to his personal status. Instead of engaging in any punitive expeditions himself, he left that drudgery to his legates while he set up headquarters on the island of Lesbos, where he received ambassadors from eastern kings.

Whatever the real motive for Agrippa's eastern mission, the struggle over the succession collapsed before the end of the year. Marcellus died at the age of nineteen. Some suspected that Livia had poisoned him.[35] Such a possibility cannot be entirely discounted, but it needs to be put in perspective now that the theory has entered popular mythology, thanks to Robert Graves's use of it as a major plot-line in his novel *I Claudius*, where Livia is portrayed as apparently disposing of more than one member of the family to clear a path for her son

Tiberius. The overwhelming probability is that, in a city where the average age at death is estimated to have been twenty-nine, Marcellus died of natural causes. Like so many others that momentous year, he may simply have caught the plague.

The young man was buried in the massive family mausoleum which Octavian had been building for himself,[36] perhaps as a prominent reminder on the Roman townscape that he, unlike his fallen rival Antony, had no intention of leaving his bones anywhere else. For reasons that are not entirely clear, but which indicate the seriousness of the succession crisis now past, Octavian felt the need to offer to read out his will to the Senate, proving that Marcellus had not figured prominently in it. The Senate, not surprisingly, did not insist, and agreed to take his word for it.[37] The death of Marcellus left the sixteen-year-old Julia a childless widow, and Agrippa the obvious front-runner for the succession. It would not be too long before Octavian yielded to the logic of the situation and consented to marry his daughter to him. Tiberius would find himself sidelined again.

In the wake of all these events of the year 23 came the discovery of a conspiracy to assassinate the Princeps.[38] Until very recently, it was the conventional belief among historians that Dio, our basic (but inadequate) source for the plot, had wrongly dated it to the year 22, and that it had actually preceded the constitutional settlement of 23, and had therefore been to some extent responsible for it. Modern research and analysis has vindicated the probable accuracy of Dio's original dating, which puts a totally different perspective on the situation. The conspiracy is now seen to have been a likely consequence of the granting of new powers to Octavian, not the cause of his decision to seek them; and the succession crisis is evidently linked to it.

The first indication of something radically wrong occurred during the trial of a former Governor of Macedonia, Marcus Primus, who was accused of having invaded Thrace without the Senate's orders. His defence, conducted by Maecenas's brother-in-law Varro Murena, was that his orders had come from the Princeps. Primus also claimed, apparently at a later stage of the proceedings, that young Marcellus (now conveniently dead) had given him the instructions. Octavian, without being called as a witness, turned up at the hearing and denied that he himself had done so. Murena demanded to know why Octavian had come there; he replied that he had come in the public interest.

The implications of these disclosures and exchanges were multifarious and alarming. But was the underlying allegation true or false? Had someone perhaps misled Primus with a bogus message with the intention of smearing Octavian, who at that time ought not to have intervened in a senatorial province without good cause and certainly not without informing the Senate. Or had Marcellus been taking a leaf out of his uncle's book by committing Roman troops to battle while he was still a teenager? If so, did he do it on his own initiative, or had he been acting for somebody else? Was that somebody Octavian? And why, unless he believed that Octavian was holding something back, did Murena have the effrontery to question him so pointedly?

Dio gives us one further clue but without drawing any conclusion from it. In spite of the Princeps's sworn testimony, some members of the jury voted to acquit Primus. Would they really have stuck their necks out that far unless it had been obvious to them that Octavian was being economical with the truth? The next thing we hear is that, apparently arising out of the trial, the plot against Octavian's life is discovered. The leader is said to be Fannius Caepio, a republican, but otherwise unknown to history. A number of other men are alleged to have been involved, but the only one named is Murena.

The plot, indeed, thickens. None of the accused are arrested immediately. Instead, a court is convened in their absence, with Tiberius acting as prosecutor.[39] The jury finds them guilty, but once again the verdict is not unanimous.

They are sentenced to death for treason, and each one is executed as soon as he is caught, including Murena, so nobody ever hears their side of the story in court. It smells like a cover-up, and probably was. The explanation for the confused state of the surviving evidence may well be a crude attempt at censorship. Monarchical regimes are typically secretive, especially when they are pretending to be 'People's Republics', and we have already seen examples of Octavian's efforts to keep inconvenient news from the public.

Suetonius says that Maecenas fell from favour because he had told his wife Terentia that her brother was to be put on trial.[40] It was her tip-off to Murena that supposedly led to his initial escape and explained his absence from the trial at which Tiberius prosecuted. If Maecenas did sink in Octavian's estimation, it cannot have been for long, because we next hear of him still in position as a trusted associate, advising the Princeps that he has promoted Agrippa to such heights that he will either have to marry him to his daughter – or kill him.[41] Terentia, in any case, is known to have been Octavian's lover for some years.[42] Maecenas's lover was an actor.

Perhaps Marcellus was murdered, after all. But would it really have been Livia who dispensed the poison?

EIGHTEEN

THE STRUGGLE FOR THE SUCCESSION

From the time he left Rome at the age of thirty-one to fight Mark Antony, until his fiftieth year in 13 BC, Octavian spent all or part of fifteen calendar years outside Italy. Then the pattern changed. For the remaining twenty-six years of his Principate, except for an occasional brief foray, he stayed within Italy, sending a succession of members of his family out around the empire to carry on where he had left off. Great changes continued to occur. During that total span of forty-five years, for instance, the provinces of the empire increased enormously in number and size. We can list the territories that were added[1] but we have only a vague idea of how that amazing feat was accomplished. Very much the same lack of information restricts our knowledge of the public career and private life of the Princeps himself.

In circumstances where a whole year may pass without our knowing anything signficant that happened to him, there is plainly no longer any possibility of constructing a continuous narrative. Fortunately there are beacons of light amid the encircling gloom, which can lead us to some worthwhile conclusions, so long as we recognize that the depradations of time and chance are not the only reasons for the paucity of material. The withholding of information by an increasingly secretive regime also plays its part, along with misinformation that in some cases may have been deliberately planted to hoodwink or confuse those outside the inner circle of government.

In the specific case of the outstanding military

achievements of the period, the meagre sources often make it seem as if almost all of it was the work of the Princeps himself, his son-in-law Agrippa, and his two stepsons Tiberius and Drusus. A limited number of names of other generals have filtered through the censorship process, which was evidently designed to ensure that whatever glory was going went to members of the imperial family, with a trifle to spare for a few court favourites. The last triumph by a non-family member to be held in Rome took place as early as 19 BC. Even Agrippa wisely declined offers of triumphs, knowing by then that the Princeps wanted him for the secondary, and slightly insulting, role of possible future regent to his own sons, simply and solely because they were Octavian's grandsons and carried his diluted streak of Julian blood.

His marriage to Julia[2] in 21 was specifically intended for him to beget those grandsons on her fertile body. Where Marcellus failed, Agrippa succeeded – three times, and with two girls added for good measure. Julia's personal feelings were irrelevant in the context of the obsessive dynastic drive to guarantee the continuing supremacy of Octavian's genes beyond the grave. So were the even more injured feelings of Octavia's daughter, Marcella, whom Agrippa had to divorce before he could marry her cousin. Octavia is said to have approved of the arrangement, but that sounds a prime example of misinformation. What mother would want her daughter to be cast aside like a puppet by any man, let alone the one deemed most likely to be the next Princeps if Octavian should suddenly die?

Still in Rome for a few more months after the thwarting of the Caepio/Murena plot, the ruling Princeps continued to enjoy the backing of the plebs. Against a background of plague, floods and a grain shortage, popular superstition asserted that all those natural phenomena were really due to disapproval in Heaven of the fact that Octavian was no longer consul. A fanatical mob besieged the Senate House, demanding of the trembling occupants that he be given the consulship not just for that year but in perpetuity. Octavian declined the offer but shouldered the task of restoring adequate food supplies, which he managed to achieve in only a few days, no doubt by knocking heads together and opening the warehouses of hoarders.[3]

After he left for Sicily, at the start of a projected eastern tour, the electorate sulkily refused to vote in more than one consul so that the vacancy could be saved for him. But Octavian stayed abroad for the whole of 21 and 20, first in Greece, later in Asia, Bithynia and Syria. His great coup in 20 was to scare Phraates, whose hold on the Parthian throne had become shaky, into giving back the legionary standards that had been captured at different times from the former triumvirs Crassus and Antony during their abortive invasions. He and Tiberius led converging armies towards the Parthian border in a show of strength, and it was Livia's son who was lucky enough to take physical delivery of the trophies, along with some surviving prisoners of war.[4]

Octavian had proved to the doubters back home that armed diplomacy could succeed against Parthia where actual fighting had failed – and might easily have failed again. The Parthians were not too serious a threat to their neighbours because they had not yet developed a large-scale standing army that could operate all year round, and they had problems defending their eastern borders against the nomadic tribes of central Asia and the powerful civilizations of northern India. A further boost to Octavian's prestige came from his reception of envoys from India, seeking to negotiate a trade agreement for the spice route via the Red Sea and Egypt. His earlier efforts to take over part of the trade, by a hostile incursion into Arabia Felix (Yemen), had proved an expensive failure.[5]

Meanwhile, the voters in Rome continued obstinately to try to force Octavian's return. Again, only one consul, Sentius Saturninus, was elected for 19 BC. He ran into trouble when a serving praetor, Egnatius Rufus, made an illegal bid to stand for the consulship before the due period. Rufus had earlier won popular support as an aedile by organizing a fairly efficient but small fire brigade. Octavian, ever anxious to curb rival populists whose successes might detract from his own prestige, had squelched him by forming a bigger and better fire brigade to take over from his. When Saturninus refused to accept his candidacy, Rufus started a riot; the Senate passed its 'ultimate' decree, and Saturninus executed him.[6]

Feelings continued to run high, and a senatorial deputation went east to plead for the return of the Princeps. He appointed a member of the deputation as a consular colleague for Saturninus, and sent him post-haste back to the capital while he himself followed at a leisurely pace. It may be that he was secretly pleased at the mess the republican senators had got themselves into after years of agitating for him to stop hogging the consulship. The day of his return, 12 October, was decreed by the Senate to be celebrated ever after as an annual holiday, the Augustalia. More importantly, they also voted him consular *imperium* for life, rendering his prized tribunician powers largely superfluous.[7] That effective admission that they could no longer manage without him to run affairs in Rome, represented a final collapse of serious senatorial opposition. From now on they would cooperate tamely, if not always enthusiastically, in his dynastic schemes, as well as buckling down to the job of helping him to run the Empire on his terms.

Tiberius, now aged twenty-three, was given praetorian rank; his brother Drusus, three years younger, received the right to stand for magisterial office five years earlier than the law permitted to others. While rejecting the Senate's offer of an official role as the guardian of public and private morality, Octavian embarked on a raft of legislation to curb conspicuous extravagance by aristocrats and *nouveaux riches* alike. He also made provision for financial incentives for marriage among citizens and the procreation of children, and imposed severe penalties for adultery, especially if committed by members of the upper classes. The master race, such as it was, had to remain as pure as practicable.[8] He also found time to revise once more the senatorial rolls, cutting membership to 600.

Antiquarian researchers among the priestly colleges produced an outdated but welcome proposal for holding so-called Secular Games, which had last been celebrated as long ago as 146 BC. These were not 'secular' in the modern sense of the word, but derive their name from the Latin *saeculum*, meaning (in that context) an age lasting a century or more; the essential requirement for their celebration was that everybody who had been alive at the date of the previous event must now be dead. Nor were they 'games', as usually understood. The *Ludi Saecularis* were a combination of all-night prayer meetings and daytime theatrical performances, whose basic purpose was to mark a new beginning in the endless cycle of the ages.

They proved to be a splendid showcase, in 17 BC, for contrasting the benefits of Octavian's paternalistic and peaceful welfare regime with the instability typical of the earlier form of republicanism which it had replaced. All good citizens were supposed to attend at least once during the festival, but we are not told how they managed to cope with the logistics, now that the census showed there were more than four million of them. The notably pious Princeps kept three all-night vigils, when sacrifices were offered to the Fates and Mother Earth; happier prayers arose during the day to Apollo, the god now especially associated with Octavian, and to the divine couple Jupiter and Juno, who traditionally kept a benevolent eye on Rome through their sanctuaries on the heights of the Capitol.[9]

By this year of the games, Julia had produced two grandsons for the Princeps, which was no doubt something extra for the festive crowds to celebrate. Gaius Julius Caesar, aged three, and the newly born Lucius Julius Caesar, were both adopted by him as his sons, hence their Julian names.

Their natural father's ultra-plebeian clan name of Vipsanius would never have done for young men of such great expectations. Their future and that of the Principate seemed assured, so long as Octavian or Agrippa – now the undisputed heir-apparent, with grants of tribunician power and proconsular *maius imperium* – survived until the boys came of age. If Octavian were to die first, Agrippa, as the new Princeps, would be bound to designate either Gaius or Lucius as his successor. For the moment, however, Agrippa was consolidating Rome's grip on the provinces of the East. Julia must have joined him abroad, because she was to produce three more children for him.

Octavian left his capital again in 16 for what turned out to be his last major foreign tour, starting in Gaul. He would be away for three years, during which, as commander-in-chief of the legions led by Tiberius and Drusus, he masterminded the conquest of huge areas of the central and eastern Alpine regions, which became the provinces of Raetia (Tyrol, plus parts of Switzerland and Bavaria) and Noricum (east of Raetia and south of the Danube). The triumphal monument, of which some pillars and a pediment still stand today, on the heights above Monaco, record the defeat of forty-eight tribes, chiefly in the *Alpes Maritimes* region of what is now modern France.[10]

Both Octavian and Agrippa returned in 13 BC to Rome, where Tiberius, at the age of twenty-nine, was serving as consul. It was probably the first time the two old campaigners had met for several years. Agrippa, the rapidly ageing war-horse, had to leave again before the end of the year, charged with subduing a revolt in Pannonia, the future Balkans province east of Noricum. It was one winter campaign too many in that snow-bound graveyard of armies. After restoring some sort of temporary order, Agrippa made it back to Italy but not in time to take his farewell of Octavian. He died in mid-February before the Princeps had time to reach him.[11]

Only the death of Octavian could have delivered a greater

blow to the regime. He himself felt the loss of Agrippa deeply. It was more than thirty years since they had set out together from Apollonia on their great adventure. He gave his friend a state funeral, and delivered personally the speech of *laudatio* in the Forum. He was laid to rest in the Augustan mausoleum, whose echoing empty spaces he now shared with Marcellus, that other heir-apparent who failed to survive long enough to make it to the top. Unforgivably, a significant number of the Roman *nobiles* boycotted the funeral games of this outstanding Roman hero, presumably because his humble origins made him unworthy of their attention.[12] In addition to his military achievements, Agrippa had transformed the daily lives of tens of thousands of his fellow-citizens by his construction of new aqueducts and drainage systems; now he bequeathed to them free public baths and gardens. The rest of his vast estate he left to Octavian.

The latest honour for the Princeps was a commission by the Senate for the creation of what would become perhaps the greatest work of fine art ever produced under the auspices of Roman civilization, usually so derivative of Greek originals in that field. This was the *Ara Pacis Augustae*, the much venerated Altar of the Augustan Peace.[13] It would take four years to complete, and shows Octavian as a human rather than a god-like figure, sculpted among his family and his People on the relief panels that surround all four sides. After its excavation in 1937 under Mussolini's regime, the altar was reassembled, incorporating pieces which had been dug up earlier and had found their way into museums elsewhere in Europe.

Agrippa's third son by Julia was born after his death, and so became known as Agrippa Postumus. He would outlive his brothers but suffer a wretched life because of his personal inadequacies. His mother was no sooner free of that fifth pregnancy than she had to prepare herself, at the age of twenty-seven, to marry again for the sake of her father's plans to fix the succession ever more securely on one or other of those three grandsons. Once again she had no choice in the matter. This time the groom was to be Tiberius – who was deeply unwilling. Few men have been accorded the doubtful privilege of marrying their mother-in-law. Livia's elder son was contentedly married to Agrippa's daughter; now he was forced to marry his widow.[14] Tiberius's well-attested reluctance to divorce Vipsania calls for a degree of scepticism in judging the assertion that he and Julia were happy together at first, even if they fell out so spectacularly later.

Knowing his stepson's fondness for his first wife, Octavian deliberately kept them apart after the divorce. They did, however, meet once by chance, not very long after his wedding to Julia in 11 BC. Witnesses reported seeing tears in his eyes as they finally parted.[15] It may not be too much of an exaggeration to say that swapping Vipsania for Julia blighted the rest of his life. As emperor he was to suffer from depressions which may, at least partly, have had their origin in the knowledge that he ought to have outfaced the Princeps; subsequent events showed that he gained nothing from compliance that he would not have gained anyway. The marriage was to poison relations within the family, which was currently mourning the death, in her mid-50s, of the loving and selfless Octavia. Julia had a baby by Tiberius, but it died in early infancy. After that blow, they appear to have abandoned marital relations.

For the present, Tiberius resolved his problem by undertaking a long and bloody struggle in the Balkans, against the Pannonians and Dalmatians, to extend the imperial frontier to a further long stretch of the Danube. Then he was off again, after the death of his younger brother in a riding accident, to try to complete Drusus's unfinished task of attempting to push the hostile border with Germany forward from the Rhine to the Elbe, an objective which would ultimately prove unattainable.[16] During those years of unrelenting military campaigning, the political news from Rome would have fed his resentment at the increasingly blatant promotion of Gaius and Lucius as if they were princes of a royal house, fit to succeed to absolute rule whatever their age, merit, experience or previous service to the state.

That policy was offensive to Tiberius's aristocratic principles, which would never be entirely eradicated. He admired Octavian as a great national leader but looked down on him socially. His Claudian ancestry was more distinguished, in terms of consuls in his family tree, than that of Julius Caesar himself, let alone the plebeian stock of Octavian's natural father. Upper-class Romans were close students of bloodlines. Tiberius's was 100 per cent proof, as both his parents were Claudians. Octavian, as the grandson of Julius Caesar's sister, was only one-eighth Julian and not in the direct male line; his own grandsons would be able to claim about three per cent Julian blood each.[17]

When Tiberius eventually returned from the wars in 7 BC to celebrate the first triumph to have been seen in Rome for twelve years, his outrage could scarcely be suppressed when he experienced for himself how Octavian's indulgence towards the two boys had spoilt their character by giving them too high a sense of their own importance at such an impressionable age, a feeling exacerbated by the adulation shown towards them by others, who evidently hoped to ingratiate themselves at this early stage with the two rising powers in the land. Tiberius must have complained about them to his mother, always his strongest supporter. She would surely have warned him on no account to oppose them publicly, or even she would not be able to answer for his safety. No doubt she advised him to keep quiet and stick it out, even if the boys, formerly his own stepchildren, did treat him disrespectfully.[18]

Tiberius, however, also seething at the rumoured infidelities of his second wife, had had enough. The next time the Princeps offered him a foreign command, in 6 BC, he replied that he was tired of war and public affairs and wanted to retire to private life on the Greek island of Rhodes at the eastern end of the Mediterranean.[19] We may imagine

Octavian's incredulous response and the subsequent interviews with his advisers and with Livia, demanding to know what had got into her son and what he ought to do about it. The diplomatic Maecenas was no longer available to patch up a compromise, having died two years earlier. It may well have been Livia who advised her furious husband to award tribunician power to Tiberius; one of the mysteries of the year 6 is the conferral of that coveted honour on her 36-year-old son just before he actually quit.

Nothing Octavian chose to do or say was sufficient to placate Tiberius, who eventually went on hunger-strike to get his way. Anyone else but Livia's son would no doubt have been left to get on with it and die. After four days it was the Princeps who cracked first. Tiberius took ship, but lingered for a while off the Italian coast because a serious illness was rumoured to be afflicting his stepfather. It might have been paroxysms of thwarted rage. Eventually Tiberius sailed on to Rhodes, where he was to spend the next seven years, leaving behind him a whiff of scandal and much speculation over his true motives, speculation which continues to this day.

When, four years after his departure, Julia was arrested for immorality in a new scandal that rocked the nation,[20] people decided that the real reason Tiberius had retired to Rhodes was because he could no longer tolerate his wife's affairs with her numerous alleged lovers, just because she was the only child of the Princeps. Octavian himself might well have approved of that convenient fiction, as a means of diverting attention from the real reason behind both scandals – that they represented direct political threats to his regime by people who were dangerously close to the centre of power. In both cases the threats arose because his personal dynastic plans for the succession were an affront to them. Rome was not yet an established monarchy, even though it may at times have felt like one.

Tiberius, sensitive, isolated, with a high sense of duty to his class and for the integrity of the state, would not have thrown away his career over a resentful and impetuous woman. The idea that he would starve himself to death just to get away from Julia is ludicrous. Apart from any other consideration, Octavian, in those circumstances, would surely have risked Livia's hatred by calling his bluff for rather longer than four days. He knew that her obstinate and high-minded son was ready to die for his country, even though his conception of it was sadly out of date. When, one day, Tiberius himself would be offered the Principate, he would accede to power only reluctantly, more in contempt at the abject servility of those urging him to accept it than from a desire to rule the world. He shunned the responsibility but knew that if he were to reject it, the tainted prize would go to an even less worthy contender than he, who might damage or destroy the matchless Augustan legacy.

The early career and behaviour of young Gaius confirmed Tiberius in the rightness of his decision to escape to Rhodes. At the age of twelve, the boy had been shown to the legions in Gaul by Octavian himself, during a brief excursion when he paid the troops a bonus in Gaius's name – no danger there of not making his message clear. In his fifteenth year Gaius donned the *toga virilis*, and a compliant Senate voted to let him attend their meetings as an honoured guest.[21] By that time, Tiberius had settled down in a modest property on Rhodes and had begun a course of astrological studies, no doubt anxious to know what else the stars might have in store for him.

Octavian went on to accept the Senate's decision to nominate Gaius as consul-designate for appointment five years hence, when he should have reached the age of twenty. While waiting for that promotion, he was to be known as *Princeps Iuventutis* ('Prince of Youth'), a title so closely related to Octavian's own as to demonstrate that the Princeps was no longer troubling to conceal his long-term monarchical intentions. Some of the provinces showed their enthusiasm by sending the boy their loyal greetings. Tiberius, still kicking his heels at Rhodes, added a course in Greek philosophy to his daily round, as a consolatory second string to his attempts to foretell the future.[22]

In 2 BC Octavian considered he had reached the pinnacle of his career when the Senate awarded him the title of *Pater Patriae* ('Father of his Country'), which the plebs and the knights had long been urging them to do. He was deeply moved by the thought that it represented the genuine opinion of all sections of society, and he would record the honour in the closing paragraph of his *Res Gestae* as a fitting climax to the inscriptions setting out his achievements.[23] But hard on the heels of this moment of well-merited national applause came the scandal that ruined his daughter Julia and would tarnish his own reputation as a strict but loving *paterfamilias* in the tradition that he himself had done so much to uphold – and to enforce on other people.

Julia was thirty-six. Like most Roman women she had spent her life doing very much as she was told, chiefly by her father and step-mother but also by her three successive husbands, none of whom she had been permitted to veto as suitors, much less choose anyone for herself. Having been deserted by the last of her spouses and left, at least to a limited extent, to her own devices, she had marked her new sense of freedom by going out on the town and getting drunk with some of her classy friends. She was spotted staggering around the Forum with a group of men, and larking about on the rostra from which her father made his dignified speeches to the citizens.[24]

Among her fellow-revellers was Iullus Antonius, surviving son of Mark Antony and Fulvia, who had been brought up within the imperial circle by Octavia, whose elder daughter, Claudia Marcella, he had married in 21 after Agrippa had been obliged to divorce her in order to wed Julia herself. As husband of the Princeps's niece, whom he could not have married without his firm consent, Antonius had gone on to enjoy a fine career, becoming consul in 33 and senatorial governor of the rich and highly civilized province of Asia three years later. He was also an accomplished poet. At the time of his arrest he was forty-one, only five years older than Julia and probably her current boy-friend.

Antonius was accused with a number of other men, including four from well-known senatorial families: Tiberius Sempronius Gracchus, Appius Claudius Pulcher, Cornelius Scipio and Titus Quinctius Crispinus. One or two may have been in and out of Julia's bed, but surely not all. Their names sound more like a roll-call of the discredited republican opposition. According to Velleius Paterculus, a partisan of Tiberius but also a devoted admirer of Octavian, Julia had not refrained from any sexual act possible to a woman, and had allowed herself to be debauched by all of them.[25] That is so implausible, especially in the context of a society where wealthy aristocrats could keep any number of mistresses or household slaves for sexual purposes, as scarcely to be worth consideration.

If Antonius had indeed been her lover, he would surely not have wanted to share her with so many others. The same reluctance would have applied to men with such proud, historic names as Scipio, Gracchus, Claudius and Quinctius. Tacitus, writing more than a century later, claims that Gracchus first seduced Julia while she was Agrippa's wife; but he states in another context that although the offences of those arrested had been sexual, Octavian put them on trial for treason. To many historians it makes better sense to assume a more straightforward explanation of the charge – that they were put on trial for treason because the Princeps suspected them of treason. Judging by the vindictive punishment he inflicted on his daughter, he probably suspected her of plotting against him, too.

As a proconsular member of the Princeps's family, from which his most influential and trusted advisers were drawn, Antonius ought to have been well informed about Octavian's policies and prejudices. As a close friend of the mother of

The Struggle for the Succession

Gaius, Lucius and Agrippa Postumus, he would have been especially aware of his plans for the succession, as well as Julia's personal views – perhaps when she was topped up with wine – on how much her father's decisions had blighted her life. Finally, as the son of Mark Antony, he had a name that might yet rouse a cheer from the ranks of Tuscany, where his father did once have many supporters. If Octavian were to die suddenly, with Tiberius out of touch and vulnerable to a swift order for his execution, what would stop Antonius, backed by his senatorial allies, from marrying Julia in order to take over the Principate and deny it to Gaius, who was still only eighteen. Julia would then become the first lady of Rome. If they waited until Gaius became consul at twenty, it would be too late: Julia would go from daughter to dowager at a stroke.

All that is speculation. What complicates the affair further, and adds to its fascination, is that it was Octavian himself who went to the Senate and denounced his daughter.[26] Many of the senators must surely have thought he was becoming unhinged in his old age. Why wash the First Family's dirty linen in public, when he could so easily have fallen back on his rights as *paterfamilias* to keep her under restraint privately, while taking his revenge on her supposed paramours in some other way? As it was, the obedient Senate sprang into action, condemning the accused men to banishment or death; Antonius alone seems to have found the time to commit suicide.

Julia herself was sent to the offshore prison island of Pandateria, where the warders were instructed not to let her have wine. Her mother, Octavian's second wife Scribonia, showed her opinion of the verdict by voluntarily following her daughter into exile.[27] In the explanatory letter he wrote to her husband, Octavian informed him that he had sent a bill of divorce to Julia in Tiberius's name. The latter responded by writing frequent letters to the Princeps, suggesting a reconciliation between father and daughter. Octavian did allow her to return to the mainland after about two years, but she

315

remained in closely supervised confinement until her death fourteen years later.

Lucius Caesar qualified for his *toga virilis* in the same year as the trial, and was voted the same rights his brother Gaius had received three years earlier. Gaius himself was sent to the East the following year, in company with an experienced general, to gain military and diplomatic experience. Among other errands, he was instructed to negotiate on various issues with the Parthians. He seems to have acquitted himself well and made a generally good impression, although to what extent he was helped by his minders is not disclosed. Suetonius reports that once, at dinner, a man (not named) offered to go to Rhodes on his behalf and bring back the head of Tiberius. Gaius did not take him up on it.[28]

By that time Tiberius's tribunician powers had expired, and Octavian, pointedly, did not renew them. The Princeps also refused all requests, either from him or his mother, for him to be allowed to return to Rome to live as a private citizen. It cannot have been a happy time at the imperial household on the Palatine, and may help to some extent to explain the well-known story that Octavian got into the habit of writing down in advance whatever he had to say to Livia on important topics.[29] Tiberius wrote to tell him, perhaps on Livia's advice, that his true reason for going to Rhodes had been to avoid any hint of rivalry with Gaius and Lucius while they were growing up; now they were older and destined for the highest positions in the state, he said, that former consideration no longer applied. Eventually, Octavian allowed him back, in AD 2, but made no move to restore him to favour.[30]

In less than two years, Octavian's carefully nurtured plans for his grandsons came to grief. Shortly after Tiberius's return, Lucius fell ill while travelling to take up his first command with the army in Spain, and died at Massilia (Marseilles). The following year Gaius, who had become consul while serving abroad, received a head wound when besieging the minor fortress of Artagia in Armenia. Although he succeeded in capturing Artagia, the wound seems to have affected his brain. He began to babble about not wanting to return to Rome but to spend the rest of his life in some remote corner of the world. He was being escorted back home through Lycia when he died, in February AD 4, presumably as a result of the injury.[31]

It was too late to start all over again. With the two young men lying in the mausoleum with their father and their cousin, Octavian, at the age of sixty, was forced to reconsider his other options. His own precipitate actions had ruled out Julia. Her reputation was now so blackened that even if he found a new husband for her, any child she conceived (she was in her forty-second year) would be the subject of rumours about its parentage. Her surviving son, Agrippa Postumus, was by all accounts a brutish lout, perhaps of limited intelligence, but certainly inclined to be rebellious. He, too, would later be packed off to a prison island. That left Tiberius. Livia had achieved her goal at last.

Octavian imposed one condition: Tiberius would have to pass over his own son, Drusus, in favour of Germanicus, grandson of Octavia and Mark Antony. That way a fraction, however, small, of his family blood would have a chance of maintaining its superiority through future generations. Tiberius refused to comply; Octavian waited. This time it was the younger man who caved in. No doubt Livia advised him that once he became Princeps he would be able to reverse the decision, but Octavian could be reasonably confident that her son's oath, once given, would be kept. He adopted Tiberius as his son and chief heir, restoring to him both the powers of a tribune and a complementary proconsular *imperium*.[32]

The effects of Octavian's harsh treatment of his daughter could not be confined to her own generation among the imperial family. Everyone was affected. Agrippa Postumus was only ten when his mother was snatched away. His reported misbehaviour as a teenager was no doubt linked to that early emotional disturbance. He was given a minor administrative job, but either gave it up or was sacked. When he was about eighteen or nineteen he was exiled for unacceptable behaviour, which is not precisely specified in the sources beyond an assertion that he was brutish.[33] Not long afterwards, in AD 8, his sister Julia (the Younger) was sent to a prison island in the Adriatic, where she gave birth to an illegitimate child.

The baby was exposed, on Octavian's orders.[34] Exposure of infants, especially of girls, was not considered a criminal act if sanctioned by a *paterfamilias*. The custom was for a new-born baby to be laid at the feet of its father; if he picked it up he signified acceptance of responsibility for it and for its upbringing, but if he rejected it, the child could legally be exposed. In the case of Julia the Younger, her husband, Lucius Aemilius Paullus, had been in exile for a number of years on a charge of conspiring against the Princeps. The baby's natural father, Junius Silanus, hitherto a friend of Octavian, left the country voluntarily, but suffered no further punishment.

The actions of the Princeps, now nearly seventy years old, thus led to a situation where his only daughter, his only surviving grandson and one of his two granddaughters were living in exile, separated from each other, while his own great-grandchild had been deliberately left to starve to death. Could any family be more dysfunctional? But was there a hidden reason for his otherwise inexplicable severity? Scholars are generally agreed that some sort of 'palace revolt' lies beneath the surface of events, even though the banishing of Julia the Younger can be firmly attributed to adultery, punishable under legislation inspired by the Princeps himself.

The earlier succession crisis had been resolved in AD 4 by the designation of Tiberius as the main heir, a move that would scarcely have been acceptable to Octavian's three remaining grandchildren. The claims of Agrippa Postumus could not have been spurned more contemptuously. Did his mother's disgrace lead Octavian to believe the boy was illegitimate? If so, did Livia put that idea in his head? Paullus, who was consul for AD 1, had been exiled for conspiracy but, unlike Mark Antony's son, he had not been made to die for it. Why not? As the proconsular husband of Octavian's granddaughter he would have had a stronger claim to the succession than Germanicus, husband of the Princeps's other granddaughter Agrippina, if Tiberius were to fall by the wayside. Perhaps Paullus had not plotted directly against Octavian but against Tiberius.

Throughout the entire ten years that separated the successive disgraces of the two Julias, mother and daughter, Livia had been in charge of the Princeps's household on the Palatine. Before the first crisis her son Tiberius had been in exile for years, while her stepdaughter Julia's five children lorded it in Rome; after the second crisis, Tiberius was the Princeps's trusted deputy, while four of the five children were dead or exiled. Germanicus's wife Agrippina was the only one of them still in favour, and she had just provided Octavian with two legitimate great-grandsons, to compensate for the baby he had wantonly sacrificed. Nobody seriously believes that throughout that period Livia was just an innocent bystander, but proof of malign intervention is lacking.

Another prominent victim of the year of Julia the Younger's exile was the poet Ovid (Publius Ovidius Naso), who is generally believed to have been involved in the same scandal in a minor way. Octavian banished him to the primitive coastal town of Tomis (Costanza) on the Black Sea, where he spent the remaining nine years of his life writing vainly for permission to return to Rome, and composing verses much less light and amusing than those earlier ones on which his reputation rests. In *Tristia* ('Miseries') he confesses that his 'two crimes were a poem and a blunder *(carmen et error)*'.[35] The poem he refers to is usually identified as being the *Ars Amatoria* (The Art of Love), which Octavian disapproved of as potentially corruptive of Roman morals. By modern standards it hardly ranks as pornography, but it does offer cynical advice to women on how to please men, as well as tips for men on how to seduce women.

A problem with that theory is that the *Ars Amatoria* had been circulating in Rome for some seven or eight years before Ovid's fall from grace, and Octavian must have been fully aware of it before his granddaughter apparently decided to put some of his recommendations into practice. Both Virgil and Horace were long dead, and Ovid had deservedly become the most highly regarded poet of his generation. Snippets from the *Ars Amatoria* have been found on walls at Pompeii, attesting to its wide popularity. As for the 'blunder', nobody knows what it was. Only Ovid himself reports it; no other relevant ancient source even mentions his exile.

A rival theory, which is perhaps more profound than true, holds that Octavian punished him for his *Metamorphoses*, written immediately before his exile and dealing with mythological examples of humans being transformed into animals, plants, stars or 101 other things. The American scholar S.G. Nugent believes that behind his use of such myths, Ovid was really describing 'a world in which individual human agents are helpless before the wilful and apparently boundless power of the Olympians, whose affinity to the inhabitants of the Palatine Ovid made every effort to stress'.[36] It seems doubtful whether Octavian would have recognized such a sub-text, but the theory makes us confront the issue of tyranny. No legal process was apparently required to ruin Ovid's life – merely one man's displeasure, expressed by unchallengeable *fiat*. That represents the blinkered, self-righteous aspect of Octavian's paternalism. Banning Ovid's books probably helped to preserve them. No Roman poet was to have more influence than he on the literature of the European Middle Ages and the art of the Renaissance.

From the time of his restoration to favour in AD 4, Tiberius would have ten years to wait before becoming the next Princeps. During that time his new adoptive father would extract the maximum value from his services. At the first opportunity, he sent him off to fight in Germany again, then for four gruelling years to deal with a revolt by the

Pannonians and Dalmatians. That border crisis proved so serious that for a while it caused panic in Rome, where many slaves were freed so that they could be called up, presumably to defend Italy. The outcome was the ruthless pacification[37] of those huge territories south of the Danube, stretching as far as the Euxine (Black Sea), with important long-term consequences for freedom of movement by land between the Eastern and Western halves of the empire. Jews, Christians and other refugees would migrate along those routes in the following centuries.

The cost of maintaining the legions and paying off the troops on discharge was becoming too much for existing revenues, even when amplified from Octavian's deep pocket; the treasure of the Ptolemies was plainly beginning to run out. He set up a special demobilization fund, financed largely by a 5 per cent inheritance tax on large estates. From now on, soldiers who had served the full term of 20 years in the ranks would get 12,000 sesterces instead of a parcel of land, so the old problem of robbing existing landowners to accommodate veterans would not recur. The men were also to be discharged at manageable intervals instead of large numbers being released, all at the same time.[38]

The worst military disaster of the reign occurred in AD 9 when Quinctius Varus, at the head of three legions, was lured into an ambush in the Teutoberg Forest in central Germany. They were wiped out almost to a man by a grand alliance of many tribes, brought together for the purpose by a German chieftain, Arminius, who had formerly served as an auxiliary soldier under Roman command, and knew that their sophisticated battlefield manoeuvres worked only in open country, not in dense woods. Tiberius was sent to do what he could to retrieve a fairly hopeless situation, but after two years of campaigning, accompanied by his adoptive son Germanicus, he withdrew to the west bank of the Rhine.[39]

Octavian's response to the losses showed his failing powers. For months after the initial disaster he would sometimes bang his head and call out: 'Varus! Give me back my legions!'[40] Eventually he wrote instructions to Tiberius that, if he should succeed him, he must defend the existing frontiers of the Empire and not attempt to expand them further.[41] By AD 13 it became plain that the end was near for the ageing Princeps when he made Tiberius his effective co-ruler, with equal powers of command. The following summer, largely reconciled now to each other, the two men made a final trip together as Octavian accompanied his adopted son on the first stage of Tiberius's proposed visit to Illyricum. He turned aside from the route to go to the small town of Nola.[42]

Instinct must have brought him there. He went to visit the house in which his father, plain Gaius Octavius, had spent his last hours, and decided to move into the room in which he had died. Livia realized at once what was in his mind. The moment of crisis was at hand. She dispatched messengers to gallop after her son and bring him back.

NINETEEN

THE GODFATHER OF EUROPE

Tiberius galloped back just in time to spend one last day with the dying Father of his Country. They talked privately for a long time. Nobody knows what they said to each other. Next morning, Octavian looked into his mirror, poking at his face with his fingers as if he might somehow be able to improve its shape and colour. He asked those attending him if they thought he had played his part well in the comedy of life. They hastened to assure him that he had. The date was 19 August AD 14, and he had reigned supreme for forty-four years.

He died in Livia's embrace, with Tiberius beside the bed. The formal mask did not slip. He expired as he had lived, in control of his emotions, doing his duty to the end.[1] The tears that were shed throughout his empire by thousands, perhaps millions, of people who had never met him or had seen him only from a distance, could no longer compensate the man himself for any lack of fondness among what remained of his dysfunctional family. His grandson, Agrippa Postumus, was killed by imperial *fiat* as soon as an executioner could reach him on his prison island.[2] Did Octavian sign the warrant as his final act? We do not know. It may well have been the first act of Tiberius – or a tidying-up of loose ends by his mother.

All Rome came to a halt on the day of his funeral, which he had meticulously planned. The small, thin body in its coffin was driven in solemn procession to the Forum, where Tiberius and his disinherited son Drusus gave the orations from the rostra amid the ceremonial formality that had marked his own appearances there in life. The coffin was carried to the Field of Mars and placed on a pyre near the giant obelisk he had brought back from Egypt to serve as a sundial, and which, at sunrise on his birthday, would cast its long shadow directly onto the sculpted representation of himself on what was his truest monument, the *Ara Pacis Augustae*, Altar of the Augustan Peace.

His idea of peace was different from some modern definitions. For him, the *Pax Romana* was inextricably related to war and conquest. It was not the peace that passeth all understanding, but one based on a rational calculation of the material benefits to be derived from ruling subject peoples who would work and pay taxes, and fight (against Rome's enemies) only when told to by Augustus and his successors. It had nothing to do with ethical principles such as 'love your neighbour as yourself'; it was closer to 'control your neighbour – and help and protect yourself'. The latter formulation can still be applied in modern times. That was the attitude of the former Soviet Union towards Eastern Europe, and it evidently underpins current American operations in Iraq (once part of the Parthian Empire) and elsewhere in the Middle East. Unlike his modern counterparts, Octavian was perfectly frank in describing his greatest achievement as 'Peace through victories' *(Parta victoriis Pax)*.[3]

Peace as a concept could not, for a Roman, be dissociated from the virtues traditionally fostered by the *mos maiorum* ('moral stance of the majority'), where the majority is understood to include the best of all those citizens who are dead as well as the best of those still living – whose responsibility, in turn, is to pass on the virtues unsullied to the following generation. Courage and patriotism head the list, with *pietas* not far behind. Once again, there are significant differences from our concept of piety. To Octavian, who made a point of publicly emphasizing his own *pietas*, it does not simply describe someone of a religious disposition who avoids sin and does good works. It had a much broader meaning in terms of reciprocal loyalty and social responsibility within the context of the *mos maiorum*.

The pious Roman was one who was always on the side of Rome and her gods, and who fought to maintain her supremacy and the honour of his family. Octavian would have regarded unbroken peace as posing a threat to traditional Roman morals, leading to loss of energy, self-indulgence and decadence. That was one reason why he added more lands to the empire by warfare than anyone before or after him, and expected his followers to devote their careers to administering and protecting it. He maintained a legionary army of about 150,000 (backed by a roughly equal number of provincial auxiliaries), mostly on or near the frontiers, which was enough to enforce internal peace and deter invaders, as well as permitting carefully planned expeditions to acquire fresh lands.

The glory of the *Pax Augusta*, however, was that it permitted the arts of peace to flourish untroubled within a larger area of the earth than had ever been possible before. Trade flourished between member countries, and also with distant parts of the known world. Huge tracts of land which had never known the plough were brought into cultivation as the population expanded. Honest travellers could move in safety from Europe to Africa via Asia, and just as safely return, so long as they stayed within Roman-protected territory. Not only material goods but ideas and even religions could move with them. Roman ways spread outwards, and in many cases were eagerly adopted by provincials, especially in the barbarian regions of the West. For Rome itself, the Augustan years gave its citizens a new sense of moral and social direction.

While Octavian's boasted 'restoration' of the Republic was fraudulent at the higher levels of political decision-making, at a deeper level it was true in the way that a creative work of art is 'true', even though it may be fictional in its details. What he genuinely tried to restore was not a particular combination of constitutional laws and practices, but a system of traditional values that placed the public good of all citizens before the individualistic strivings of a privileged few. His own compulsive quest for power had not been founded in cynicism. Once he had achieved eminence his policies became motivated to an increasing degree by love for the spirit and ways of earlier generations of Romans – at least, so far as these could be adduced from the legends of the past, which provided examples of the sort of conduct that had made the nation great and raised it above all others.

That spirit (whether it ever existed or not) has never been expressed more eloquently and succinctly than in the famous lines, too often derided as sentimental, by Lord Macaulay, a nineteenth-century British Cabinet minister, addressing a later imperial people:

> Then none was for a party;
> Then all were for the state;
> Then the great man helped the poor,
> And the poor man loved the great;
> Then lands were fairly portioned;
> Then spoils were fairly sold:
> The Romans were like brothers
> In the brave days of old.[4]

None of that, of course, is literally accurate. How could it ever have been, among fallible human beings? It represents, for Macaulay as for Octavian, a yearning to believe that, once upon a time, before money and luxuries and rampant personal ambition came along to spoil things, a Golden Age of brotherhood and heroism had really existed. That was the *Res Publica* which Octavian dreamed of restoring, or, at least, of holding up to the citizens as the example they should try to emulate. It was a country of the mind, a symbol rather than a fact, perhaps more potent for being so.

In pursuit of his notion of the common good, Octavian was prepared to sacrifice his own claims to personal happiness, just as those legendary exemplars of heroic times had willingly laid down their lives for Rome. He sacrificed his only daughter and two of his grandchildren when their conduct prejudiced the realization of his self-appointed task of reforming the character of citizens by a combination of stricter moral laws and personal example on the part of the imperial family. Those reforms, like his *Pax Augusta*, were not derived from disinterested ethical principles, but were based on the perceived needs of the state, *his* state, one which was greater than himself and which demanded from a true Roman not less than everything.

It involved an unashamed appeal to nationalism, even to racism, except that almost nobody in ancient Rome would have seen any shame in that. It was also a call to international duty, one that found an answering echo, miraculously, in the subjugated provinces. The semi-professionalized administrations he supplied, under strictly accountable governors, helped to improve Rome's image as a colonialist power. Taxes were still demanded, of course, but the process of assessment and collection became more rational, less extortionate. Some backward provinces learned to appreciate the benefits that cooperation with a more advanced civilization could bring, at least to their local elites.

Just as Italian towns had copied Roman originals, each with its own new senate house and forum – even, in some cases, identical street names – so provincial cities underwent a building boom as they vied with each other to catch up with and mimic the ways and manners of the envied capital. When Octavian was born, the tribal warriors of Gaul had waged fairly constant warfare against each other; they chopped off the heads of fallen enemies to hang as decorations from the eaves of their primitive huts or from branches in druidic groves. When he was a small boy and Julius Caesar was fighting the Gauls, the Roman army built a camp at the confluence of the Rhône and Saône. By the time he came to power, the camp had developed into a thriving administrative centre, destined for a great future.

Under his reign the settlement became a boom town, Lugdunum, boasting public baths and marble temples, theatres and an aqueduct, rows of workshops for manufacturing fine ceramics, and weatherproof housing of brick and concrete and stone, from which no severed heads were permitted to dangle. Octavian forbade the practice of druidism to anyone who wanted to become a Roman citizen, and the young and ambitious longed above all for the citizenship. Before his death, Lugdunum became the capital of Roman Gaul, hub of a system of wide roads, laid down in stone by legionary soldiers to link the Mediterranean with the Atlantic coast and the North Sea, opening up the entire country to trade and a postal service. Today we know it as Lyons,[5] heart of a conurbation of 1,260,000 people, second city (after Paris) of France, and claimed by many who have sampled the delights of its triple-rosette restaurants to be the gastronomic capital of the world.

That postal system was another Augustan development that helped to unify the empire, although its original and primary purpose was to get information, especially military intelligence, as quickly as possible from the provinces to the capital. Republican Rome already had a private postal network of messengers (in constant use by Cicero and Atticus). Octavian set up a public system for the entire empire, with stable blocks, horses and relay riders at intervals on major roads. It was meant, officially, for public business and confined to men holding senior appointments, but often enough they managed to get the letters of their wives and friends carried, too, rather as non-official mail today somehow finds its way into diplomatic bags. A more efficient and widespread system than Octavian's had to await the building of the railways in the mid-nineteenth century.

Lugdunum is not an isolated example of the Augustan building boom that underlay the rapid spread of urbanization. Many smaller towns and cities sprang up from small beginnings in Gaul and Spain, in North Africa and the Balkans. Some

Augustan foundations, especially numerous in Gaul, can be easily detected by their ancient names: Augustobona (Troyes), Augustodunum (Autun), Augustodurum (Bayeux), Augustonemetum (Clermont Ferrand), to name but a few. Archaeologists, digging up the bones of ancient Gauls, have noted a marked change in grave-goods before and after the reign of Augustus. For centuries, the typical buried artefacts had been weapons and primitive pottery; afterwards, luxuries such as mirrors, ceramics, perfume bottles and oil-lamps tend to predominate. Another great change was also under way, as tribes of beer-drinkers began to switch to wine. No doubt the Romans took the view that the Gauls had never had it so good.

On coming to power, Octavian had begun restoration work on the many decaying temples of Rome. As his reign progressed, new temples were built under his auspices around the empire, often paid for by local worthies who begged for permission to do so. Perhaps the most beautiful, and certainly the best preserved, is the Maison Carrée at Nemausus (Nimes), another Augustan foundation in southern Gaul. It was built in imitation of the Temple of Apollo, which Octavian had erected next to his own home on the Palatine, and includes in its decoration a pattern of carved acanthus leaves taken from his Altar of Peace. Early in the nineteenth century, the Maison Carrée inspired the construction, on a monumental scale, of the church of the Madeleine in Paris. By such means the cultural revolution of Augustus migrated both geographically and temporally, the first helping to bring unity to his empire, the second to link him with modern times.

His iconography even survives among the regalia of English monarchs. When Octavian dedicated Caesar's temple in Rome, he provided a statue of his adoptive father holding a globe in his hand, to represent the universe, not merely the earth. On top of this globe was a tiny figure of Victory. Fourth-century Christians persuaded the emperor of the day to replace the figure with a small cross. Throughout the Middle Ages, a globe surmounted by a cross served as an internationally recognized emblem of kingship. Queen Elizabeth II held just such an orb in her hand at her coronation ceremony in 1953.

Examples could be multiplied. As everyone knows, Julius Caesar, shortly before his assassination, reformed the Roman calendar to fix the length of a year at 365 days, with leap year adjustments. It was Octavian who applied it to the whole empire as a unifying measure, and one that removed control from various local priesthoods, whose power had partly derived from their unscientific decisions about the measurement of seasons and the dates of important festivals. That power was now surrendered to the laws of mathematics, as applied by experts subject to Augustus, instead of by elites responsible only to themselves. Our modern, scientific world works that way, too.

The mourners at Octavian's funeral knew that a remarkable man had passed from them, but few could have imagined that two millennia later his influence would still be so pervasive, in so many ways, great and small, though often quite unrecognized by the general public. As the flames mounted up to consume his earthly remains, a senator claimed to see his spirit rising into the sky to join the other gods in Heaven. He was later rewarded by Livia with a million sesterces for a sworn statement to that effect. She herself returned to the cold pyre five days later to retrieve his bones and some of the ashes, which she transferred to his great, circular mausoleum, from whose dome his own giant statue now looked down.[6]

Throughout the capital, prayers continued to be offered up for years afterwards in the 265 wards into which, for administrative purposes, he had divided the sprawling city, because each ward contained a room or niche in which reposed a cult statuette of himself, which he had thoughtfully provided during the closing years of his reign. Nobody prays to Caesar Augustus any more. More than a billion people, however, pray to one of his former non-Roman subjects, born about eighteen years before his death, whose earthly father was registered with Augustus to pay tax, and who had reason to be thankful for the *Pax Romana* that allowed him to travel in comparative safety with his wife, her new-born child and a donkey to Egypt, where today pious Christians will point out in a suburb of Cairo one of the spots where Mary, Joseph and baby Jesus are said to have rested, now marked by a Coptic church.

That same Augustan peace facilitated the later missionary efforts of St Paul during the reign of the Emperor Nero; without its protection, the man from Macedonia, whom the saint saw in a dream, might have beckoned in vain to the Apostle of the Gentiles to cross from Asia to preach the good news to Europe. The possible consequences are almost unthinkable. Would St Peter have been able to make it all the way to Rome? Would the West have remained sunk in pagan superstition for many centuries? And we must not forget that if the political system of Augustus had not proved so durable, the Roman Empire could not have become nominally Christian so suddenly in the fourth century, as it did under Constantine, because only an absolute ruler could have imposed conformity over such a vast area.

Octavian was far from being the noblest Roman of them all, but he was the Roman who made the greatest contribution to Western civilization. His political system continued to hold much of Europe together for about four centuries after his death, and would inspire the successive ambitions of Charlemagne, Renaissance princes, Enlightenment kings, Napoleon Bonaparte and twentieth-century dictators. Popes would take over his title of *Pontifex Maximus*, and both the Kaiser of Germany and the Czar of all the Russias would inherit his name of Caesar as a synonym for monarchy.

Today, the European Union, sprung from a new Treaty of Rome, follows a methodology not wholly alien to Octavian's, having claimed at intervals during its growth to be no more than a grouping of sovereign states, while pursuing a veiled agenda of aggregating more and greater political power to itself as it gradually expands across the continent. On the other side of the Atlantic, the only country in the world today which can stand comparison with the Augustan Empire, in terms of relative power, debates all issues of war and peace in its own version of the Senate on its own Capitol Hill in Washington, while its current ruler threatens to impose a *Pax Americana* on sovereign nations whom he considers to be rogue states.

Shades of Octavian! He was a man of his own times, of course, not of ours. And he was certainly not a god. But he surely qualifies as a godfather, in both senses of that word. He rose to power by criminal methods at the head of an organization which sometimes acted as if it were a state within a state. People who crossed him died. His peace was more important than the blood of the martyrs in facilitating the spread of the Gospel and the growth of the Christian Church. He and his secretive, family-led organization subverted the Republic by force and fraud, making a series of offers the Senate could not refuse. He sheltered behind aliases. Whether as Caesar or Augustus, Imperator or Princeps, *Divi Filius* or just plain Gaius, the multifaceted Octavian was the Godfather of Europe.

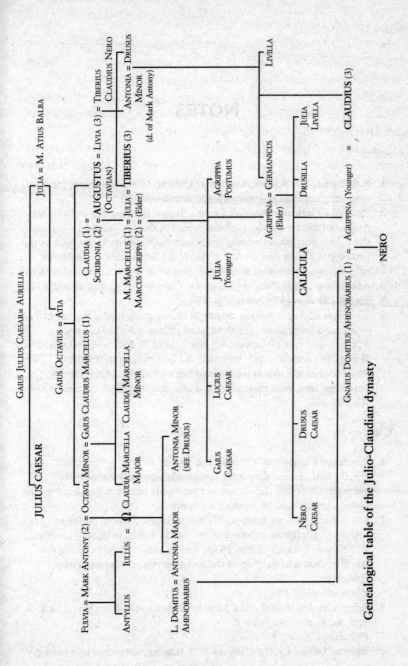

Genealogical table of the Julio-Claudian dynasty

NOTES

Preface

1. R.A. Syme, *The Roman Revolution* (Oxford, 1939). All quotations are from the (corrected) 1960 paperback edition.
2. Professor Galinsky says that Syme's *Roman Revolution* 'was to be an Augustan mirror for the political events of the 1920s and 1930s' on the Continent, where among historians Augustus had 'emerged as the prototypal *Fuhrer* and *Duce* . . . Syme cast him in exactly the same role, though, of course, from a perspective of reprobation rather than admiration'. Karl Galinsky, *Augustan Culture* (Princeton, 1996), p. 3.
3. Syme, *The Roman Revolution*, p. 184.
4. The slave had accused his master of hiding gold, which Brutus had demanded from all the inhabitants of Patara, Lycia (Kelemis, Turkey), in order to support his war against Antony and Octavian. When the accused man's wife said she had hidden it, the slave retorted that she was lying (to save her husband). Brutus let the couple go free, with their gold, and crucified the slave. Appian, *Civil Wars* IV. 81.

Chapter One

1. The legend of Aeneas's escape and voyage to Italy is the subject of Virgil's epic *Aeneid*. Dryden's seventeenth-century translation, although obviously dated, has not yet been entirely superseded by the various leaden-footed modern alternatives.
2. Legend and fact are inextricably mixed in the first ten books of Livy's history (from the foundation of the city to 9 BC), originally totalling 142 books of which all but 35 are lost. None of those covering the late Republic and the rise of Octavian survive, except as brief epitomes.
3. Virgil, *Aeneid* V. 851–3.
4. Julius Caesar claimed to be personally descended from Venus and Aeneas. Suetonius, *Julius* 6.
5. Plutarch, *Caesar* 15.
6. Marcus Tullius Cicero (106–44 BC), scholar, statesman and orator,

left a vast collection of his writings and speeches, including works on philosophy, politics and morality that profoundly influenced the Christian Middle Ages. His letters give an intimate picture of his life and times unequalled by any other writer of antiquity. The most accessible modern biography is by Antony Everitt, *Cicero: A Turbulent Life* (London, 2001).

7. The fullest account of Caesar's intervention and the reaction to it is in Sallust, *Catiline*, 49–55. See also Plutarch, *Cicero* 20–2; Suetonius, *Julius* 14.

8. Suetonius, *Augustus* 2–4.

9. *Ibid.* 2.

10. *Ibid.* 7.

11. *Ibid.*

12. *Ibid.* 4

13. The key modern work is Henrik Mouritsen, *Plebs and Politics in the Late Roman Republic* (Cambridge, 2001).

14. *Ibid.*, pp. 18–37, on measurements of excavated voting areas and estimates of capacity and time taken to vote.

15. '*optimates*', a word derived from *optimus*, the Latin superlative of *bonus* ('good'), is the descriptive term (applied by themselves to themselves) for conservative politicians who claimed ancestral rights to rule according to traditional ways in the Roman Republic.

16. Sallust, *Jugurtha* 41.

17. Matthew 9:11 (Authorized Version).

18. P.A. Brunt, *Social Conflicts in the Roman Republic* (London, 1971), p. 17.

19. 'Debauched by demagogues and largesse, the Roman People was ready for the Empire and the dispensation of bread and games.' Syme, *Roman Revolution*, p. 100.

Chapter Two

1. The most detailed accounts of the Gracchan era are by Greek historians and date from the second century AD, some 250 years after the events described. Plutarch, *Lives of Tiberius and Gaius Gracchus*, and Appian *Civil Wars*, I. 9–26.

2. Plutarch, *Tiberius Gracchus* 10.

3. *Ibid.* 12; Appian. *Civil Wars* I. 12.

4. Plutarch, *Tiberius Gracchus* 17–19; Appian, *Civil Wars* I. 15–16.

5. Plutarch, *Tiberius Gracchus* 20; Appian, *Civil Wars* I. 17.

6. Plutarch, *Gaius Gracchus* 12–17; Appian, *Civil Wars* I. 26.

7. Plutarch, *Sulla* 30.

8. The cult of Vesta, goddess of the hearth, was the only one in Rome to

be served by a female priesthood. Each of the six virgins was appointed, by lot, as a child and had to serve for at least thirty years. Loss of virginity was punishable by being buried alive. Their sanctuary contained the Palladium, a wooden carving of the goddess Athena, said to have been brought from Troy by Aeneas; only the chief vestal was permitted to see it.

9. Suetonius, *Julius* 1.
10. Appian, *Civil Wars* I. 35–6.
11. Aulus Gellius, X. 3. Quoted in the readily accessible collection of translated documents edited by the late A.H.M. Jones, *A History of Rome through the Fifth Century*, Vol. 1 'The Republic' (London, 1968).
12. Appian, *Civil Wars* I. 38–54.
13. Appian, *Civil Wars* I. 55–60.
14. When they sacked Athens, for instance, so many Greeks were killed it was impossible to count them – they could be estimated only by the extent of ground drenched in blood. Plutarch, *Sulla* 14.
15. Plutarch, *Marius* 39; Appian, *Civil Wars* I. 61.
16. Plutarch, *Sulla* 2, 6; *Pompey* 2. One of Pompey's early lovers, Flora, said she never left his bed without his bite marks on her.
17. Plutarch, *Sulla* 31.
18. Cicero, *Pro Sestius* 96–7; *Republic* I. 31.
19. e.g., Livy III. 54–5.
20. Livy, *Epitome* 97; Plutarch, *Pompey* 21–2; Velleius Paterculus, II. 30.
21. Sallust, *Catiline* 55.
22. The *de facto* rule of Pompey, Crassus and Caesar was not known as a triumvirate ('group of three men') at the time; that is a conventional label fixed later. Among many hostile references in his letters, Cicero described the triumviral regime as 'the most infamous ever' – *Ad Atticum* II. 19. Other sources include Suetonius, *Julius* 19–22; Plutarch, *Caesar* 13–14; *Pompey* 47–8; Appian, *Civil Wars* II. 9–14.
23. The long, raised speakers' platform in the Forum. It was decorated with ships' prows *(rostra)*. Our modern term 'rostrum' is the singular form.
24. The crowd emptied a bucket of manure over Bibulus's head when he tried to obstruct Caesar's legislation. He retreated to his house for the rest of his year of office, issuing warnings almost daily of inauspicious omens that would have invalidated all public business if they had been heeded.
25. The provinces of Illyricum, Southern Gaul and northern Italy.

Notes

Chapter Three

1. Suetonius, *Augustus* 6.
2. Cato was a great-grandson of Cato the Censor (234–149 BC), who was still a byword for severe morality and parsimony and whom Cato tried to emulate.
3. A proconsular governor automatically forfeited his *imperium* by entering the capital.
4. After Luca, Cicero changed sides temporarily to support the triumvirs, writing to Atticus: 'As the powerless deny me their love, my task now is to get it from those in power.' *Ad Atticum* IV. 5.
5. The same rule that prevented Caesar from returning to the city (see note 3 above) forced Pompey to leave it.
6. Crassus would try to conquer Parthia, while Caesar would invade Britain.
7. Britain did not become a Roman province until the Emperor Claudius added it to the empire in AD 43.
8. Octavian's full sister Octavia, daughter of Atia, must be distinguished from his much older half-sister of the same name, also a daughter of Gaius Octavius but by his first wife.
9. Octavia's husband had two cousins, also named Claudius Marcellus, who were brothers – one with the same *praenomen*, Gaius, as himself, the other with the *praenomen* Marcus. They are a fertile source of confusion for historians: Marcus would be consul in 51, Octavia's husband consul in 50, and the other Gaius consul in 49. Ancient writers tend to refer to each of them simply as 'Marcellus', so that often only the date identifies the individual.
10. Since the death of Crassus, Caesar had perforce to finance the street gang which had looked after their interests at the rough end of Roman politics. Their leader, Clodius, had been murdered by Milo, head of a rival gang paid by Pompey. After the Senate put Pompey in charge of stamping out street violence, Caesar's gang fades from the record.
11. The uprising was the last large-scale attempt by the Gauls to shake off Roman rule. Vercingetorix was kept alive in Rome until Caesar's triumph in 46 BC, when he was executed, in accordance with Roman tradition, after the procession ended.
12. While he held office, Caesar was immune from prosecution. Suetonius (*Julius* 30) says that Cato vowed to impeach him as soon as he reverted to being a private citizen.
13. For instance, Caesar's own foundation of Novum Comum (Como), an important garrison town among the North Italian lakes, birthplace of both the Elder and Younger Pliny. The Senate cancelled its

citizenship rights during the clash with Caesar, who restored them after he came to sole power.

14. In the great aristocratic houses of Rome, the masks were kept as venerated objects in a room set aside for the purpose, as part of the family cult.

15. Appian, *Civil Wars* II. 30; Plutarch, *Pompey* 58; *Caesar*, 30.

16. Cicero, *Ad Atticum* VII. 6. See also *Ad Atticum* VIII. 9 for Caesar's options.

17. Plutarch, *Caesar* 34; Caesar, *Civil War* I. 16–23; Cicero, *Ad Atticum* VIII. 12A, B, C & D (for Pompey's letters about Corfinium), IX. 16 (for Caesar's clemency).

18. Among many letters on Pompey's retreat and Caesar's pursuit, see especially Cicero *Ad Atticum* VII. 2, VIII. 1, 3, 7, 11, IX. 6, 13, 14. Caesar, *Civil War* I. 24–9.

19. Plutarch, *Caesar* 35; Caesar, *Civil War* I. 29.

20. Appian, *Civil Wars* II. 70; Caesar, *Civil War* III. 85–96.

21. Suetonius, *Julius* 30; Plutarch, *Caesar* 46.

22. Appian, *Civil Wars* II. 112. The belief that Brutus was Caesar's son by Servilia is based on nothing stronger than malicious gossip – he would have been about fifteen when Brutus was born.

23. Suetonius, *Augustus* 94.

24. Nicolaus was the same age as Octavian; before serving Herod he was tutor to the children of Antony and Cleopatra in his home city Alexandria. Little survives of his prolific writings, which included works of philosophy, plays and a universal history in 144 books.

25. Cleopatra VII of Egypt was a descendant of one of Alexander the Great's generals, Ptolemaeus, a Macedonian who became the Pharaoh Ptolemy in the late fourth century BC. She is said to have been the first of the Greek-speaking Ptolemies to learn to converse in the Egyptian language.

26. Plutarch, *Pompey* 76–80; *Caesar* 48; Suetonius, *Julius* 35; Appian, *Civil Wars* II. 84–6; Caesar, *Civil War* III. 103–4.

27. Plutarch, *Caesar* 49.

28. Suetonius, *Julius* 37; Dio, XLIII. 21–2; Appian, *Civil Wars* II. 101.

29. Life expectancy in Rome is estimated to have averaged twenty-nine years, taking into account the high mortality rate among infants and mothers in childbirth.

30. Plutarch, *Caesar* 56.

31. Velleius Paterculus, II. 59; Suetonius, *Augustus* 8.

32. Velleius Paterculus, II. 59.

33. Plutarch, *Caesar* 28.

34. Dio XLIII. 43–5; XLIV. 4–6; Appian, *Civil Wars* II. 106; Suetonius, *Julius* 79. The evidence is treated exhaustively in Stefan Weinstock, *Divus Julius* (Oxford, 1971).

35. Dio XLV. 1; Suetonius, *Augustus* 94.
36. Weinstock, *Divus Julius*, p. 14.
37. Suetonius, *Augustus* 94.
38. Suetonius, *Julius* 86.
39. *Ibid.*, 77.
40. *Ibid.*, 78.
41. Plutarch, *Antony* 11.
42. *Ibid.*, 13.
43. Suetonius, *Julius* 83.
44. *Ibid.*, 79; Appian, *Civil Wars* II. 108.
45. Cicero, *Philippics* III. 12; Suetonius, *Julius* 79; Appian, *Civil Wars* II. 109.
46. Dio, XLIV. 6.
47. Weinstock, *Divus Julius*, p. 286.
48. Appian, *Civil Wars* II. 110. The rumour was made plausible by the qualification that Caesar need not, for that purpose, be named king of Rome, but simply be given permission to use the title of king in the relevant eastern provinces.
49. Plutarch, *Caesar* 63; Suetonius, *Julius* 87.
50. Appian, *Civil Wars*, 115; Plutarch, *Caesar* 63.
51. Plutarch, *Caesar* 66.
52. Many sources, notably Plutarch, *Caesar* 66, *Brutus* 13–17; Dio XLIV. 16–19; Appian, *Civil Wars* II. 111, 117.

Chapter Four

1. For the immediate aftermath of the assassination, see Plutarch, *Caesar* 67; Dio XLIV. 20; Appian, *Civil Wars* II. 118; Cicero, *Philippics* II. 28–30.
2. As Master of Horse at the time of the assassination, Marcus Aemilius Lepidus, the future triumvir, was officially Caesar's second-in-command by military rank. The death of Caesar automatically deprived him of that office, leaving Antony, the surviving consul, as temporary head of state.
3. Plutarch, *Antony* 14; Dio, XLIV. 22. The first occasion on which Antony disguised himself as a slave was when he escaped from Rome to join Caesar before the crossing of the Rubicon.
4. The actions of the conspirators after leaving the Senate until nightfall on the Ides are described in Plutarch, *Brutus* 18, *Caesar* 67; Velleius Paterculus, II. 58; Appian, *Civil Wars* II. 118–23; Dio XLIV. 21–2; Suetonius, *Julius* 82.
5. Lucius Cornelius Balbus, a wealthy Spaniard from Gades (Cadiz), was Caesar's chief agent at the time of the assassination, with

responsibilities for diplomatic, financial and secretarial matters. See Chapter 5.

6. Plutarch, *Antony* 15; Appian, *Civil Wars* II. 125.
7. Cicero, *Philippics* II. 71; Dio XLIV. 53.
8. Plutarch, *Antony* 13.
9. Dio XLIV. 35; Suetonius, *Julius* 82.
10. Velleius Paterculus II. 58; Plutarch, *Cicero* 42, *Brutus* 19.
11. Plutarch, *Brutus* 19; Dio XLIV. 34.
12. Suetonius, *Julius* 83.
13. Plutarch, *Caesar* 68; Suetonius, *Julius* 83.
14. Appian, *Civil Wars* II. 146–8; Cicero, *Philippics* 91; Dio, XLIV. 50. Plutarch, *Caesar* 68, *Cicero* 42, *Antony* 14, *Brutus* 20; Suetonius, *Julius* 84.
15. Suetonius, *Julius* 85; Appian, *Civil Wars* II. 126; Plutarch, *Caesar* 68, *Brutus* 20; Dio, XLIV. 50.
16. Cicero, *Ad Atticum* XIV. 5.
17. Dio XLIV. 51; Appian, *Civil Wars* III. 2.
18. Cicero, *Ad Atticum* XIV. 4.
19. Cicero, *Ad Familiares* XI. 1.
20. Quintus Caecilius Bassus, who had fought under Pompey, refused to surrender after the defeat at Pharsalus. He took over a fortified position in Syria, which he defended for several years until he eventually handed over command of his troops to Cassius.

Chapter Five

1. Appian, *Civil Wars* III. 9–10; Dio XLV. 3.
2. Velleius Paterculus II. 59.
3. Appian, *Civil Wars* III. 11.
4. Cicero owned eight such properties in or near Rome and in Campania. By contrast, Octavian, even at the height of his power, owned three, none of which demonstrated ostentatious use of his great wealth.
5. Cicero, *Ad Atticum* XIV. 5.
6. Appian, *Civil Wars* III. 11; Velleius Paterculus II. 60.
7. Cicero, *Philippics* XIII. 24–5.
8. Appian, *Civil Wars* III. 13.
9. Appian, *Civil Wars* III. 14.
10. Cicero, *Ad Atticum* XIV. 11.
11. *Ibid.* XIV. 12.
12. Dio XLIV. 53.
13. Cicero, *Ad Atticum* 15, 16, 17A, 19.
14. Cicero, *Ad Familiares* XII. 1.

15. Cicero, *Ad Atticum* XIV. 13A.
16. *Ibid*. XIV. 13B.
17. *Ibid*. XIV. 13, XV. 18.
18. Plutarch, *Antony* 16, *Brutus* 22; Velleius Paterculus II. 59; Dio, XLV. 4; Appian, *Civil Wars* III. 12.
19. Appian, *Civil Wars* III. 5.
20. Cicero, *Ad Familiares* XII. 1.
21. Cicero, *Ad Atticum* XIV. 21.
22. *Ibid*.
23. Plutarch, *Antony* 16; *Cicero* 43; Dio XLV. 5; Appian, *Civil Wars* III. 15–20.
24. Appian, *Civil Wars* III. 22.
25. Plutarch, *Antony* 16.
26. Dio XLV. 7.
27. Appian, *Civil Wars* III. 21, 28.
28. Velleius Paterculus II. 60; Cicero, *Ad Atticum* XIV. 14; Dio XLIV. 53.
29. Plutarch, *Cicero* 43; Cicero, *Ad Atticum* XV. 11.
30. Cicero, *Ad Atticum* XV. 4.
31. Dio XLV. 8; Appian, *Civil Wars* III. 30; Plutarch, *Antony* 16.
32. Appian, *Civil Wars* III. 30.

Chapter Six

1. Appian, *Civil Wars* III. 28.
2. Cicero, *Ad Atticum* XV. 11.
3. *Ibid*.
4. Appian, *Civil Wars* III. 23–4; Plutarch, *Brutus* 21.
5. Suetonius, *Augustus* 10; Appian, *Civil Wars* III. 31.
6. Dio XLV. 6–7.
7. Cicero, *Philippics* I. 8.
8. Cicero, *Ad Atticum* XVI. 7.
9. Velleius Paterculus II. 62.
10. Cicero, *Ad Familiares* XI. 3.
11. Cicero, *Ad Atticum* XV. 12.
12. Cicero, *Ad Familiares* XI. 3
13. Cicero, *Ad Atticum* XVI. 7.
14. Plutarch, *Cicero* 43.
15. Cicero himself named as 'Philippics' his series of fourteen speeches (not all of them delivered) against Antony, to invite comparison with those of the Athenian orator Demosthenes in the fourth century BC against Philip of Macedon, father of Alexander the Great.
16. Cicero, *Ad Familiares* XII. 2.

17. Plutarch, *Cicero* 44.
18. Appian, *Civil Wars* III. 32–9; Plutarch, *Antony* 16.
19. Cicero, *Ad Familiares* XII. 3.
20. Suetonius, *Augustus* 10; Plutarch, *Antony* 16; Appian, *Civil Wars* III. 39.
21. Cicero, *Ad Familiares* XII. 23.
22. *Ibid*; Dio XLV. 12; Appian, *Civil Wars* III. 40.

Chapter Seven

1. Cicero, *Ad Atticum* XV. 13; Plutarch, *Brutus* 24; Appian, *Civil Wars* III. 26.
2. Cicero, *Ad Brutum* 11; Plutarch, *Brutus* 24, *Cicero* 45.
3. Cicero, *Ad Familiares* XI. 7.
4. Appian, *Civil Wars* III. 31; Suetonius, *Augustus* 10; Dio XLV. 12; Plutarch, *Antony* 16.
5. Velleius Paterculus II. 61; Appian, *Civil Wars* III. 40; Dio XLV. 12; Plutarch, *Antony* 16.
6. See below, p. 99.
7. Appian, *Civil Wars* III. 43; Dio XLV. 13.
8. Fulvia had been the widow, successively, of Publius Clodius (organizer of politicized street violence in support of the First Triumvirate), and Scribonius Curio, who proposed the key Senate motion for both Pompey and Caesar to disarm. Antony was her third husband. As his wife, according to Professor Bauman, she became 'the first empress in all but name'. P.A. Bauman, *Women and Politics in Ancient Rome* (London and New York), p. 89.
9. Appian, *Civil Wars* III. 44.
10. Cicero, Ad Atticum XVI. 8; Plutarch, Cicero 45.
11. Cicero, Ad Atticum XVI. 8.
12. *Ibid*. XVI. 9.
13. *Ibid*. XVI. 11.
14. Appian, Civil Wars III. 41; Dio XLV. 6.
15. Appian, Civil Wars III. 41.
16. *Ibid*. III. 42.
17. *Ibid*. III. 45.
18. *Ibid*; Dio XLV. 13.
19. Velleius Paterculus II. 61; Dio XLV. 13.
20. Dio XLV. 9.
21. Appian, *Civil Wars* III. 46; Dio XLV. 13.

Notes

1. Cicero's two speeches on 20 December are recorded in *Philippics* III and IV, but those are almost certainly versions polished up after the event for future publication. The orator's pride in them is clearly reflected in letters he wrote shortly afterwards: *Ad Familiares* X. 28, XI. 6A, XII. 22A. Dio XLV. 18–47.
2. Cicero, *Ad Atticum* XVI. 15. This is his last surviving letter to Atticus. He plainly wrote others to him during the deepening crisis, but they may have been destroyed by later censors if, as seems likely, some of them attacked Octavian.
3. Cicero, *Philippics* III. 2.
4. Cicero, *Ad Familiares*, 20, 21; Suetonius, *Augustus* 12; Velleius Paterculus II. 62. The witticism turns on the double meaning of the Latin *'tollendum'*, which may be translated as 'fit to be exalted' or 'fit to be cast aside', even 'fit to be killed'. Octavian was not amused.
5. Appian, *Civil Wars* III. 47; Velleius Paterculus II. 62; Cicero, *Philippics* III.
6. Cicero, *Philippics* IV. 2.
7. Appian, *Civil Wars* III. 48.
8. Cicero, *Philippics* V. 43, 51; Dio XLV. 18–47, XLVI. 1–29. Suetonius, *Augustus* 10; Plutarch, *Cicero* 45; Appian, *Civil Wars* 50–1.
9. Cicero, *Philippics* II. 44.
10. *Ibid*. III. 4, V. 22, XIII. 18.
11. Appian, *Civil Wars* III. 50, 54–60.
12. *Ibid*. III. 51
13. Cicero, *Philippics* VI. 16–17.
14. *Ibid*. VIII.
15. Appian, *Civil Wars* III. 61–3; Dio XLVI. 30–1.
16. Cicero, *Ad Familiares* XII. 4.
17. *Ibid*. XII. 5.
18. Cicero, *Philippics* X. 14–15, 23–6.
19. Plutarch, *Brutus* 25–6.
20. Cicero, *Ad Familiares* XII. 11; Dio XLVI. 26–8.
21. Appian, *Civil Wars* III. 65; Dio XLVI. 36.
22. Appian, *Civil Wars* 65.
23. *Ibid*. III. 61; Dio XLVII. 29; Cicero, *Philippics* XI.
24. Cicero, *Philippics* XIII.
25. Cicero, *Ad Familiares* X. 27.
26. Cicero, *Ad Brutum* 9.
27. Cicero, *Philippics* X. 25–6; Plutarch, *Brutus* 27; Dio XLVII. 29.

Chapter Nine

1. Suetonius, *Augustus* 10.
2. Dio XLVI. 38.
3. Cicero, *Ad Familiares* X. 30, *Philippics* 26–8, 36–8; Suetonius, *Augustus* 10; Appian, *Civil Wars* III. 66–70; Dio XLVI. 37–8.
4. Appian, *Civil Wars* III. 70.
5. Cicero, *Philippics* XIV. 14–16.
6. Cicero, *Ad Brutum* 7.
7. Appian, *Civil Wars* III. 71.
8. Plutarch, *Antony* 17; Appian, *Civil Wars* III. 72.
9. Appian, *Civil Wars* 75–6.
10. *Ibid.* III. 73; Cicero, *Ad Familiares* XI. 9 (this letter from Decimus on 29 April shows he understood the true military/political situation much more clearly than did Cicero), XI. 10, 11, 13.
11. Dio XLVI. 39–40; Velleius Paterculus II. 62; Appian, *Civil Wars* III. 80; Cicero, *Ad Brutum* 24.
12. Cicero, *Ad Brutum* 11, 17.
13. Dio XLVI. 41; Appian, *Civil Wars* III. 74.
14. Plutarch, *Antony* 18; Appian, *Civil Wars* 83–4; Velleius Paterculus II. 63.
15. Cicero, *Ad Familiares* XI. 10.
16. Appian, *Civil Wars* IV. 64.
17. *Ibid.* III. 97–8; Dio XLVI. 53; Velleius Paterculus II. 64.
18. Plutarch, *Cicero* 45–6; Appian, *Civil Wars* III. 82; Dio XLVI. 42.
19. Cicero, *Ad Brutum* 11.
20. Cicero, *Ad Familiares* XI. 14.
21. Cicero, *Ad Brutum* 26.
22. Dio XLVI. 43; Appian, *Civil Wars* III. 86–8; Suetonius, *Augustus* 26.
23. Dio XLVI. 44; Appian, *Civil Wars* 90–2.
24. Appian, *Civil Wars* III. 92.
25. *Ibid.* III. 93.
26. Dio XLVI. 46.
27. Appian, *Civil Wars* III. 94.
28. *Ibid.* III. 95–6; Dio XLVI. 48–9.
29. Syme, *The Roman Revolution*, p. 177.
30. Cicero, *Philippics* XIII. 40.

Chapter Ten

1. Appian, *Civil Wars* 2; Plutarch, *Antony* 19; Dio XLVI. 54–6.
2. Velleius Paterculus II. 66; Plutarch, *Cicero* 46.
3. Appian, *Civil Wars* IV. 5; Livy, *Periochae* 120; Plutarch, *Cicero* 46, *Brutus* 27, *Antony* 20; Suetonius, *Augustus* 27.

4. Appian, *Civil Wars* IV. 3, 86.
5. Plutarch, *Antony* 20; Dio XLVI. 56.
6. Velleius Paterculus II. 67; Appian, *Civil Wars* IV. 6–16; Dio XLVII. 3.
7. Appian, *Civil Wars* IV. 17.
8. *Ibid*. IV. 11.
9. Plutarch, *Antony* 19–20; Dio XLVII. 6–8.
10. Appian, *Civil Wars* IV. 23.
11. *Ibid*. IV. 25.
12. *Ibid*.
13. *Ibid*. IV. 43.
14. *Ibid*. IV. 45.
15. Plutarch, *Cicero* 47–9; Appian, *Civil Wars* IV. 19–20; Dio XLVII. 8.
16. Appian, *Civil Wars* IV. 5, 34; Dio XLVII. 14–17.
17. Appian, *Civil Wars* IV. 32–4.
18. Velleius Paterculus II. 69; Plutarch, *Brutus* 29–32, 34–5; Dio XLVII. 31–6.
19. Appian, *Civil Wars* IV. 84–6; Dio XLVII. 36–7.
20. Appian, *Civil Wars* IV. 63.
21. *Ibid*. IV. 65, 87, 106; Dio XLVII. 37.
22. Plutarch, *Brutus* 38–9; Appian, Civil Wars IV. 87–106; Dio XLVII. 38.
23. Plutarch, *Brutus* 40–2, *Antony* 22; Appian, *Civil Wars* 107–12; Dio XLVII. 39, 42–6.
24. Plutarch, *Brutus* 43–4, *Antony* 22; Velleius Paterculus II. 70; Appian, *Civil Wars* IV. 113–14; Dio XLVII. 46.
25. Plutarch, *Antony* 22; Dio XLVII. 41, 46; Velleius Paterculus II. 70.
26. Plutarch, *Brutus* 47; Appian, *Civil Wars* IV. 115–16; Dio XLVII. 47.
27. Plutarch, *Brutus* 36, 48.
28. *Ibid*. 37.
29. *Ibid*. 53; cf. Dio XLVII. 49.
30. Plutarch, *Brutus* 46–8; Appian, *Civil Wars* 122–5; Dio XLVII. 48.
31. Suetonius, *Augustus* 13; Velleius Paterculus II. 70–1; Plutarch, *Brutus* 49–52, *Antony* 22; Appian, *Civil Wars* 126–31, 135–8; Dio XLVII. 49.

Chapter Eleven

1. The most detailed information comes from Appian, writing almost 200 years after the events he describes, and the even later history of Dio Cassius in the early third century AD. Plutarch's life of Antony and Suetonius's life of Augustus, each dating from the early second century, are brilliant but flawed, and more biographical than historical. The surviving work of the contemporary chronicler Velleius Paterculus is part of a less-than-satisfactory attempt (by a partisan of Octavian and

his successor Tiberius) to summarize the main incidents of Roman history for an audience of ordinary citizens. Octavian's own *Res Gestae* is vital but necessarily brief as it survived only as an inscription. The only other substantial contemporary references are to be found in the laudatory and historically unreliable verses of Augustan poets, four of whom (Virgil, Horace, Propertius and Tibullus) were among those dispossessed in Octavian's land resettlement programme.

2. Appian, *Civil Wars* V. 27; Velleius Paterculus II. 74.
3. Suetonius, *Augustus* 13; Appian V. 3–5; Dio XLVIII. 2.
4. Dio XLVIII. 1–2.
5. *Ibid*. 3; Appian, *Civil Wars* V. 12.
6. Syme, *The Roman Revolution*, p. 208. See also Dio XLVIII. 4.
7. Dio XLVIII. 9–10.
8. Appian, *Civil Wars* V. 12.
9. *Ibid*.
10. *Ibid*. V. 13.
11. *Ibid*. V. 14; Dio XLVIII. 6.
12. Suetonius, *Augustus* 14; Appian, *Civil Wars* V. 14.
13. Appian, *Civil Wars* V. 16.
14. *Ibid*. V. 19.
15. *Ibid*. V. 4–5.
16. *Ibid*. V. 7.
17. *Ibid*. V. 8–9; Plutarch, *Antony* 25–7.
18. Suetonius, *Augustus* 62; Dio XLVIII. 5.
19. Appian, *Civil Wars* V. 13, 27.
20. Dio XLVIII. 10.
21. *Ibid*. 12; Appian, *Civil Wars* V. 20.
22. Dio XLVIII. 12; Appian, *Civil Wars* V. 23.
23. Dio XLVIII. 13.
24. Appian, *Civil Wars* V. 31.
25. *Ibid*. V. 32; Dio, XLVIII. 14.
26. Appian, *Civil Wars* V. 33.
27. *Ibid*. V. 34–7.
28. *Ibid*. V. 46–8; Dio XLVIII. 14; Velleius Paterculus II. 74.
29. Suetonius, *Augustus* 15; Dio XLVIII. 14. This story of alleged 'human sacrifice' became so well known that nearly a century later Seneca, in his essay *de Clementia* 'On Mercy' (written for the teenage Emperor Nero), referred to it without need of further explanation as *post Perusinas aras et proscriptiones* ('after the Perugian altars and the proscriptions'). Seneca evidently believed it, taking the view that Augustus recognized the great value of being merciful only when he was fully mature. *De Clementia*, I. 11.
30. Velleius Paterculus II. 76; Appian, *Civil Wars* V. 50–1; Dio XLVIII. 48.

Notes

Chapter Twelve

1. Plutarch, *Antony* 28, 30; Appian, *Civil Wars* V. 52, 55, 59; Dio XLVIII. 16, 24–7.
2. Appian, *Civil Wars* V. 60.
3. *Ibid.* V. 55–6; Dio XLVIII. 27–8.
4. Appian, *Civil Wars* V. 56–7; Dio XLVIII. 30.
5. *Appian* V. 58–9.
6. *Ibid.* V. 59; Plutarch, *Antony* 30; Dio XLVIII. 28.
7. Appian, *Civil Wars* V. 60–3.
8. *Ibid.* V. 64.
9. Velleius Paterculus II. 78; Appian, *Civil Wars* V. 64; Plutarch, *Antony* 31 (wrongly states that Antony is to marry Octavian's half-sister, also Octavia).
10. Appian, *Civil Wars* V. 65; Plutarch, *Antony* 30; Velleius Paterculus II. 76; Dio XLVIII. 28–9.
11. Dio XLVIII. 35.
12. Plutarch, *Antony* 3113. Dio XLVIII. 16.
13. Suetonius, *Augustus* 62; Appian, *Civil Wars* V. 53.
14. Suetonius, *Augustus* 62.
15. See below, Chapter 18.
16. Appian, *Civil Wars* V. 66; Dio XLVIII. 31.
17. Appian, *Civil Wars* 66; Dio XLVIII. 33; Valeius Paterculus II. 76.
18. Suetonius, *Augustus* 66.
19. Dio XLVIII. 30.
20. Suetonius, *Augustus* 70.
21. *Ibid.* 71.
22. Appian, *Civil Wars* V. 68; Dio XLVIII. 31.
23. Appian, *Civil Wars* V. 67. The notices were not, of course, made of paper but of wood.
24. *Ibid.* V. 69–73; Dio XLVIII. 36.
25. Appian, *Civil Wars* V. 70; Dio XLVIII. 19; Velleius Paterculus II. 77.
26. Appian, *Civil Wars* V. 72; Dio XLVIII. 36; Velleius Paterculus II. 77; Plutarch, *Antony* 32.
27. Dio XLVIII. 37.
28. Appian, *Civil Wars* V. 73; Dio XLVIII. 38; Plutarch, *Antony* 32.
29. Livia's first husband was the direct ancestor of the four successive emperors after Augustus, being the father of Tiberius, great-grandfather of Caligula, grandfather of Claudius and great-great-grandfather of Nero.

Chapter Thirteen

1. Suetonius, *Tiberius* 4, *Augustus* 15.
2. Suetonius, *Tiberius* 6; Velleius Paterculus II. 75.
3. See above, p. 18.
4. Suetonius, *Tiberius* 4.
5. Anthony A. Barrett, *Livia: First Lady of Imperial Rome* (New Haven and London, 2002), p. 21.
6. Suetonius, *Augustus* 69.
7. Suetonius, *Caligula* 25.
8. Velleius Paterculus II. 75.
9. Tacitus, *Annals* I. 10, V. 1.
10. Dio XLVIII. 44.
11. *Ibid.* 34.
12. *Ibid.* 44.
13. Plutarch, *Antony* 34; Dio XLVIII. 39–41, XLIX. 19–21.
14. Appian, *Civil Wars* V. 77; Dio XLVIII. 46.
15. Suetonius, *Augustus* 74; Dio XLVIII. 45.
16. Appian, *Civil Wars* V. 78–9; Dio XLVIII. 46.
17. Appian, *Civil Wars* V. 84–7; Dio XLVIII. 47–8.
18. Suetonius, *Augustus* 25.
19. Appian, *Civil Wars* V. 88–92; Dio XLVIII. 49–51; Suetonius, *Augustus* 16; Velleius Paterculus II. 79.
20. Appian, *Civil Wars* V. 93; Dio XLVIII. 54; Plutarch, *Antony* 35.
21. Appian, *Civil Wars* 94.
22. *Ibid.* 95.
23. Plutarch, *Antony* 36; Dio XLVIII. 54.
24. Appian, *Civil Wars* V. 96–9; Velleius Paterculus II. 79; Suetonius, *Augustus* 16.
25. Appian, *Civil Wars* V. 109–12; Dio XLIX. 1–5.
26. Appian, *Civil Wars* V. 118–22, 142–4; Dio XLIX. 8–11, 18; Velleius Paterculus II. 79.
27. Appian, Civil Wars V. 123–6; Dio XLIX. 11–12; Velleius Paterculus II. 80; Suetonius, *Augustus* 16.
28. Appian, *Civil Wars* V. 131; Dio XLIX. 12; Augustus, *Res Gestae* 25.
29. Appian, *Civil Wars* V. 130, 132; Dio XLIX. 15.
30. Plutarch, *Antony* 36; Dio XLIX. 32.
31. See above, pp. 167–8.

Chapter Fourteen

1. Velleius Paterculus II. 82; Plutarch, *Antony* 37; Dio XLIX. 24.
2. Plutarch, *Antony* 38; Dio XLIX. 25.

3. Plutarch, *Antony* 39; Dio XLIX. 26.
4. Velleius Paterculus II. 82; Plutarch, *Antony* 40–50; Dio XLIX. 27–9, 31; Livy, *Periochae* 130.
5. Plutarch, *Antony* 51; Dio XLIX. 31.
6. Plutarch, *Antony* 53–4; Dio XLIX. 33.
7. Dio XLIX. 34, L. 24–6.
8. Dio L. 5.
9. Seneca, *Epistulae Morales* LXXXIII. 25.
10. Plutarch, *Antony* 52–3.
11. Suetonius, *Augustus* 20; Dio XLIX. 34–8.
12. Dio XLIX. 39–40; Velleius Paterculus II. 82.
13. Plutarch, *Antony* 54; Dio XLIX. 41.
14. Suetonius, *Julius* 52.
15. Plutarch, *Antony* 55; Dio L. 1.
16. Suetonius, *Augustus* 69.
17. *Ibid*, 37; Dio XLIX. 42–3.
18. Dio, XLVIII. 42.
19. Dio XLIX. 43.
20. Dio L. 2.
21. *Ibid*. 2–3; Plutarch, *Antony* 57.
22. Plutarch, *Antony* 58; Dio L. 3; Velleius Paterculus II. 83; Suetonius, *Augustus* 17.
23. Dio L. 4.
24. Augustus, *Res Gestae* 25.
25. Plutarch, *Antony* 60; Dio L. 4.

Chapter Fifteen

1. Plutarch, *Antony* 56, 60; Dio L. 6–7.
2. Josephus, *Jewish Wars* 20. 1.
3. Plutarch, *Antony* 61–2; Dio L. 23, 29; Velleius Paterculus II. 84.
4. Plutarch, *Antony* 62; Dio L. 11.
5. Dio L. 11.
6. Plutarch, *Antony* 58; Dio L. 10.
7. Plutarch, *Antony* 62; Dio L. 11–12.
8. Dio L. 13; Velleius Paterculus II. 84.
9. Plutarch, *Antony* 68.
10. Plutarch, *Antony* 63; Dio L. 13; Velleius Paterculus II. 84.
11. Plutarch, *Antony* 63–4; Dio L. 14–22.
12. Plutarch, *Antony* 66; Dio L. 33.
13. Plutarch, *Antony* 64–8; Velleius Paterculus II. 85; Dio L. 31–5. Dio's vivid account of the battle continuing long after Antony and Cleopatra had fled appears to be no more than a rhetorical fantasy.

14. Plutarch, *Antony* 68.
15. Dio LI. 5.
16. Horace, *Odes* I. 37. 5–10.
17. *Ibid.* I. 37. 21.
18. Plutarch, *Antony* 68; Dio LI. 4.
19. Velleius Paterculus II. 88.
20. Plutarch, *Antony* 72–3; Josephus, *Jewish Wars* 20. 3–4; Dio LI. 6, 8.
21. Plutarch, *Antony* 74–6; Dio LI. 9–10; Velleius Paterculus II. 87.
22. Plutarch, *Antony* 74, 77.
23. *Ibid.* 78.
24. *Ibid.* 78–9, 83; Dio LI. 11–13.
25. Plutarch, *Antony* 85; Dio LI. 14.
26. Shakespeare, *Antony and Cleopatra* V. 2. 282–3. Sir Thomas North translated Plutarch in 1579, not from the original Greek but from a celebrated French version of 1559 by Jacques Amyot. It was Shakespeare's source for both *Julius Caesar* and *Antony and Cleopatra*. See T.J.B. Spencer, *Shakespeare's Plutarch* (London, 1964), which prints North's English text with interpolated passages from the plays.
27. *Ibid.* V. 2. 303–5.
28. *Ibid.* V. 2. 328–9 (derived from Plutarch, *Antony* 85).
29. Plutarch, *Antony* 81–2, 86; Dio LI. 6.

Chapter Sixteen

1. Suetonius, *Augustus* 18; Dio LI. 16.
2. Suetonius, *Virgil* 27.
3. Dio LI. 19–20.
4. Suetonius, *Augustus* 41; Dio 51. 21.
5. Augustus, *Res Gestae* 34.
6. Pliny, *Natural History* XI. 54.
7. Velleius Paterculus II. 89.
8. Dio LII. 42.
9. The precise qualification for inclusion in the census is uncertain. See the essay under 'population, Roman' in the *Oxford Classical Dictionary* (3rd edn, 1996).
10. Suetonius, *Augustus* 52.
11. Dio LII. 1–40; Suetonius, *Augustus* 28. Dio's account is in the form of imagined speeches by Agrippa and Maecenas, which set out Octavian's various options.
12. *Ibid.* LIII. 3–10.
13. *Ibid.* LIII. 11.
14. *Ibid.* LIII. 12–15.
15. *Ibid.* LIII. 17.

16. *Ibid*. LIII. 16; Velleius Paterculus II. 91.
17. Livy II. 10.
18. Horace, *Odes* III. 2. 12.
19. Wilfred Owen (1893–1918), describing a gas attack when one of his men failed to put on his gas-mask in time, writes that anyone who witnessed the scene 'Would not tell with such high zest/To children ardent for some desperate glory/The old Lie: *Dulce et decorum est/Pro patria mori*.' Owen was killed in action, leading his platoon, a week before the Armistice.
20. Horace, *Odes* III. 6. 33–41.
21. Horace, *Epistles* II. 2. 51–2.
22. Horace, *Odes* II. 18. 1–14; I. 9. 5–8, 18–24.
23. *Ibid*. III. 5. 2–4.
24. Propertius II. 31.
25. *Ibid*. IV. 1. 55–7.
26. When Aeneas goes down to the Underworld (beneath the Sibyl's cave) the ghost of his dead father, Anchises, prophesies that 'this man, Augustus Caesar, son of a god, shall establish an age of gold in Latium'. Virgil, *Aeneid* VI. 792–4.
27. 'A democracy cannot rule an empire. Neither can one man, though empire may appear to presuppose monarchy. There is always an oligarchy somewhere, open or concealed.' Syme, *The Roman Revolution*, 346.
28. Dio 53. 21; Suetonius, *Augustus* 35.
29. Dio LI. 23–4.
30. *Ibid*. LI. 24–5.
31. *Ibid*. LIII. 23–4.

Chapter Seventeen

1. Suetonius, *Augustus* 71.
2. Dio LVIII. 2.
3. Suetonius, *Augustus* 45, 83.
4. *Ibid*. 72.
5. Macrobius II. 4. 11.
6. *Ibid*. 4. 20.
7. *Ibid*. 4. 1.
8. Seneca, *de Clementia* I. 18, *de Ira* III. 40; Dio LIV. 23.
9. Suetonius, *Augustus* 64, 73.
10. *Ibid*. 45.
11. *Ibid*. 40.
12. *Ibid*. 44.
13. *Ibid*. 76–7.

14. *Ibid.* 42.
15. *Ibid.* 72.
16. Macrobius II. 4. 18.
17. Suetonius, Augustus 74.
18. *Ibid.* 53.
19. *Ibid.* 55.
20. *Ibid.* 85.
21. *Ibid.* 92–3.
22. *Ibid.* 90–1.
23. *Ibid.* 33.
24. *Ibid.* 45.
25. *Ibid.* 27.
26. *Ibid.* 36.
27. *Ibid.* 53.
28. See above, Chapter 16.
29. Dio LIII. 25.
30. *Ibid.* 27.
31. *Ibid.* 28.
32. *Ibid.* 30.
33. *Ibid.* 32.
34. *Ibid.*; Suetonius, *Augustus* 34.
35. Dio LIII. 33; Velleius Paterculus II. 93.
36. Dio LIII. 30; see Plate 9.
37. Dio LIII. 31.
38. Dio LIV. 3; Velleius Paterculus II. 91.
39. Suetonius, *Tiberius* 8.
40. Suetonius, *Augustus* 66.
41. Dio LIV. 6.
42. Dio LIV. 19.

Chapter Eighteen

1. Among the more important are Egypt; the Alpine provinces of Raeta and Noricum; the Balkan provinces of Pannonia and Moesia; the Near East provinces of Galatia and Judaea; and large parts of Spain and North Africa.
2. Dio LIV. 6.
3. *Ibid.* LIV. 1.
4. *Ibid.* LIV. 7–8; Augustus, *Res Gestae* 29; Velleius Paterculus II. 91; Suetonius, *Augustus* 21.
5. Dio LIII. 29, LIV. 9; Suetonius, *Augustus* 21.
6. Velleius Paterculus II. 91; Suetonius, *Augustus* 19; Dio LIII. 24.
7. Dio LIV. 10.

Notes

8. Suetonius, *Augustus* 27, 34; Dio LIV. 10, 16, 30; LVI. 1–10; Augustus, *Res Gestae* 6.

9. Velleius Paterculus II. 18.

10. *Ibid*.II. 95; Dio LIV. 22, 24.

11. Velleius Paterculus II. 96; Dio LIV. 28–9.

12. Dio LIV. 29, LV. 8.

13. See Plate 11.

14. Dio LIV. 31, 35; Velleius Paterculus II. 96; Suetonius, *Augustus* 63.

15. Suetonius, *Tiberius* 7.

16. Velleius Paterculus II. 97; Dio LIV. 31, 34, 36; LV. 1–2, 6.

17. See family tree, p. 277.

18. Dio LIV. 27.

19. Suetonius, *Tiberius* 10; Dio LV. 9; Velleius Paterculus II. 99.

20. Velleius Paterculus II. 100; Suetonius, *Augustus* 65; Pliny, *Natural History* VII. 149.

21. Dio LV. 9.

22. *Ibid*. LV. 11.

23. *Ibid*. LV. 10; Augustus, *Res Gestae* 35; Suetonius, *Augustus* 58.

24. Dio LV. 10.

25. Velleius Paterculus II. 100.

26. Dio LV. 10; Suetonius, *Augustus* 65, Tiberius 11.

27. Velleius Paterculus II. 100; Tacitus, *Annals* III. 24, IV. 71.

28. Suetonius, *Tiberius* 13.

29. *Ibid*., *Augustus* 84.

30. Velleius Paterculus II. 103.

31. *Ibid*. II. 102; Dio LV. 10; Suetonius, *Augustus* 65; Tacitus, *Annals* I. 3.

32. Dio LV. 13.

33. *Ibid*. LV. 32; Suetonius, *Augustus* 65; Tacitus, *Annals* I. 3.

34. Suetonius, *Augustus* 65.

35. Ovid, *Tristia* II. 207.

36. S.G. Nugent, 'Ovid and Augustus', in K.A. Raaflaub and M. Toher (eds) *Between Republic and Empire* (Berkeley and London, 1990), p. 256.

37. Velleius Paterculus II. 110–16; Dio LV. 28–34, LVI. 11–17; Suetonius, *Tiberius* 16–19.

38. Dio LV. 23–5; Suetonius, *Augustus* 49.

39. Velleius Paterculus II. 117–20; Dio LVI. 18–24.

40. Suetonius, *Augustus* 23.

41. Dio LVI. 33; Tacitus, *Annals* I. 11.

42. Suetonius, *Augustus* 97–8; Velleius Paterculus II. 123; Dio LVI. 29–30.

Chapter Nineteen

1. Suetonius, *Augustus* 99–100; Velleius Paterculus II. 123; Dio LVI. 31; Tacitus, *Annals* I. 5.
2. Tacitus, Annals I. 6; cf. Velleius Paterculus II. 112.
3. Augustus, *Res Gestae* 13.
4. Lord Macaulay, *Horatius* 32.
5. For a recent assessment of the early development of Roman Gaul, in the light of archaeological research, see Ramsay MacMullen, *Romanization in the Time of Augustus* (New Haven and London, 2000), pp. 85–123.
6. Dio LVI. 34–42, 45–6.

SELECT BIBLIOGRAPHY

Adam, Jeane-Pierre, *La Construction Romaine: Materiaux et Techniques*, Paris, 1989; Eng. transl. *Roman Buildings: Materials and Techniques*, London, 1994 (copiously illustrated)

d'Ambra, Eve, *Art and Identity in the Roman World*, London, 1998

Barrett, Anthony A., *Livia: First Lady of Imperial Rome*, New Haven/London, 2002

Bauman, Richard A., *Women and Politics in Ancient Rome*, London/New York, 1993

Brunt, P.A., *Social Conflicts in the Roman Republic*, London, 1971

——, *The Fall of the Roman Republic*, Oxford, 1988

——, and Moore, J.M., (eds), *Res Gestae Divi Augusti*, Oxford, 1967

Carter, John M., *Suetonius: Divus Augustus*, (Latin text, introduction and notes), Bristol, 1982

Charles-Picard, Gilbert, *Auguste et Néron*, Paris, 1962; Eng. transl., *Augustus and Nero*, 1982

Chisholm, Kitty and Ferguson, John (eds), *Rome: The Augustan Age*, Oxford, 1981

Claridge, Amanda, *Rome*, Oxford Archaeological Guides, 1998

Cunliffe, Barry, *Rome and her Empire*, London, 1978

Eck, Werner, *Augustus und seine Zeit*, Munich, 1998; Eng, trans. *Augustus*, Oxford, 2003

Everitt, Anthony, *Cicero: A Turbulent Life*, London, 2001

Fantham, Elaine, *Roman Literary Culture: From Cicero to Apuleius*, Johns Hopkins UP, 1996

Galinsky, Karl, *Augustan Culture*, Princeton, 1996

Grant, Michael, *The Roman Forum*, London, 1970 (many colour photographs)

Gruen, Erich S., *The Last Generation of the Roman Republic*, Berkeley, 1974

Habinek, Thomas and Schiesaro, Alessando (eds), *The Roman Cultural Revolution*, Cambridge/New York, 1997

Hopkins, Keith, *Conquerors and Slaves*, Cambridge, 1978

Jones, A.H.M., *Augustus*, London, 1970

Levick, Barbara, *The Government of the Roman Empire: A Sourcebook*, London, 1985

Lindsay, Jack, *Cleopatra*, London, 1971

Lintott, Andrew, *Imperium Romanum: Politics and Administration*, London/New York, 1993

Lyne, R.O.A.M., *Horace: Behind the Public Poetry*, New Haven/London, 1995

MacMullen, Ramsay, *Romanization in the Time of Augustus*, New Haven/London, 2000

Millar, Fergus, *A Study of Cassius Dio*, Oxford, 1964

——, *The Crowd in the Late Republic*, Ann Arbor, 1998

——, and Segal, E. (eds), *Caesar Augustus: Seven Aspects*, Oxford, 1984

Mouritsen, Henrik, *Plebs and Politics in the Late Roman Republic*, Cambridge, 2001

Raaflaub, Kurt and Toher, Mark (eds), *Between Republic and Empire*, Berkeley/London, 1990

Ramage, Nancy and Ramage, Andrew, *Roman Art*, Cambridge, 1991

Shotter, David, *Augustus*, Lancaster Pamphlet, London/New York, 1991.

Shuckburgh, E.S., *Augustus*, London, 1905

Southern, Pat, *Augustus*, London/New York, 1998

Syme, Ronald, *The Roman Revolution*, Oxford, 1939

Wallace-Hadrill, A., *Augustan Rome*, London, 1993

——, 'The Imperial Court', in *Cambridge Ancient History*, vol 10, 1996

Wells, Colin, *The Roman Empire* (2nd edn), London, 1992

Zanker, Paul, *Augustus und die Macht der Bilder*, Munich 1987; Eng. trans., *The Power of Images in the Age of Augustus*, Ann Arbor, 1998

INDEX

Notes: Major entries are in chronological order, where appropriate. Italic page numbers indicate maps or figures; numbers in brackets preceded by *n* are note numbers.

Index

Index

Libo, Lucius Scribonius 203,
        207, 209
Livia Drusilla 210, 211–15, 241,
        294, 298–9, 316, 323
    influence on Octavian 285,
        311, 319
Livy (Titus Livius, historian)
        162, 276, 278
Luca 33
Lucius (Antony's brother) 161,
        179–80, 182–3
    in opposition to Octavian
        184–5, 186–7, 193–4
    in siege of Perusia 188–91
Lucretius 289
Ludi, Secularis 306
Lugdunum (Lyons) 327–8
Lupercalia rite 49

Macauley, Lord 326
Macedonia 31, 38, 46, 59, 73–4,
        88, 102–3, 109, 122,
        274
    struggle for governorship 136,
        137
Macrobius 286–7, 288
Maecenas, Gaius 113, 218, 223,
        242, 277, 278, 294, 301
magistrates *see* consuls
Maison Carrée 329
Manius (Antony's agent) 179,
        183, 205
Marcella 303
Marcellus, Gaius Claudius 34,
        36, 38, 105, 199
Marcellus (Octavian's nephew)
        293–4, 295, 298–9
Marius (general) 22
Mark Antony (Marcus Antonius)
        xi, 23
    and Army 109–10, 112–15,

        121–2, 149–50, 195,
        230–1
    desertions 253, 256
    at Philippi 169–71, 174–5
    and Brutus/Cassius 93–7, 100,
        102–3, 108–9, 133
    and Caesar 36, 45, 47, 49–50,
        51
    in aftermath of murder
        54–64, 66–8, 69
        left out of will 67–8
        as priest of Caesar cult 167
    character 62–3, 112, 114–15,
        183, 197, 230, 266
    drinking/womanizing 62,
        183, 236, 248
    and Cicero 83, 99–100,
        103–5, 130–1, 158
    and Cleopatra *see under*
        Cleopatra
    as consul 70–2, 82, 84–5,
        108–10
    manipulates constitution
        110–11, 122–3
    opponents of 108–11
    invades Parthia 228, 229–34
    marriage to Octavia 200, 202,
        204, 222, 234–5, 245
    military tactics 249–51, 253–4
    errors in 125, 193–4, 197–8,
        232, 253
    and Octavian 4, 5–7, 63, 80,
        85–7, 90–1, 179–80, 184
    agreements between 186,
        198–9
    at Tarentum 218–22
    battles with 142–5, 195–6,
        248–57
    diplomacy between 194,
        198, 219–21, 222
    political struggle with 92–3,
        98–107, 114, 121–3,

Index

Index